MW01181621

INTERNATIONAL LAW AND ITS DISCONTENTS

In *Civilization and Its Discontents*, Sigmund Freud argued that civilization itself is the major source of human unhappiness, inhibiting instincts and generating guilt. In *Globalization and Its Discontents*, Joseph Stiglitz shows how the "economic architecture" that produced globalization has also driven the backlash against it. This book brings together some of international law's most outspoken "discontents," those who situate their malaise in international law itself. Their shared objective is to expose international law's complicity in the ongoing economic and financial global crises and to assess its capacity – and its will – to address them constructively.

Some, like Freud, view that which holds us together as an inevitable source of discontent. Others, like Stiglitz, draw on the energy of the backlash. How have these crises affected particular groups, sovereign states, and international law itself? How have they responded? When does crisis serve as a catalyst, and for what?

Barbara Stark is Professor of Law at Hofstra University. She has published dozens of articles in the California and UCLA law reviews and the Yale, Stanford, Virginia, Vanderbilt, Pennsylvania, and Michigan journals of international law, among others. Since joining the Hofstra faculty in 2005, she has published five books.

International Law and Its Discontents

CONFRONTING CRISES

Edited by

Barbara Stark

Hofstra University School of Law

CAMBRIDGE
UNIVERSITY PRESS

32 Avenue of the Americas, New York, NY 10013-2473, USA

Cambridge University Press is part of the University of Cambridge.

It furthers the University's mission by disseminating knowledge in the pursuit of
education, learning, and research at the highest international levels of excellence.

www.cambridge.org
Information on this title: www.cambridge.org/9781107047501

First published 2015

A catalog record for this publication is available from the British Library.

Library of Congress Cataloging in Publication Data
International law and its discontents : confronting crises / edited by Barbara Stark.
    pages   cm
Includes bibliographical references and index.
ISBN 978-1-107-04750-1 (Hardback)
1. Law–Social aspects.   2. Law–Economic aspects.   3. Comparative law.   4. International law
and human rights.   I. Stark, Barbara, 1952– editor.
K561.I57 2015
341–dc23   2014045664

ISBN 978-1-107-04750-1 Hardback

CONTENTS

List of Contributors .... *page* vii

Acknowledgments xi

Introduction: The Discontents Confront Crisis

Barbara Stark 1

PART I   THE ENVIRONMENT

1   Binge Development in the Age of Fear: Scarcity,
    Consumption, Inequality, and the Environmental Crisis
    Ileana Porras 25

2   International Law as a War Against Nature? Reflections
    on the Ambivalence of International Environmental Law
    Karin Mickelson 84

PART II   GENDER

3   Decoding Crisis in International Law: A Queer Feminist
    Perspective
    Dianne Otto 115

4   The Incredible Shrinking Women
    Barbara Stark 137

PART III   SOVEREIGN STATES

5   Corporate Power and Instrumental States: Toward a
    Critical Reassessment of the Role of Firms, States, and
    Regulation in Global Governance
    Dan Danielsen 171

6   Global Economic Inequality and the Potential for Global
     Democracy: A Functionalist Analysis
     Andrew Strauss 194

PART IV   INTERNATIONAL POLITICAL CRISIS

7   A Bolivarian Alternative? The New Latin American
     Populism Confronts the Global Order
     Brad R. Roth and Sharon F. Lean 221

8   Global Crisis and the Law of War
     Jeanne M. Woods 249

Index 287

CONTRIBUTORS

Dan Danielsen is Professor of Law at Northeastern University. Professor Danielsen's current research focuses on the role of corporate actors in transnational regulation and governance. His work identifies regulatory strategies to shape and harness corporate power to improve social welfare and increase economic development around the globe. Recent publications include: "Economic Approaches to Global Regulation: Expanding the International Law and Economics Paradigm," *J. Int'l Bus. & L.*, 10 (2011), p. 23; "Local Rules and a Global Economy: An Economic Policy Perspective," *Transnational Legal Theory*, 1 (2010), p. 49.

Sharon F. Lean is Associate Professor and Graduate Director in the Department of Political Science at Wayne State University. Her specialty is Latin American politics. Her current research considers the impact of accountability institutions such as human rights commissions and election administration bodies on the quality of democracy. She is author of *Civil Society and Electoral Accountability in Latin America* (Palgrave Macmillan, 2012), which includes a chapter on the electoral underpinnings of Venezuela's Bolivarian Revolution. She is contributing coeditor with Thomas Legler and Dexter S. Boniface of *Promoting Democracy in the Americas* (Johns Hopkins University Press, 2007).

Karin Mickelson is Associate Professor at the University of British Columbia Faculty of Law. Her research activities focus on the South-North dimension of international law, and she has been actively involved in TWAIL (Third World Approaches to International Law). She has analyzed the failure of international environmental law to respond to the concerns of the South in "South, North, International Environmental Law, and International Environmental Lawyers," *Yearbook of International Environmental Law*, 11 (2000), p. 52; recent publications include "The Maps of International Law: Perceptions of Nature in the Classification of Territory," *Leiden Journal of International Law*, 27 (2014), p. 621, and "Between Crisis and

Complacency: Seeking Commitment in International Environmental Law,"
Netherlands Yearbook of International Law, 44 (2013), p. 139.

Dianne Otto holds the Francine V. McNiff Chair in Human Rights Law at
Melbourne Law School and is the Director of the Institute for International
Law and the Humanities (IILAH). Professor Otto's research interests include
addressing gender, sexuality, and race inequalities in the context of international human rights law, the UN Security Council's peacekeeping work,
the technologies of global "crisis governance," and other threats to economic,
social, and cultural rights, as well as the transformative potential of people's
tribunals and other NGO initiatives. Recent publications include *Rethinking
Peacekeeping, Gender Equality and Collective Security* (edited with Gina Heath-
cote, Palgrave, 2014) and three edited volumes, *Gender Issues and Human
Rights* (Edward Elgar Publishing, 2013). She also authored a bibliographic
chapter, "Feminist Approaches," in *Oxford Bibliographies Online: International Law*, ed. Tony Carty (Oxford University Press, 2012).

Ileana Porras is the Associate Dean of Academic Affairs at the University of
Miami School of Law. Professor Porras teaches in the fields of international
law (including international legal theory, European Union law, the international law of sustainable development, international environmental law,
and trade and environment) and property law. She was the founding Director
of the Brown International Advanced Research Institutes and has been a
Visiting Professor at the Watson Institute–Brown University, Sandra Day
O'Connor College of Law, Arizona State University, and Boston College
Law School. Her scholarship has been primarily concerned with issues of
violence, colonialism, trade, and the environment. Most recently her work
has focused on the subject of the city and sustainable development. She is the
author of "The City and International Law: In Pursuit of Sustainable Development," *Fordham Urban Law Journal*, 36 (2009), p. 537; "Appropriating
Nature: Commerce, Property and the Commodification of Nature in the Law
of Nations," *Leiden Journal of International Law*, 27:3 (September 2014),
pp. 641–60; "Liberal Cosmopolitanism or Cosmopolitan Liberalism? Notes
from International Law," in *Parochialism, Cosmopolitanism, and the Foundations of International Law*, ed. Mortimer Sellers (Cambridge University Press,
2011); and "Constructing International Law in the East Indian Seas: Property, Sovereignty, Commerce and War in Hugo Grotius' '*De Iure Praedae*' –
The Law of Prize and Booty, or 'On How to Distinguish Merchants from
Pirates,'" *Brooklyn Journal of International Law*, 31 (2006), p. 741.

Brad R. Roth is Professor of Law and Political Science at Wayne State University. His scholarship applies political theory to problems in international

and comparative public law. He is the author of *Sovereign Equality and Moral Disagreement* (Oxford University Press, 2011), *Governmental Illegitimacy in International Law* (Oxford University Press, 1999), and numerous articles and book chapters on sovereignty, human rights, and international criminal justice, as well as the coeditor, with Gregory H. Fox, of *Democratic Governance and International Law* (Cambridge University Press, 2000).

Barbara Stark is Professor of Law at the Maurice A. Deane School of Law, Hofstra University. Her work has appeared in the California, UCLA, and Hastings law reviews and the Yale, Stanford, Michigan, Virginia, and Vanderbilt journals of international law, among others. Her recent publications include: "International Law from the Bottom Up: Fragmentation and Transformation," *University of Pennsylvania Journal of International Law*, 34 (2013), p. 687; "Jam Tomorrow: A Critique of International Economic Law," in eds. Chios Carmody et al., *Distributive Justice and International Economic Law* (Cambridge, 2012); "What's Left?" (reviewing *International Law on the Left: Re-Examining Marxist Legacies* (Susan Marks, ed., Cambridge University Press, 2008) *George Washington International Law Review*, 42 (2011), p. 191; "Theories of Poverty/The Poverty of Theory," *BYU Law Review* (2009), p. 381; and *Family Law in the World Community* (with Marianne Blair et al., 2009).

Andrew Strauss is Professor of Law and Associate Dean for Faculty Research and Strategic Initiatives at Widener University School of Law. He specializes in international law. Professor Strauss has been a Visiting Professor at the University of Notre Dame Law School, Rutgers Camden Law School, and the European Peace University. Strauss is coauthor (with Burns Weston, Richard Falk, and Hilary Charlesworth) of the fourth edition of *International Law and World Order,* a standard international law textbook. Recent publications include "Cutting the Gordian Knot: How and Why the United Nations Should Vest the International Court of Justice with Referral Jurisdiction," *Cornell International Law Journal* (2011) and *A Global Parliament: Essays and Articles* (with Richard Falk) (2011).

Jeanne M. Woods is the Ted and Louana Frois Distinguished Professor of International Studies at Loyola University College of Law in New Orleans. She teaches Public International Law, International Trade, International Human Rights, and Law and Poverty. In 2004, she was a Fulbright Lecturer at the China University of Political Science and Law in Beijing, Peoples' Republic of China. Her publications include *Human Rights and the Global Marketplace: Economic, Social and Cultural Dimensions* (Transnational Publishers/Brill, 2005) (with Hope Lewis).

ACKNOWLEDGMENTS

This book began as a roundtable at the Annual Meeting of the American Society of International Law, and I am grateful to the Society for its efforts to stimulate critical debate. The Institute for Global Law and Policy at Harvard Law School provided a forum for the contributors at the half-way point, and we are deeply indebted to its Faculty Director, David Kennedy. The comments of those who joined that panel, including Kerry Rittich, Fran Ansley, Jennifer Rosenblum, and Alvaro Santos, were very much appreciated.

Finally, my warmest gratitude to those at Hofstra for their sustained support: to the law school for its generous research grants; to Deans Eric Lane and Ron Colombo for their steadfast support for faculty scholarship; to my indefatigable research librarian, Patricia Kastings; to my research assistant Christina Pingaro, who assumed major responsibility for the index; to Mary Ruggilo and Teresa Harrington, for their coordination of staff support; and especially to my assistant Joyce Amore Cox, for her years of patience, skill, and hard work.

John Berger has been a kind and wise editor, and we are happy to join the long list of distinguished legal scholarship that would not exist without him.

INTRODUCTION: THE DISCONTENTS CONFRONT CRISIS

Barbara Stark

I INTRODUCTION

In *Civilization and its Discontents*, Sigmund Freud argues that civilization itself is the major source of human unhappiness, inhibiting instincts and generating guilt. In *Globalization and Its Discontents*, Nobel prize-winning economist Joseph Stiglitz shows how the "economic architecture" which has produced globalization has also driven the backlash against it. This book brings together some of international law's most outspoken "discontents"; those who situate their malaise in international law itself. Their shared objective here is to expose international law's complicity in the ongoing economic and financial global crises and to assess its capacity – and its will – to address them constructively.

Some, like Freud, view that which holds us together as an inevitable source of discontent. Others, like Stiglitz, draw on the energy of the backlash to address urgent needs with radical pragmatism. Some are frustrated; others are angry; all are thoughtful and provocative.

This project began as a roundtable at the 2012 Annual Meeting of the American Society of International Law. The participants were invited to consider international law's "discontents" in relation to the Annual Meeting's theme, *Confronting Complexity*. Do its discontents generate "complexity" in international law? Do they resolve or even

I am deeply grateful to the Maurice A. Deane School of Law, Hofstra University, for its generous support of this project and to Joyce Amore Cox, for her patience and skill in preparing the manuscripts.

exploit it? To what effect? Under what circumstances does complexity disrupt what Antony Anghie has called the "civilizing mission [of the] imperial encounter?"

The speakers brought unexpected energy and originality to the session. They challenged the premises of the conference theme as well as the characterization of the 2008 economic and financial "crises" as somehow more significant than those that have affected the developing world more, and the developed world less. They questioned the constructs of "developed" and "developing," rejecting them along with "Global north and global south," "First and Third Worlds," and "the West and the Rest." They rejected the structure of the roundtable itself, appropriating for themselves (and an increasingly involved audience), the roles of interlocutors.

In this volume, three of the original participants are joined by six similarly prominent, cutting-edge international law scholars. They are a diverse and unruly group, tethered together by their shared focus on the ongoing global crises – their causes and consequences – and the transformative potential of international law.

A The Great Recession

The Great Recession has impacted more people worldwide than any crisis since the Great Depression. Rooted in bad government policy and worse corporate behavior in the United States, the American financial meltdown was globalized with devastating consequences, raising fundamental questions about global capitalism.

In 2007, the subprime mortgage market collapsed in the United States. Because lenders, such as Countrywide, made their money from the fees generated by transactions, they had been encouraging unqualified buyers to assume mortgage obligations that they would never be able to pay off. Subprime lending was not that risky, it was thought, as long as the residential real estate market remained strong and housing costs continued to grow. Homeowners also invested in the bubble, by taking out low-interest mortgage equity loans that enabled them to spend despite stagnant income.

The subprime mortgages themselves were sold to investment firms and repackaged. They were sliced and diced and rebundled into derivatives, complex securities created by investment banks and hedge funds. Because many of these "innovative" new instruments were unregulated, there was no legal obligation to secure them. Because there was no legal obligation, there were no reserves backing them when they failed. Even those that were regulated were highly leveraged; investors' debt was allowed to be as much as thirty times their equity. Ratings agencies, such as Standard & Poors, whose fees were paid by the investment banks, still gave them triple A ratings.[1] Government regulators, like everyone else, were unconcerned.

Then the housing bubble burst and the entire market tumbled. The now-underwater mortgages, the "toxic assets," were impossible to isolate because no one knew how to unbundle the complex new derivatives. So the bottom fell out, and once venerable investment firms like Bear Sterns and Lehman Brothers collapsed. Markets panicked, triggering a global recession.

As Stiglitz explains in *Freefall*,[2] the United States economy constitutes such a large proportion of the global economy that when it dives, it takes the rest of the world with it. In addition, the United States exported its recession because it had already exported its philosophy of deregulation. One quarter of the inadequately secured United States mortgages were held by foreign banks.

Those in low income states were especially vulnerable. They were quickly hit by the collapse in global demand.[3] Remittances – which dwarf foreign aid – from the United States and Europe plummeted.[4] The crises also spread rapidly because of policies long-foisted on developing states by the United States and the International Monetary Fund (IMF).[5]

---

[1] Joseph Stiglitz, *Freefall: America, Free Markets and the Sinking of the World Economy* (New York: W. W. Norton, 2010), p. 23.

[2] Ibid.   [3] Ibid., p. 23.

[4] Ibid., p. 24. Remittances were further reduced because the money transfer companies that enabled families to send money to keep their children in school were often the same companies that were used to send money to terrorist groups, such as the Shabab in Somalia. Nicholas Kulish, "Somalis Face a Snag in Lifelines From Abroad," *New York Times*, August 4, 2013.

[5] Ibid.

B Inequality

The Great Recession spread like wildfire because globalization had already eliminated the barriers that might have slowed it down. But the impact of the Great Recession has been skewed. As economist Branko Milanovic explains, "[F]rom a global perspective, two decades of globalization have produced what 'seems like a fairly benign outcome.' If you look at the world as a single nation, income inequality has, in fact, declined. Income in the middle has grown faster than at the top."[6] But inequality persists among countries, as Princeton economist Angus Deaton notes: "For every country with a catch-up story there has been a country with a left-behind story."[7]

Inequality *within* states, in fact, has increased almost everywhere. According to French economist Thomas Piketty, author of *Capital in the Twenty-First Century*, income inequality is increasing.[8] In terms of salary and compensation packages, Piketty shows that inequality in the United States is "probably higher than in any other society at any time in the past, anywhere in the world."[9] As set out in the Equilar 100 CEO Pay Study, conducted for the *New York Times*, the median compensation for a chief executive in 2013 was a stunning $13.9 million, up 9 percent from 2012. Piketty attributes two-thirds of the increase in American inequality over the past forty years to the growth of such "supersalaries."[10]

Even the IMF has noted, for the first time, that inequality threatens global stability. In a recent study, the IMF concluded that: "A flatter distribution of income contributes more to sustainable economic growth than the quality of a country's political institutions, its foreign debt and openness to trade, its foreign investment and

---

[6] Eduardo Porter, "A Global Boom, But Only For Some," *New York Times*, March 19, 2014, p. B1.

[7] John Cassidy, "Forces of Divergence," *The New Yorker*, March 31, 2014, p. 69.

[8] Thomas Piketty, *Capital in the Twenty-First Century* (2014).

[9] Cassidy, "Forces of Divergence," p. 70.

[10] Peter Eavis, "Executive Pay: Invasion of the Supersalaries," *New York Times*, April 13, 2014, p. BU1.

whether its exchange rate is competitive." Reducing income inequality is now explicitly part of the IMF's core mandate.[11]

The crises may be easing for some,[12] but even in the United States they continue for many.[13] The wealth divide among races in the United States has deepened.[14] A study by the Urban Institute showed that in 2010 whites on average had twice the income of blacks and Hispanics, but six times the wealth.[15] Europe, similarly, was hit hard. In May 2013, unemployment in the Eurozone reached a new high.[16] Spaniards foraged in dumpsters for food.[17] Greek children went hungry.[18] While industrial output in Germany rose 2.5 percent in June 2013, it declined 1.5 percent in France.[19] While some analysts

[11] Eduardo Porter, "In New Tack, I.M.F. Aims At Income Inequality," *New York Times*, April 9, 2014, p. B1.

[12] See for example Danielle Costello, "The Drought Is Over (at Least for CEOs's)," *New York Times*, April 11, 2011, www.nytimes.com/2011/04/10/business/10comp.html?pagewanted=all (noting that the median pay for top executives at 200 major companies was $9.6 million in 2010). Annie Lowrey, "Incomes Flat In Recovery, But Not For the 1%," *New York Times*, February 16, 2013, p. B1 (noting that "Incomes rose more than 11 percent for the top 1 percent of earners during the economic recovery, but not at all for everybody else, according to new data").

[13] Motoko Rich, "Feeble Job Numbers Show Recovery Starting to Stall," *New York Times*, July 9, 2011, p. A1 (noting new Labor Department statistics showing an increase in unemployment, up to 9.2 percent).

[14] Signe-Mary McKernan, et al., *Less Than Equal: Racial Disparities in Wealth Accumulation*, The Urban Institute, 2012 http://urban.org

[15] Ibid.

[16] David Jolly, "In Continuing Sign of Weakness, Unemployment Hits New High in the Euro Zone," *New York Times*, May 1, 2013, p. B2.

[17] Suzanne Daley, "Spain Recoils as Its Hungry Forage Trash Bins for a Next Meal," *New York Times*, September 25, 2012, p. A6 (describing "survival tactics" where "unemployment rose over 50 percent among young people and more and more households have adults without jobs").

[18] Liz Alderman, "More Children in Greece Start to Go Hungry," *New York Times*, April 17, 2013, p. A1 (citing "2012 Unicef report showing that among the poorest Greek households with children, more than 26 percent had an economically weak diet").

[19] David Jolly, "Rising Output in Factories Hints at Growth in Europe," *New York Times*, August 14, 2013.

were encouraged by rising output in factories, twenty-six million Europeans remain unemployed.[20] In 2014, the European Union finally took a step back from German-inspired austerity, entering into a new budget pact allowing debt-burdened states such as Greece and Italy some much-needed leeway.[21]

The issues rending Europe, such as disappearing pensions and shrinking social safety nets,[22] remain unimaginable luxuries in the developing states. As set out in the *UN Resolution on the World Economic Crisis*:[23]

> Developing countries, which did not cause the global economic and financial crisis, are nonetheless severely affected by it. The economic and social progress achieved during recent years, in particular on internationally agreed development goals, including the Millennium Development Goals, is now being threatened in developing countries, particularly least developed countries ... Women also face greater income insecurity and increased burdens of family care.[24]

Since May of 2013, moreover, capital has been fleeing emerging markets as their currencies and stock markets plunge.[25]

C The Crises in Developing States

Recent reports from the Bank, somewhat surprisingly, "show a broad reduction in extreme poverty."[26] In part, this reflects the fact that the world's poorest had no jobs, housing, savings, benefits, or pensions to

---

[20] Ibid.

[21] Ian Wishart, "Renzi Prods Merkel into Shift as EU Eases Austerity Focus," *Bloomberg News*, June 27, 2014.

[22] David C. Unger, "Europe's Social Contract, Lying in Pieces," *New York Times*, June 9, 2013; Jack Ewing, "A Recession's Daunting Reach," *New York Times*, April 26, 2013.

[23] G.A. Res. 63/303, UN GAOR, 63rd Sess., Agenda Itm 48, UN Doc. A/Res/ 63/303 (2009).

[24] Ibid., p. 2.

[25] Paul Krugman, "This Age of Bubbles," *New York Times*, August 23, 2013, p. A27.

[26] Annie Lowrey, "Extreme Poverty in Developing World is Down Despite the Recession, Report Says," *New York Times*, March 7, 2012, p. A4.

lose. Closer analysis shows that while there has been "a small drop in the number of people living below $2 per day ... the number of people living *between* $1.25 and $2 almost doubled from 648 million to 1.18 billion between 1981 and 2008."[27]

But questions have been raised about the validity of the benchmark for "extreme poverty" itself.[28] The Bank assumes an improvement in "poverty" using the $1.25 per day standards of the poorest 10–20 countries. As critics note, this is barely subsistence. Many also question the usefulness of GNP or per capita expenditure as meaningful indicators.[29] Amartya Sen and Martha Nussbaum, for example, have set out an alternative to GNP that focuses on "*human capabilities* ... what people are actually able to do and be."[30]

Half of the decline in the extreme poverty rate, moreover, is attributable to China,[31] where growth is slowing.[32] Nor do the bank reports take into account the costs of that growth, including environmental degradation.[33] According to *The Lancet*, China's outdoor pollution contributed to 1.2 million premature deaths in 2010, or 40 percent of the worldwide total.[34] An American science journal reported in July 2013 that life expectancy in northern China had fallen by five years because of air pollution.[35]

---

[27] Ibid.

[28] Annie Lowrey, "Movin' On Up," *New York Times Magazine*, May 5, 2013, p. 18.

[29] See for example Martha C. Nussbaum, *Women and Human Development: The Capabilities Approach* (2006), pp. 5–6.

[30] Ibid.   [31] Lowrey, "Movin' On Up," p. 16.

[32] Keith Bradsher, "Easy Credit Dries Up, Choking Growth in China," *New York Times*, April 16, 2013, p. A1; Keith Bradsher, "China Says Lending Put Growth Rate at 7.5 Percent," *New York Times*, July 16, 2014, p. B2 (noting that heavy lending by the central bank "appears to have headed off or at least delayed a widely expected broader slowdown of the Chinese economy").

[33] See for example Edward Wong, "Life in a Toxic Country," *New York Times*, August 4, 2013, p. SRI.

[34] Ted Alcorn, "China's Skies: A Complex Recipe for Pollution with No Quick Fix," *The Lancet* 1973, 1973–1974 (2013), p. 381.

[35] Yuyu Chen et al., "Evidence on the Impact of Sustained Exposure to Air Pollution on Life Expectancy from China's Huai River Policy," *Proc. Nat'l Acad. Sci. USA* 12936, 12936–12941 n. 32 (2013), p. 110.

Investment banks and hedge funds, meanwhile, continue to exploit ad hoc arrangements and resist the "global economic governance" called for by the UN Commission of Experts on Reforms of the International Monetary and Financial System. The G20 ignored calls by Miguel d'Escoto, President of the General Assembly, for "new global institutions, authorities and advisory boards." Absent such reforms, as Stiglitz explains, countries with lax regulation compete to attract financial services in a crippling "race to the bottom."

II THE DISCONTENTS

The essays here focus on the impact of the crises on particular groups, sovereign states and international law itself. How have states, non-state actors and international law responded? What roles has international law played in the ongoing debacle? When and where does crisis serve as a catalyst, and for whom?

A International Environmental Law

The first section describes the global environmental crisis from two very different perspectives. In "Binge Development in the Age of Fear: Scarcity, Consumption, Inequality and the Environmental Crisis," Ileana Porras sets the tone with King Lear's bitter complaint, "Allow not nature more than nature needs, Man's life's as cheap as beast's."[36] Like Lear, Porras explains, those of us in the overdeveloped West have come to see our extravagant way of life as absolutely necessary. We cannot imagine living without cheap energy, new clothes, new cars, new electronic devices, and unlimited clean water on demand. Alarmed by scientists warning of shrinking resources and irreparable environmental degradation, we respond by buying bottled spring water and organic produce flown in from the Southern Hemisphere, delivered to our door. Porras draws on the recent work of

---

[36] William Shakespeare, *King Lear* (Act 2, Sc. 4).

Harvard economist Sendhil Mullainathan and Princeton psychologist Eldar Shafir[37] to explain why:

> The evidence of drought and depleted reservoirs, the knowledge that there is less available abundance, produce an outsize feeling of insecurity. The fact that the community may have to reconsider both its short term and long term usage priorities, that non-critical uses may have to be severely restricted or prohibited, and that other uses may need to be better monitored and possibly reduced, are experienced not as necessary adjustments but as existential threats.

We cannot bear to contemplate scarcity, let alone deal with it rationally. Or, as Lear exclaims, "O reason not the need!"

Even if we were somehow able to cope with our collective pathology, Porras continues, international law is unlikely to offer useful templates because of its own commitment to, and investment in, global trade. As Philip Alston observes, "International lawyers have served as the handmaidens of globalization."[38] Indeed, Porras reminds us, "from its inception in the sixteenth century international law has had an overriding affinity for international commerce."

As she explains in her introduction, this affinity has only been deepened by the ongoing crises.

> The response of bureaucrats, policy pundits, and politicians at the national, regional, and international levels has been variously to call for more or better regulation and oversight of transnational banks and corporations; to demand the massive infusion of stimulus capital into local and national economies; or to insist on the necessity of adopting austerity measures. All agreed, however, that the way out of the global economic crisis was national economic growth.

No one argued in favor of shrinking national economies, or even of limiting growth to "green growth." Confronted with economic crises, world leaders quickly put the environment on the back

---

[37] Sendhil Mullainathan and Eldar Shafir, *Scarcity: Why Having Too Little Means So Much* (2013).

[38] Philip Alson, "The Myopia of the Handmaidens: International Lawyers and Globalization," *EJIL* 435 (1997), p. 3.

burner. Even the EU backed away from its earlier commitments to limit carbon emissions. International law, Porras shows, is not only ill-equipped to counter deep psychological drives for abundance, superfluidity, and growth; it is the *product*, and a key facilitator, of these same drives.

In "International Law as a War Against Nature? Reflections on the Ambivalence of International Environmental Law," Karin Mickelson analyzes the role of international environmental law itself in the ongoing environmental crises. Mickelson undertakes a daunting project:

> Looking back on more than two decades of lost opportunities with regard to climate change, and many more decades of partially successful or failed attempts to come to terms with other environmental harms associated with industrialization, how do we account for the fact that we keep falling short of the mark?

Mickelson begins by quoting Freud: "The principal task of civilization, its actual *raison d'être*, is to defend us against nature." The essence of modern environmentalism, Mickelson suggests, could be seen as a rejection of this view and its replacement with a depiction of nature as that which must be defended against civilization. Environmental law, whether in its domestic or international form, is expected to play an equalizing role, placing limits on the exploitation of nature while allowing for the supposedly rational pursuit of economic development. Increasingly, however, many question whether the mainstream understanding of economic growth and prosperity is fundamentally inconsistent with environmental sustainability. Given that this understanding is deeply embedded in the structures and principles of international law, international law effectively justifies a war against nature.

This chapter explores both the possibilities and the limitations of this portrayal of international environmental law, drawing on TWAIL (Third World Approaches to International Law) scholarship. Mickelson also resurrects the uncompromising work of Murray Bookchin, an early ecologist. Finally, Mickelson draws on the concept of "environmental justice" developed by social movements, to stress that:

> [D]isproportionate burden of environmental harm has fallen on those who are already marginalized by racial, class and gender inequality. But while reminding mainstream environmentalism that it should pay attention to the ways in which environmental burdens are unequally distributed, environmental justice has also insisted that demands for decent housing and safe working conditions must also be seen as part of the environmental platform every bit as significant as the demand for clean air and water and wilderness conservation.

International environmentalists, she rather literally suggests, should go *outside* – meaning both "outside" the dominant model, and "outside" into the natural world. Like Porras, Mickelson suggests no "big idea" to replace "sustainable development." Instead of a new pattern, she urges multiple new ways of understanding patterns, pointing out, "communities all over the world . . . [which] are creating new ways to interacting with the natural world, or retaining (or reclaiming) old ways that offer insights and values that the dominant model has lost sight of, or coming up with innovative fusions of the two."

B Gender in Crises

The next two chapters draw on a different set of critical tools, from feminist and queer theory. In *Decoding Crisis in International Law: A Queer Feminist Perspective*, Dianne Otto focuses on the ways in which "crises" are themselves constructs, created and exploited to justify systems of control. This includes vague definitions of "terrorism" used to justify measures targeting those who do not conform to traditional gender roles. This chapter draws on feminist and queer dissatisfactions with the assumptions, conceptual underpinnings and vocabularies of international law. While claiming to be objective and universal, these constructs order the way that we think about the international community, maintaining exclusionary normative conceptions of who is fully human, and who is not.

Otto considers it an open question whether "women" can ever be recognized as full subjects of the law, and whether it is possible to use the law to move beyond dualistic conceptions of gender (male/

female) and sexuality (hetero/homo), embracing both gender and sexuality as social, multiple, and fluid categories. As her vivid examples demonstrate, such moves are necessary to liberate the legal imagination from the bondage of patriarchal and heteronormative frames of thinking. They open the possibility that law can promote gender and sexual multiplicities and freedoms. Such moves are also "dangerous," Otto notes, because they are always susceptible to cooptation and reincorporation into mainstream assumptions. "Like others of critical faith," Otto explains, she understands international law as a discipline of "dangerous possibilities" for promoting more inclusive notions of humanity, community, justice, and equality. In *The Incredible Shrinking Women*, I explain how the ongoing global economic and financial crises exacerbate women's relative impoverishment, even among the poorest populations. This chapter draws on a recent study by the Harvard School of Public Health, which measured poor women in 54 poor and middle-income countries over a forty-year period. Noting that changes in average height have long been relied upon by researchers as a proxy for changes in the group's standard of living, the study describes the decline and stagnation in average heights among women born in the last two decades in these countries, compared to their mothers and grandmothers. For these women, the world is "not getting to be a better place ... For them, it's getting worse."

This chapter describes the ongoing failure of international human rights law, including women's human rights law, to protect these women. It further explains why international financial and economic reforms are crucial to their well-being. Such reforms, including the regulation of investment banks and the elimination of tax havens, might have prevented the last major crises and, experts warn, are necessary to prevent the next. These reforms are opposed by a savvy $700 trillion-dollar derivatives industry, however, with their armies of lawyers, and the shrinking women are not on the agenda. While economists debate about who benefits most from rising tides, there is no question that the smallest craft are the first to be swamped in tumultuous seas. Hedge funds in New York may be able to ride out market volatility, and even thrive, but the shrinking women can't.

C Crises and Global Governance

In the next section, Dan Danielsen and Andrew Strauss question the state's role in these crises. In "Corporate Power and Instrumental States: Toward A Critical Reassessment of the Role of Firms, States, and Regulation in Global Governance," Danielsen critically examines the view, widely held among political liberals and conservatives alike, of the nation-state as the primary institutional safeguard against economic instability. From this perspective, "economic crises" are primarily the result of "regulatory failure," either in the form of too much or too little oversight by states over the economy. This chapter builds on Danielsen's recent work exploring the "global economic order" as a complex co-production of states and economic actors, bargaining over and adapting in relation to the rules that govern them. Danielsen also draws on his earlier work looking at the challenges of securing positive welfare effects, whether domestic or global, through national rules in a global economy.

To Danielsen, the modern nation state looks more like a participant and enabler of capitalist exploitation than its regulator. In this view, state regulatory deference to "private" market ordering, along with market deference to limited state regulatory authority, comprises a regime of global political and economic governance, rather than the failure of the political sphere to appropriately govern the economic sphere.

The chapter then explores some of the ramifications of this revised understanding of the relation between the state and the economy, including the role of states and regulation in economic crises. The author revisits theorists such as Locke, Marx, Veblen, and others to suggest a critical lineage to the justifications for – as well as the critique of – the instrumental state and the primacy of private ordering. At the same time, he resists simple narratives of "state capture" or "conspiracies of capital" as explanations or justifications for the current global order. Danielsen concludes his detailed and rigorous analysis with an anarchic gleam in his eye, suggesting that the very complexity and ungovernability of the global system as a "system" may provide the best hope for its progressive transformation.

In "Global Economic Governance: Why Democracy Matters," Andrew Strauss draws on his work with Richard Falk on democratizing the international system to analyze the relationship between the global economic crises and the "democracy deficit." Unlike most of the other contributors, Strauss shows how global inequality contributed to the economic and financial crisis rather than the other way around. The author then applies the social science literature that correlates democratic governance to sustained – and equitable – economic growth to the international system. He also examines the applicability to the current global order of theories regarding the relationship between capital and democracy. This analysis demonstrates that the concentration of capital associated with non-democratic societies, where workers lack significant political power, undermines the ability of the economy to sustain adequate purchasing power.

Strauss makes it clear that he is not advocating any "grand legalist schemes for comprehensive world government." His project is more modest, but also more radical. He, and those who support a Global Parliamentary Assembly (GPA), have in mind a "single functionalist institution of limited powers." Its symbolic significance, like its potential for empowering the disenfranchised, is tantalizingly open-ended. As Strauss explains:

> GPA would facilitate citizens' ability to organize transnationally... Able to coalesce in the parliament's democratic space, supporters of greater economic equality could petition the organization to endorse their programs ... Not only would the organized citizenry be inclined toward supporting the legal force of legislative results that were fashioned in response to their input, but an existing GPA could powerfully lobby governments on behalf of expanding its own powers. In a world where democratic elections have become the litmus test for legitimate governance ... GPA's claim to exercise increasing authority in the name of the global citizenry would be hard to resist.

The GPA is not merely an academic theory; it has received strong support from major international institutions, including the United Nations General Assembly[39] and the United Nations Human Rights Council.

---

[39] Citing Resolution 68/175 (December 20, 2013), declaring that everyone "is entitled to a democratic and equitable international order, which requires the

D International Political Crises

The final two chapters situate the current crises in a broader political context. In "A Bolivarian Alternative? The New Latin American Populism Confronts the Global Order," Brad Roth and Sharon F. Lean analyze attempts by the Bolivarian Alternative for the Americas (ALBA) – spearheaded by Venezuelan President Hugo Chavez with the participation of the governments of Bolivia, Ecuador, Nicaragua, and Cuba – to challenge the terms of the global economic, political, and legal order. The theme of the chapter is a critical evaluation of the ALBA countries' efforts to push back against Western hegemony on several fronts, in the name of a "twenty-first century socialism." The chapter discusses the ALBA system's trade and aid flows, international investment disputes, human rights controversies, and the effort to reassert non-intervention norms. The authors describe former Nicaraguan Foreign Minister Miguel d'Escoto's short-lived initiatives as UN General Assembly President in 2008–9, and the 2009 *coup d'etat* that removed Honduras from the alliance. They conclude with a sharp critique of the backlash in Venezuela after Chavez's death, noting the role of his charisma in the ALBA movement, and questioning whether – and in what form – it can survive without him.

In "Global Crisis and the Law of War," Jeanne M. Woods examines the relationships among late-stage capitalism, military hegemony, and the law of armed conflict. Informed by the pioneering work of Tony Anghie, the chapter probes the pre-Westphalian norms of war articulated by theorists such as Vitoria and Grotius. These norms facilitated the accumulation of wealth by European naval powers; the conquest of the peoples of Asia, Africa, and the Americas; and laid the foundation for global capitalism. Woods compares these early doctrines with the law of war as it continues to evolve in a global order characterized by "chronic, simultaneous, existential crises."

The chapter explores the dialectical interplay between the systemic crises of late-stage capitalism and the devolution of the global

right to equitable participation of all, without any discrimination, in domestic and global decision-making."

hegemony of the United States and what Woods characterizes as "the corporate take-over of all aspects of life (including the environment)" and growing militarism. She explains how the law of war is manipulated to legitimize the domination of global powers over the natural resources of the earth. She concludes by suggesting some of the ways in which human rights norms can be reclaimed in the service of popular resistance and renewal. While she recognizes that these norms have become tools of the dominant international legal discourse, it is precisely *because* of their appropriation that she views them as so useful. They have become part of the zeitgeist, and even international capital must take them into account.

III CONFRONTING CRISES

The chapters reflect and incorporate the tumultuous times. Even as the authors of the first two chapters on international environmental law were editing their chapters, between September 2013 and April 2014 the UN Climate Panel issued three reports. The first, released in Stockholm, found a certainty of "95 percent or greater" that humans were the main cause of global warming. The second, released in Yokohama, noted that "profound effects were already being felt around the world, and were likely to get much worse."[40] The third, issued in New York, observed that efforts were "falling short."[41] In May 2014, American scientists issued the National Climate Assessment, a comprehensive study finding that the United States climate has already changed dramatically. These reports confirm the sober conclusions of the chapters' authors; if international environmental law promised "sustainable development," it has already failed.

The chapters on gender, similarly, tell a more complicated story than that of human progress through human rights. Despite multiple laws, on the national, regional, and international levels, gender

[40] Justin Gillis, "Climate Efforts Falling Short, U.N. Panel Says," *New York Times*, April 14, 2014, p. A1.
[41] Ibid.

equality remains far beyond the reach of most women and unimaginable to many. Indeed, "gender and sexual panics" proliferate, and are used to justify "emergency laws that are never rescinded." Gender is where seething cultural tensions, temporarily subsumed in globalization, erupt.

The chapters on sovereign states also expose failed paradigms. The restrictive theory of sovereign immunity has long recognized that states often function in a "commercial" capacity, for example, and that states cannot rely on traditional notions of sovereign immunity when they act like private entities. This doctrine was recently expanded by the United States Supreme Court in *Argentina* v. *NML Capital Ltd.*,[42] in which the Court denied Argentina's appeal against "vulture capital" hedge funds, which rejected debt restructuring that had been accepted by holders of 92 percent of Argentina's bonds.[43]

Yet in the regulatory context, states are still assumed to promote the public welfare. Worse, they are *depended* upon for that purpose. Thus, as Danielsen sharply observes: "The conception of a (mostly public) regulatory system charged with and responsible for securing ... the functioning of a global economy driven by (mostly private) self-interested economic actors," neither accurately describes the actual operation of the global economy nor explains why a public global order intended to promote general welfare instead leads to unprecedented inequality. Rather, it is clear that "states," and "markets" cannot be depended upon to hold each other in check, or to cooperate for some "greater good."

This reflects, in part, the hollowness of the institutions of global governance and the need for democratic participation to revitalize them. But as Strauss explains, international law is created by states and "the interstate system does not facilitate opportunities for citizens to formally participate in the law-making process. Without any institutional structure for bringing disparate communities together, language, ethnicity, religion, culture, nationalist ideology, and distance all conspire to make a collective response on behalf of common economic interests extremely difficult."

---

[42] No. 12–842, decided June 16, 2014.   [43] Ibid.

Transnational solidarity is problematic for states, as well as for individuals, resisting neoliberalism. As Roth and Lean show, the impediments to deep and lasting structural reform are many, including the limited alternatives to global markets and capital investment. Even transnational peace – the mere *absence* of armed conflict, which was the paramount objective of the UN Charter[44] – is increasingly elusive. As Woods grimly suggests, "As late-stage capitalism confronts multiple intersecting crises – of debt, energy, climate, inequality – it has reconstructed a paradigm of permanent war." The chapters addressing international political crises raise profound questions about the capacities and the parameters of international law. Does it permit or preclude alternatives to neoliberalism? Does it even aspire "to save succeeding generations from the scourge of war,"[45] as set out in the UN Charter? Like the other contributors, the authors confront hard questions with candor, rigor and imagination.

For the most part, the authors collected here eschew the soaring rhetoric of earlier generations of internationalists. Unlike their predecessors, they are skeptical of metanarratives, including that of neoliberalism, which they see as a cover for hegemony. But a bright thread ties them all together: the simple, but recently neglected insight, that law is produced by political choices, rather than immutable forces (or uncontrollable markets). As Mickelson reminds us:

> [E]conomic models do not exist in a Platonic ether, beyond the purview of mere mortals. The dominant model of economic prosperity is not an ideal that has informed human thinking about progress and well-being throughout human history. It is the product of a particular time and place, a set of assumptions and choices that can and should be challenged.

The task for the discontents, accordingly, is to create, or discover, what Otto aptly calls "strategies of disruption," while retaining what she has referred to elsewhere as "critical faith."

---

[44] Louis Henkin, *Politics, Values, Functions* (1990).
[45] Preamble, UN Charter.

A Strategies of Disruption

For some, these strategies begin with reconceptualization. After a modest and disarming disclaimer ("I do not have a plan. I offer no more than fragments"), Porras suggests we jettison everything we think we know about our own "needs and wants": "We must attend to and reevaluate the construct of scarcity, which in turn requires a redefinition of needs and wants." She concedes that some of this may well be hard-wired, but refuses to let us off the hook: "However irrational it appears, we need to recognize the human desire to expend and waste in a performative manner and make space for it. This urge cannot be repressed, but it may be possible to cabin it off by channeling it into periodic rituals."[46]

Porras is even wary of "green" consumption: "Alternative consumption may drive positive trends such as fair trade, organic farming, and fair labor standards, but we must be attentive to the assumptions that underlie the producer-consumer relationship, especially when production is located in a developing country while the product is destined for western consumption." Whatever the methods, she insists, "Somehow we will need to wrench citizenship away from consumer identity."

Mickelson looks outward, drawing on

> ... the alternative understanding of human well-being that have begun to emerge in countries like Bolivia and Ecuador, where the idea of "Buen Vivir" or "Vivir Bien" (literally "to live well", but often translated as "the good life") have come to inform the discourse of both governments and social movements. The concept is often contrasted with the idea of a "better life", which is characterized as "individualistic, separate from others and even at the expense of others.

She also finds inspiration in nature, urging an alternative approach "along the lines of a fractal through which order emerges organically

---

[46] See for example Stephanie Cash, "Christian Boltanski No Man's Land,"*Art in America*, May 4, 2010 (describing installation consisting primarily of a 25 foot-tall pile of used clothing); Peter Menzel, *Material World: A Global Family Portrait* (1995) (sixteen photojournalists collaborated with families in thirty countries to produce portraits of them with their possessions).

out of what might initially appear to be chaos, the sort of design that can be perceived in crystals or ferns."

Otto, cheekily citing Milton Friedman ("notorious proponent of disaster capitalism") for the proposition that, "A crisis, whether real or imagined, always creates opportunities that did not exist before," appropriates "the opportunities created by crisis to progressive ends." *The Incredible Shrinking Women* finds similar opportunities in the fragmentation of international law itself.

Danielsen, too, urges disruption, and the open-ended possibilities it can generate. What will we learn, he asks rhetorically, "When we loosen our attachment to a stable distinction between 'public' and 'private' ... or 'legal rules' and ... 'bargaining'." Danielsen sketches an adaptable analytic metric that could be applied in most, if not all, of the contexts considered here.

B Critical Faith

Strauss, in some ways the most theoretical of the contributors, turns out to be among the most grounded, relying on well-accepted international procedures and institutions to challenge their very foundations. Roth and Lean tell a difficult story that continues to unfold (or unravel) as we go to press. Yet they strike a positive note:

> [W]hile the Alliance's efforts to achieve structural change in the
> global order are of doubtful long-term significance, the Chávez
> government and its allies can be credited with significant
> accomplishments on behalf of constituencies long left behind, and
> with helping to revive an international conversation about the
> economic and social dimensions of human rights and
> democracy.[47]

However "discontent," none of the authors here has quite given up on international law. Rather, they all retain a "critical faith" in what has been called its emancipatory potential.

Even Woods, parsing the convoluted laws of war during what one former national security aide recently characterized as "a world

---

[47] Roth and Lean; correspondence on file with the volume editor.

aflame,"[48] insists that "law is a site of resistance as well as a tool of oppression." Her conclusion resonates with those of the other contributors, and explains why we wrote this book, and why it matters:

> The innovative technologies that enable capital to penetrate markets across the globe – that made globalization possible – also connect its victims – human beings – in unprecedented ways. We can use this technology to exploit or to organize; to isolate or to unite; to retreat into our hypnotically addictive toys; or to change the world.

[48] Peter Baker, "Crises Cascade and Converge, Testing Obama," *New York Times*, July 23, 2014, p. 1.

PART I   The Environment

1 BINGE DEVELOPMENT IN THE AGE OF FEAR: SCARCITY, CONSUMPTION, INEQUALITY, AND THE ENVIRONMENTAL CRISIS

Ileana Porras

Allow not nature more than nature needs,
Man's life's as cheap as beast's.

King Lear (Act 2, Sc. 4)

INTRODUCTION

The opening act of the twenty-first century is likely to be remembered as one driven by the twin scourges of fear and crisis. Calculated to be spectacular, the attacks of September 11, 2001 became a global media sensation without precedent. Fear became the undertone underlying choice in politics, policy, and daily life. Fear of terrorism[1] engendered and justified the costly global War on Terror, while fear of the intimate strangers in our midst and new technologies coalesced to enable the new security state. Reacting to a perceived existential threat, the western liberal democracies entered into moral crisis, openly embracing the use of force, preemptive war, repressive but friendly regimes, torture, drone strikes, extrajudicial executions, indefinite detention, and the deployment of pervasive surveillance technologies.

---

[1] For a discussion of the construction of terrorism as the antithesis of liberal democracies, and of the terrorist as frightening barbaric outsider whose use of extraordinary violence must be met with extranormal means, See Ileana Porras, "On Terrorism: Reflections on Violence and the Outlaw," in D. Danielsen and K. Engle (eds.), *After Identity: A Reader in Law and Culture* (1994).

In parallel, the global economic crisis, aptly termed the Great Recession,[2] broke out in 2008. Triggered by rampant greed and excessive risk taking in the banking sector and facilitated by lax regulatory regimes in the United States and other western democracies, the Great Recession demonstrated the vulnerability of the increasingly interconnected national economies to each other's failures. The Great Recession, whose effects are still being felt in 2014, directly and indirectly affected the livelihoods of large segments of the global population. The response of bureaucrats, policy pundits, and politicians at the national, regional, and international levels has been variously to call for more or better regulation and oversight of transnational banks and corporations; to demand the massive infusion of stimulus capital into local and national economies; or to insist on the necessity of adopting austerity measures. All agreed, however, that the way out of the global economic crisis was national economic growth. Across the globe, emphasis was placed on ensuring the survival of major private economic actors; stimulating investment in the building and infrastructure sectors; shoring up industrial and manufacturing assets; job creation; and above all, on building consumer confidence, so that borrowing and spending could once again drive the global economy.

While anxieties about the new security state and the fears of economic contraction had risen to the level of crisis in the collective psyche of the early twenty-first century, efforts to highlight another looming disaster failed to gain significant purchase. Continuing attempts by environmental activists, ecological economists, climate scientists, and other experts to raise public alarm about what they considered to be the equally urgent environmental crisis were met with general indifference. It was not for lack of trying. Warnings were issued. The experts were in agreement: the scale of the environmental impact of human activity on the world's ecosystems was unprecedented and potentially dangerous. Endless reports were produced detailing a neverending litany of environmental horrors, risks, and

---

[2] The term had been widely adopted by December 2008; see Catherine Rampell, "Great Recession: A brief Etymology," March 11, 2009 at http://economix .blogs.nytimes.com/2009/03/11/great-recession-a-brief-etymology/

vulnerabilities.[3] The production, accumulation, and interpretation of expert knowledge overwhelmingly pointed in the same direction: the existence of an environmental crisis of major proportions, which required urgent attention and immediate and sustained action. None of it managed to catch the public's attention or fire up its imagination. Neither the experts' warnings nor the voluminous supporting data managed to convince the public that here was a crisis of comparable magnitude to the concurrent security crisis or the economic crisis. Thus, the environmental "crisis" never quite managed to become an effective or functional crisis, one that provokes anxiety and fear and justifies the taking of extraordinary measures.

While the experts failed to move the public to a sense of crisis around the mounting ecological risks, their concerns came to permeate the policy discourse space in the guise of the principle of sustainable development.[4] Commentators from many fields have pointed to the obvious fact that, even as the ecological situation has worsened, the pervasive talk of sustainable development in policy circles and adherence to the principle in the political sphere has failed to generate meaningful policy action at any level. In this chapter, I take this failure as a given, but seek to sharpen the critique. What intrigues me about the present moment is less the lack of concordance between the endless pronouncements and the near total absence of policy implementation,[5] but that despite our pledged allegiance to the principle of

---

[3] In addition to warning of the cross-cutting risks and potentially disastrous impacts of climate change, experts and international bodies focused their attention on an array of intersecting negative effects of human activity on the environment, including: the depletion of the ozone layer, loss of biodiversity and the extinction of species, accelerating desertification, reduction of forests, exhaustion of freshwater aquifers, plummeting fish stocks, vanishing wetlands, pollution of rivers and lakes, the improper disposal of hazardous wastes and toxic chemicals, and the degradation of arable lands through salination and erosion.

[4] For a discussion of the principle of sustainable development see Section II.

[5] See Fred Luks, "Deconstructing Economic Interpretations of Sustainable Development: Limits, Scarcity and Abundance," [Hereinafter Luks] in Lyla Mehta (ed.) *The Limits to Scarcity: Contesting the Politics of Allocation,* (2010) [Hereinafter *Limits to Scarcity*], arguing that "scarcity" in both classical

sustainable development, we are individually and collectively engaged in a mad rush to consume not less but more, not prudently but extravagantly. In other words, what intrigues me is that at a time when we have lost our innocence and are daily confronted with the ugly facts of environmental degradation and natural resource depletion, we are seemingly engaged in a form of binge development.

In reflecting on the bizarre temporal coincidence of the call to sustainable development and the advent of binge development, I have come to the conclusion, troubling, but not altogether surprising, that the two are intimately connected. Indeed, as I will try to show, binge development might be said to be an effect of sustainable development discourse in an age of fear. The main thrust of my argument is that sustainable development, with its focus on natural limits and constraints, and with its emphasis on equity, inadvertently feeds the powerful fear of scarcity that lurks in the human heart. Scarcity may be a culturally determined social construct rather than an empirically discoverable material fact,[6] yet scarcity matters. Scarcity has many contradictory faces. It is the backdrop of economics, where it serves as the theoretical condition of rational choice and value. At the same time, scarcity – the experience of not having enough – produces anxiety, a mix of tunnel vision and distraction, and leads to irrational actions. The human capability to generate new needs, and thereby multiply the possible experiences of scarcity, is the fount of human drive and creativity. Yet, scarcity has been tied to the proliferation of wants and needs and the descent into the vortex of the hyper-consumerist society.

When sustainable development touched a nerve and awakened the always latent fear of scarcity, its effects were predictable. Suddenly, everyone wanted more or wanted to grab what was there before it was gone. The severe contractions of the Great Recession cemented our already growing conviction that in reality there was not enough to go around. The desiring Other became a competitor for resources in a

---

economics and ecological economics is naturalized, and that it must instead be understood as a social construction. See also Section 1 on Scarcity, Need and Consumption.

[6] See Section I, Scarcity, Need and Consumption.

materially limited world. Need arose from an exacerbated mimetic desire.[7] The discourse of sustainable development, already replete with references to risk and uncertainty, heightened the sense of insecurity that individuals, communities, and states were navigating in the early part of the twenty-first century.[8] The resulting mindset has been conducive to neither careful management of limited resources, nor a genuine concern with equity. Thus, while ostensibly committed to the objective of sustainable development, we are awash in conspicuous consumption and engaged in binge development. Meanwhile, as though in an alternative time-space dimension, the production of policy reports and recommendations continues unabated, and seemingly every day, a new treaty, resolution, judicial opinion, constitution, or regulation endorses the principle of sustainable development.

In the remainder of this chapter I will weave together three related points, connected to one another by the theme of scarcity. First, I will

[7] I use the term mimetic desire to emphasize the extent to which human beings' desire is fueled by the perception of others' desire. We have all had the experience of a sudden rush of feeling that we need to have something, when we see another displaying their ownership of the thing. This human propensity is the basis of most effective advertising, which manufactures needs by associating products with the pleasure and lifestyle of others whom our culture encourages us to admire. Mimetic desire is exacerbated or heightened by the perception of scarcity. Examples include luxury items intentionally produced in limited quantities, but also the periodic collective madness that arises seemingly spontaneously around Christmas shopping, such as the frenzy around the infamous Cabbage Patch Dolls of 1983 or the Mighty Morphin Power Ranger scare of 1994. (See www.nytimes.com/1994/12/05/us/with -power-rangers-scarce-a-frenzied-search-by-parents.html.)

[8] The risks and uncertainties I have in mind here are what Beck refers to as self-generated risks and uncertainties that are the side effects of successful modernization. As Beck emphasizes, risk is an evaluative assessment and always bears both a cultural and a political dimension. "Risks are always *future* events that *may* occur, that *threaten* us. But because this constant danger shapes our expectations, lodges in our heads and guides our actions, it becomes a political force that transforms the world." Ulrich Beck, *World at Risk* (2009), p. 9. In the sphere of sustainable development, the precautionary principle, e.g. Principle 15 of the Rio Declaration, captures both the sense of seriousness of these self-generated risks and the degree of "not-knowing" that we now live with.

sketch out the relationship between scarcity, need, and consumption, in order to provide insights into our current context of consumption-led economic growth. Second, I will explore some possible ways in which the general focus on sustainable development since 1992 has fed the fear of scarcity and thereby contributed to the excesses of binge development. Third, I will locate the special role that the trope of scarcity has played in international law and its foundational commitment to commerce. Drawing on these three themes, I conclude that the way forward requires a reevaluation of the notion of scarcity, which in turn requires a redefinition of need. Fear of scarcity is counterproductive and leads to irrational behaviors. The call to sustainable development has fed the fear of scarcity, while failing to mobilize decision-makers to attend to either the environmental or the social justice impacts of their choices. It may therefore be time to set aside the concept of sustainable development. International law can never be fully dissociated from its commitment to international commerce nor freed of its originary biases. Despite its inherent flaws, biases and limitations, however, international law nonetheless offers an aspirational space of hope, which must not be disdained but appropriated.

I SCARCITY, NEED, AND CONSUMPTION

The idea of scarcity seems strangely familiar to those of us living amidst plenty in the affluent regions of the world. At a time when human beings in developed countries, at all income levels, are enjoying levels of consumption unimaginable even to our grandparents, and orders of magnitude greater than our peers in developing countries,[9] we still worry about scarcity. Scarcity, we feel, is always just around the corner. Even as we stand in the well-stocked aisles of a

---

[9] See William E. Rees, "Ecological Footprints and Appropriated Carrying Capacity: What Urban Economics Leaves out," *4 Env't & Urbanization* 121–30 (1992), and Mathis Wackernagel, *What We Use and What We Have: Ecological Footprint and Ecological Capacity*, Center for Sustainability Studies, Universidad Anahuac de Xalapa, Mexico (1999).

typical supermarket, we are ready to believe that scarcity is a perpetual condition of human existence. Privileged as we are, we are restless, concerned with running out, with "not-enough."[10]

What are we to make of this intimate presence of scarcity in our lives and how does it affect our choices? In the next section, I will argue that the post-1992 call for sustainable development, with its emphasis on limits and constraints, tapped into and exacerbated the fear of scarcity, and thus contributed to the rash of binge development. In this section, I will first explore the concept of scarcity and its history. On the one hand, scarcity is constructed and culturally specific. In the West, its dominant sense was forged alongside the industrial revolution and modernity, and became associated with the imperative to foment a consumer society. On the other hand, the human experience of scarcity is powerful, and in connection with its cognates, need and desire, may be said to drive the creative impulse. Scarcity has been used to explain the establishment of the polis and the urgency of economic growth. It has been used to justify international commerce and the appropriation of distant lands and resources, and it has served as the cornerstone of classical economics in the form of the scarcity postulate. In this section then, I explore the nexus between scarcity and consumption and the continuing primacy of consumption in the current global economy. Finally, I reflect on the consumer as citizen.

---

[10] There is a growing literature in consumer studies that addresses the phenomenon of the insatiable consumer from a variety of points of view. For a fascinating and nuanced exploration of consumer desire see generally R. W. Belk, G. Ger, and S. Askegaard, "The Fire of Desire: A Multisited Inquiry Into Consumer Passion," *Journal of Consumer Research*, 30 (2003), pp. 326–51. We have become a society of hoarders. At the household level consumers in North America stock up on everything, from preferred foodstuffs, to toilet paper and shampoo; even though a run to the nearby well-stocked supermarket is part of their weekly routine. The result is waste and the experience of never having enough storage space. According to a recent World Bank Report, North Americans waste food at a rate of 1520 calories per person, per day, on average, 61% of which is lost at the consumption stage – that is, it rots in the refrigerator. See Food Price Watch Issue 16 (2014) graph at 7, www.worldbank.org/content/dam/Worldbank/document/Poverty%20documents/FPW%20Feb%202014%20final.pdf.

That scarcity has become an ever-present concern even in the midst of affluence and plenty is a relatively new phenomenon. Indeed, the notion of scarcity was, according to Nicholas Xenos, born with modernity.[11] Not that hunger, insufficiency of clothing, or lack of adequate housing were unknown prior to the modern age. That some human beings have suffered from the inability to fulfill basic needs throughout history is indisputable. That cyclical famines have afflicted human societies is well attested even in the earliest written sources. Rather, Xenos's point is that the idea that scarcity is a perpetual state of the human condition is a modern idea and can be traced to the industrial revolution beginning in the eighteenth century. The industrial revolution was characterized by a newfound ability to harness energy, the invention of labor-saving machines, and the development of new modalities of transport that made markets more accessible. Fed by the fortunes made possible by foreign trade and colonization, and by the influx of natural resources brought to Europe from distant lands starting in the seventeenth century, this period saw the transition from an artisanal and subsistence-agriculture-based economy to automated production and large-scale agriculture. Already in the seventeenth century the East Indian trade, which too often resulted in intermittent gluts of similar goods flooding local markets, had produced an urgent need to expand demand for luxury items. With the industrial revolution leading to mass manufactured goods whose production required significant up-front investment, it became evident that consistent demand would need to be stimulated. The lack of consistent demand for any given product meant that manufacture would come to a standstill. To avoid economic stagnation, new markets would need to be developed, and that meant creating new needs and desires across larger sectors of society and geographies.[12] Thus was born the middle class. Each

---

[11] *See* Nicholas Xenos, *Scarcity and Modernity* (1989) [Hereinafter Xenos, *Scarcity and Modernity*]. Hans Achterhuis, "Scarcity and Sustainability," in *Global Ecology: A New Arena of Political Conflict*, W. Sachs (ed.) (1993) [Hereinafter *Global Ecology*], pp. 104–16 [Hereinafter Achterhuis: "Scarcity and Sustainability"] makes a similar point.

[12] See John Kenneth Galbraith, *The Affluent Society* (1998), p. 124 et seq.

newly created need then added to scarcity pressures on the producers, who needed to procure more materials, more labor, more energy, factories, warehouses, and so forth. Each new need created thus generated scarcity. In order to keep the engines humming, every need fulfilled would have to open up new possibilities of other needs and desires to be fulfilled, in an endless cycle. Thus was born the consumer society.

Scarcity, as Xenos reminds us, is a culturally determined construct.[13] Scarcity in the modern sense is decoupled from what we might agree are basic material human needs. Indeed basic material human needs are few, and as Shakespeare's Lear exclaims, unless we allow human beings "more than nature needs," we reduce human life to mere bio-life, or in his terms: "Man's life's as cheap as beasts."[14] Once we get beyond the basic material requirements for the continuance of bio-life, however, the range of possible needs expands infinitely. What is experienced as a need in one cultural context, is not necessarily so in another time or place. What should count as a need, and the relative importance of competing needs, will also be subject to contestation. While our intuition about scarcity suggests that it relates in some way to limits or finitude, scarcity depends neither on material finitude nor on availability as such.[15] Finitude, rather, becomes relevant only in respect of a perceived need, and only in the context of actual or imagined competition for a thing. Only that which we desire (and that we imagine others to desire) can be experienced as scarce. Thus, what constitutes scarcity is not finitude but the fear of unfulfilled desire, and the intensity of mimetic desire renders scarcity more acute.

---

[13] See Xenos, *Scarcity & Modernity*.

[14] See William Shakespeare, *King Lear*, (Act 2, sc. 4) and the epigraph of this chapter.

[15] On the construction of scarcity see Luks, and also Lyla Mehta, "The Scare, Naturalization and Politicization of Scarcity" in *Limits to Scarcity*. See also generally Xenos, "Scarcity & Modernity." For a discussion of the mechanisms by which scarcity is created by influencing the relationship between "demand end-uses" and sources of supply, see Lakshman Yapa, "Improved Seeds and Constructed Scarcity," in Richard Peet and Michael Watts (eds.), *Liberation Ecologies: Environment, Development, Social Movements* (1996), pp. 69–85. [Hereinafter *Liberation Ecologies*].

The modern notion of scarcity, then, was born not out of the fact of finitude of a thing or its not-being, but rather out of an exacerbated state of frustrated desire, or the anticipation of such.[16] The idea that we live in a perpetual state of scarcity (as a condition of human existence) was a response to the proliferation of needs in modernity: A proliferation whose genesis can be traced back to the modern economy and its dependence on the restless, ever-desirous consumer. The modern economy may have invented the notion of scarcity, and engendered a new way of being-in-the-world as consumer, but it did so by taking advantage of one of humankind's defining characteristics. Indeed, one characteristic that distinguishes human beings, as a species, from other animals is our capacity to generate new material needs and our ability to devise the means to fulfill those needs. Human beings, unlike other animals, are not satisfied with fulfilling the most basic biophysical needs. Once these inescapable fundamental needs are met, we create entirely new needs. While it might be argued that only the few basic needs are real needs, and that everything beyond that is mere superfluous want and that we can do without, this does not tally with human experience. New wants become needs, and are experienced as needs. They may not be necessary to life itself, but they do become necessary in the context of our conception of how we want to live. This need-generating characteristic of human beings may seem problematic when we observe the hyper-consuming endpoint to which affluent societies have arrived, but it must also be recognized as the engine of human creativity and imagination.[17] The capacity to continuously generate new needs and the ability to devise the means to fulfill them has been the condition of what is called human progress and civilization.[18] The

---

[16] A recent example of a consumer scare occurred after the announcement by the company Hostess that it was filing for bankruptcy. See Parija Kavilanz, "Twinkies hoarding begins!" CNN Money, Nov. 17, 2012, at http://money.cnn.com/2012/11/16/news/companies/twinkies-hoarding-hostess/.

[17] The relationship often seems to run in the opposite direction as new needs are manufactured by an industry in search of an outlet for their product while the art of marketing specialists is to create desire.

[18] See Gilbert Rist, *The History of Development: From Western Origins to Global Faith* (1997). [Hereinafter *History of Development*].

restlessness and dissatisfaction that human beings suffer from, it turns out, is also a key source of their achievement. This may be, in part, what Freud was getting at, when he famously suggested that discontent was inescapably at the heart of civilization.[19]

While the modern economy tapped into the human tendency never to be satisfied, and fed mimetic desire by multiplying the range of things that people could have and therefore could be induced to want, the root of the problem arose out of an essential human characteristic: the creative ability to generate new needs and the capacity to fulfill them. That this fundamentally creative impulse could over time serve to feed the experience of scarcity was perhaps inevitable. Once discovered, the open-ended notion of scarcity was naturalized and universalized. Scarcity became the context for theoretical reflection.

Preoccupation with the universal condition of scarcity influenced philosophical and political thought in a variety of ways, and gave powerful shape and impetus to the emerging science of economics in the eighteenth century. Taken as fact, the universal condition of scarcity could be understood as a deficiency of nature left-to-herself. Without the active and industrious intervention of man, nature was, it turned out, lacking. The state of nature was a state of scarcity. Since nature alone could not supply human needs, then it was the duty of humans to make nature produce more by subduing the earth and bringing her under cultivation. The urgency of scarcity made the

---

[19] Sigmund Freud, *Civilization and Its Discontents* (1929). Freud's insight was that discontent was not an aberration but a necessary corollary of civilization. In his view, human beings seek happiness, which means they seek experiences of intense pleasure on the one hand and aim to eliminate pain and discomfort on the other. Intense pleasure, however, could be experienced only from the satisfaction of pent-up need and waned quickly. Meanwhile, there were many sources of suffering. Civilization, according to Freud, is a Faustian bargain; civilization is human's destiny, the chosen means to reduce the sources of suffering, but in exchange it demands that humans curb their natural tendency to aggression (and give up their freedom to satisfy their pleasures freely.) The means devised by culture to curb aggression is a heightening of guilt. Since civilization can never fully eliminate suffering, human beings experience a sense of frustration, which translates into general discontent.

continued existence of uncultivated, unmodified, and therefore unproductive nature akin to a moral wrong. The preoccupation with scarcity thus provided moral justification for the appropriation of empty (mostly foreign) lands, empty because they were either not used or too lightly used. Furthermore, the universal and perpetual state of scarcity in nature became part of a common narrative about how people came to form political communities.[20] The transition from the original state of nature to the organization within polities was driven by the need to ensure security of possessions in a world where there was not enough and where the strong needed to be restrained from appropriating that which belonged to another. In a world of scarcity, property rules and contract rules became essential. A fusion of these two themes became the basis for the powerful new idea that the role of the sovereign and the purpose of political organization was to address the ever threatening reality of scarcity by managing the economy in order to grow it. Economic growth became the objective of all properly governed states.

The modern universal open-ended notion of scarcity may have been discovered in the eighteenth century in the context of an economy that needed to stimulate demand, but as we have seen, its existence was easily projected backwards in time. Meanwhile, the notion of boundless and limitless need became a cornerstone of neo-classical economic thought, in the guise of the scarcity postulate.[21] Indeed, economists in the eighteenth century theorized that rational choice was a function of scarcity. In a world without scarcity, presumably, no choice would need to be made as you could have it all. In the context of scarcity, on the other hand, there were insufficient means available, so choices between possible alternative uses

---

[20] For the argument that Hobbes and Locke both used the idea of scarcity to support their theories about the origin and nature of political communities see Achterhuis, "Scarcity and Sustainability."

[21] See Xenos, *Scarcity and Modernity*. For an incisive critique of the scarcity postulate see Karl Polanyi, "The Economy as Instituted Process," in K. Polanyi, C. M. Arensberg and H. W. Pearson (eds), *Trade and Market in the Early Empires: Economies in History and Theory* (1957). [Hereinafter "Economy as Instituted Process"].

would need to be made. Such choices would be driven by the fact of scarcity and alternative use options, and would be determined by the decision maker's preferences. Thus, value (and ultimately price) in a market economy would be based on the graded preferences of consumers, indicated by their choices, in a state of scarcity.[22] Because classical economics sought to distinguish itself from moral or political philosophy and to present itself as scientific and objective (and therefore ostensibly value neutral), it did not concern itself with the substantive basis of the actual choices. Its formal definition of rationality required only that the means chosen correspond to a stated end. Formal rationality had nothing to say about the choice of ends, treating them as all equally valid. Thus, within the field of economics, scarcity became devoid of moral valence. The discovered fact of scarcity did not inform a particular attitude about proper allocation or distribution of means, nor did it serve to encourage a pro-conservation-of-resources, anti-waste stance. The sole function of scarcity within the science of economics was to serve as the context and driver of choice.[23]

The idea of open-ended scarcity clearly has had a sweeping trajectory since its emergence in the eighteenth century and has left an indelible imprint on many fields and practices that characterize modern life. As we have seen, it is embedded in economic orthodoxy and there gave shape to the rational man of the economists; it is the substratum of the modern faith in consumption-led economic growth; it has provided fodder for the utility value view of nature; it has lent credence to the claim that the state must have a role in managing the economy; and it has bolstered the case for international commerce. The claim that scarcity (and therefore open-ended scarcity) is a culturally determined social construct, while useful and in some ways liberating, must be approached with caution. Social constructions may be malleable, but their hold can be powerful. The

---

[22] Economists later recognized that scarcity also responds to changes in price and affects supply in myriad ways.

[23] Polanyi makes the case for substantive rationality, pointing out that the choice of ends depends on values unrelated to economic logic; see "Economy as Instituted Process," p. 246.

power of scarcity arises not only because it is now entrenched in our modern mindset, but because it builds upon a vital human faculty and attaches to a human experience. As already discussed earlier, while the modern economy actively encouraged the proliferation of new wants and manufactured needs and was responsible for the invention of open-ended scarcity, nonetheless the capacity for new-need creation is an important human faculty.

Indeed, the human experience of want or scarcity has both bio-physiological and psychological dimensions that must also be taken into account.[24] The experience of scarcity is akin to an experience of pain. Recent research suggests that it has a tendency to produce two contradictory effects: On the one hand, scarcity concentrates the mind, as the urgency of addressing scarcity results in the falling away of minor distractions. On the other hand, scarcity has a distracting effect, for the acute thoughts and feelings brought up by the experience of scarcity intrude unwanted and keep us preoccupied in the midst of life's other activities and pursuits. Thus, according to economist Sendhil Mullainathan and psychologist Eldar Shafir, of *Scarcity: Why Having Too Little Means So Much*, scarcity can be shown to produce both a tunnel vision effect and a loss of bandwidth (a bandwidth tax).[25]

The global economy today is more complex and interconnected than at any time in history. Diverse economic systems co-exist within single polities, reflecting the continuation and adaptation of traditional economic practices alongside participation in globally driven economic networks that are characterized by intersecting international flows of natural resources (including energy), goods, services, investments, financial instruments, and remittances. The

---

[24] See Sendhil Mullainathan and Eldar Shafir, *Scarcity: Why Having Too Little Means So Much* (2013). The authors' objective is to study what happens to the mind under conditions of scarcity "when we feel we have too little." They conclude that scarcity is not just a physical constraint, but rather produces a universal mindset with important consequences on our choices: "Scarcity captures our attention, and this provides a narrow benefit ... But more broadly, it costs us: we neglect other concerns." *Scarcity*, p. 15.

[25] Ibid. For a discussion of the tunneling effect, see p. 19 et seq.; for a discussion of the bandwidth tax effect, see p. 38 et seq.

pervasiveness of these global flows and their magnitude has been
enabled by the emergence of the legal and institutional regimes
needed to support them. The global volume of trade in goods and
natural resources has grown dramatically in the past twenty years,[26]
reflecting not only an increase in end point consumption, but also a
transformation of both global supply chain and manufacturing practices.[27] International trade has contributed significantly to the overall
growth of the world economy. Increasingly, however, wealth and
national GDP are dependent on the gains from the various forms of
global capital flows and cross-national investments. At the same time,
growth in many developed country economies has been driven by
increased attention to the services sector, including the knowledge
and intellectual property sector, which are characterized by low
material and low energy intensity.

Consumption, in its economic sense of exchange of goods and
services in markets, is clearly the engine of the modern global
economy. Arguably, given the growing importance of financial flows
and the services industry, consumption, in its biophysical sense of
human transformation of materials and energy, might be thought to
be diminishing in relative importance. Some financial flows are
undoubtedly many layers removed from the material underpinnings
that ultimately sustain them, and fortunes may be made despite the
absence of a material referent: mortgage-backed financial instruments
packages, and currency exchange traders come to mind, as does the
avid speculation in virtual cryptocurrencies such as Bitcoins.

[26] See "Information Note: Facts and Figures on Commodities and Commodities
Trade," UNCTAD/Press/IN/2013/2.
[27] The total volume of trade reflects not only the traditional raw material and end
product flows but all the intermediate flows. These intermediate flows reflect
supply chains and manufacturing practices that have gotten increasingly
complex, as the sources of raw materials, components and sub-assemblies
have become more dispersed and further removed from the locus of final
assembly or production. The drivers for the dispersal and removal, include
outsourcing less important functions to focus on core competency,
outsourcing or simply relocating production to take advantage of lower costs
elsewhere, and outsourcing with the objective of variabilizing costs especially
in the case of cyclical businesses.

While it might appear that postmodern humans have discovered nonconsumptive ways of growing the economy, however, it remains the case that biophysical consumption is the lifeblood of the modern economy. Both national and global economies remain fundamentally dependent on continued and increased biophysical consumption. Foreign direct investment capital continues to seek investment opportunities in natural resource and energy extraction, infrastructure development, and large-scale agricultural and manufacturing production. Data centers, such as Google's, are notoriously energy intensive.[28] Even virtual trading depends ultimately on environmentally significant consumption. Bitcoin "mining," for instance, requires the proper functioning of immense amounts of computing power, which in turn requires the physical existence of networks of computers (not to mention reliable energy grids). Each computer, of course, is itself a material object, requiring for its production not just human knowledge, skill, labor, and creativity but the four traditional elements of life: earth, wind, fire, and water. The material existence of each computer requires the nontrivial expenditure of energy, water, and natural resources as inputs and denotes the nontrivial release of pollutants, including greenhouse gases, toxics, and hazardous waste that were released into the atmosphere, the land, and the water in its manufacture. The production of each component part, in addition, requires the physical occupation of land, and the physical infrastructure associated with the various stages of mining, manufacturing, waste disposal and transportation. And, ultimately, each computer will reach the end of its usable life, again consuming energy in the disposal (and hopefully at least partial recycling) process before final remnants are burned or buried as waste.

We have become accustomed to hearing that consumer confidence is what is needed to get us out of the economic slump. When consumers are confident, it means they buy more, even if they have to borrow to do it, and those purchases drive economic growth. In addition to encouraging consumer spending in general, the other

---

[28] See "Google Details, and Defends, Its Use of Electricity," James Glanz, *New York Times,* September 8, 2011 at www.nytimes.com/2011/09/09/technology/google-details-and-defends-its-use-of-electricity.html?_r=0.

urgent economic objective is growing middle classes, who will discover new needs, spend and borrow, in emerging economies. As
Henry Ford discovered in the early twentieth century, one of the
most effective ways to stimulate demand is to transform through
marketing what was once a luxury item into a necessity, while
bringing down prices so that the item is within reach. Then, when
prices come down sufficiently, consumers learn to accept that things
do not last and will have to be discarded and replaced. Furthermore,
this fits with the new logic of desire. The rapid and still increasing
rate at which fashions change (clothing, home décor and furnish-
ings, toys) and new features and functionalities are introduced
(electronics, automobiles) is such that few people wait until a product is no longer serviceable, wearable, or usable before discarding
it.[29] In western societies,[30] it is no longer sufficient to have a single
television, computer, game console, music player, or phone in a
home: instead each room and each individual must be equipped
with the latest technology. The average footprint of new homes
continues to expand. Meanwhile, fruit and vegetables are never
out of season for they can be grown in any climatically appropriate
region and shipped in from halfway across the world. The market in
bottled water is lucrative even in cities where municipal water is safe,
clean, and readily available. The programmatic objective of increasing global demand for consumer items has become so familiar that
we hardly notice that it cannot possibly be compatible with the
general imperative of sustainable development.

The principle that in order to achieve sustainable development,
states should reduce and eliminate unsustainable patterns of production

[29] For a highly readable account of one shopper's confrontation with the reality
behind the addiction, see Elizabeth L. Cline, *Overdressed: The Shockingly High
Cost of Cheap Fashion* (2012).

[30] These trends are emulated by the wealthy and the rising middle classes around
the world. For an optimistic account of how Asian global consumerism is
poised to make up for the shortfall of post-crisis U.S. consumerism see "The
Emerging Middle Class in Developing Countries," OECD Working Paper
Series (2010). For a more nuanced account of the differences among so-called
middle classes see Christophe Jaffrelot and Peter van der Veer, *Patterns of
Middle Class Consumption in India and China* (2008).

and consumption was articulated in the Rio Declaration,[31] and further developed in Agenda 21.[32] The issue of the efforts needed to achieve sustainable consumption and production was addressed with some regularity in international, regional and national fora, following Rio. The emphasis was on increasing the efficiency of resource use and reducing the pollution intensity of consumption and production.[33] Eco-efficiency and energy-efficiency became the preferred objectives. Technological advances were assumed to be a major part of the solution, while some placed great hope in the emergence of a more eco-friendly economics that incorporated negative environmental externalities and lost ecosystem services into traditional cost-benefit analysis. Nonetheless, little real progress was made, and unsustainable consumption and production continued on an upward trajectory in both developed and developing countries. In 2002, at the World Summit on Sustainable Development, in Johannesburg, the need to change unsustainable patterns of consumption and production was identified as one of the three overarching objectives and essential requirements of sustainable development.[34] Since that time,

---

[31] "To achieve sustainable development and a higher quality of life for all people, States should reduce and eliminate unsustainable patterns of production and consumption and promote appropriate demographic policies." Principle 8, Rio Declaration on Environment and Development.

[32] See Changing Consumption Patterns, Chapter 4, Agenda 21. The chapter emphasizes that the issue of changing consumption patterns is very broad and is therefore addressed throughout Agenda 21. Ibid., section 4.2.

[33] "Working Together Towards Sustainable Development: The OECD Experience," OECD 2002, p. 27. The report makes it clear that OECD countries have made little progress towards decoupling pollution and resource use from economic growth. In 2002, according to the OECD figures, with 18% of the global population, OECD countries accounted for 80% of world GDP and consumed 50% of world energy supplies. The OECD report also notes that while energy and some natural resources use is growing at a slower rate than GDP in some OECD countries, suggesting efficiency gains, absolute levels of use have continued to grow. Ibid., pp. 26–7.

[34] See Johannesburg Declaration on Sustainable Development, A/CONF.199/20, Chapter1, Resolution 1, Johannesburg, September 2002, p. 11. "Poverty eradication, changing consumption and production patterns and protecting and managing the natural resource base for economic and social development

sustainable consumption and production has become a field of inquiry and the concern of international governmental and non-governmental organizations.[35] In some respects, the blossoming of corporate social responsibility as an expected public component of a corporation's mission and commitment might be considered to be one of the field's successes. Small victories, aside, however, there is little to show for over twenty years of international "commitment" to the pursuit of sustainable consumption and production. On the contrary, across the world, environmental considerations are rarely, if ever, allowed to stand in the way of or even more than minimally alter plans for increasing production and consumption.[36] Eco-efficiency and energy-efficiency gains are lauded by environmentalists, politicians

are overarching objectives of and essential requirements for sustainable development." See also Chapter II of the Plan of Implementation of the World Summit on Sustainable Development.

[35] See for example *Trends in Sustainable Development: Towards Sustainable Consumption and Production*, UNDESA (2010); see also *Assessing the Environmental Impacts of Consumption and Production: Priority Products and Materials*, UNEP (2010).

[36] A recent example was the announcement by Australia that it was going to permit the dumping of 3 million cubic meters of dredged mud within the Great Barrier Reef Protected Zone in order to widen and deepen a shipping lane as part of an expansion project at port Abbot Point to facilitate the shipment of minerals from its mining sector. The risks that such a development might pose to the viability of the already stressed sensitive ecosystem of the UNESCO World Heritage Site were rapidly downplayed by politicians and project proponents alike, for whom the certainty of additional jobs and profits in an accelerated form simply overshadowed any other consideration. The attitude of the Governor of Queensland was straightforward, and could be summarized as: "It's the economy, stupid!" That the mineral deposits, mined at a slower rate or transported in smaller vessels, might provide longer-term social and environmental benefits was simply not relevant. That the Great Barrier Reef was a unique ecosystem that once destroyed could never be recovered, was of little concern. See Sonali Paul, "Australia permits dredge dumping near Great Barrier Reef for major coal port," Reuters, January 31, 2014 at www.reuters.com/article/2014/01/31/us-australia-reef-permit-idUSBREA0U06W20140131. See also Brian Handwerk, "Australia to Dump Dredged Sand in Great Barrier Reef Waters, Adding to Site's Mounting Woes," *National Geograpahic*, January 31, 2014 at

and corporate shareholders, so long as these gains can be shown to provide an economic return or at least cost neutrality via reduced direct and perhaps indirect production or transportation costs. Under this model, particularly when producers share a portion of the savings, everyone appears to be better off. It is a win-win situation. Producers can make their products more cheaply, and consumers may pay less. Meanwhile, if more can be made with less (the new sustainable consumption standard), then producers can increase output and more consumers will be able to acquire the goods. In addition, if consumers spend less on one item, they can be encouraged to spend what they "saved" on some other consumer product or service. The logic of consumption-led economic growth is thus preserved.

Sustainable consumption as currently defined and promoted has simply become an integral component of a global economic growth strategy. It essentially sidesteps the goal of reducing overall global consumption in favor of the efficiency goal of pursuing more with less. While the inequity of the relative consumption patterns and practices between have and have-not states is sometimes alluded to, the proposed solution is to increase consumption in the developing world. But this must be done without threatening the high standard of living in developed states, and indeed without risk to their hopes for continued improvement. The assumption is that the developed countries must take the lead in achieving efficiency gains, but not that they should reduce consumption towards levels in keeping with their share of the global population. On the contrary, the prevailing understanding of sustainable consumption is shaped by the dominant theory of how the developing world is to achieve economic growth and raise standards of living of their people: produce more and export more, until a sufficiently robust middle class develops to generate meaningful levels of in-country consumption. Which of course means that the developed world must continue to increase its consumption even as it is pursuing efficiency gains. While developing countries do worry about what they view as the excessive and inequitable

http://news.nationalgeographic.com/news/2014/01/140131-great-barrier-reef-dredge-unesco-science-coal-australia/.

consumption of energy and natural resources by developed states, they are caught in a contradiction. Their most common complaint is not that developed countries consume too much, but that they do not buy enough from them (at high enough prices).

It is no secret that one of the ways in which developed countries have achieved some degree of local improvement in terms of slowing environmental degradation is by shifting dirtier industries and manufacturing operations to developing countries. A significant proportion of what is consumed in developed countries is now produced in developing countries. There are many competing accounts of how and why this transformation has taken place, each placing the emphasis on different factors that have driven the decision to shift manufacturing away from its historical home. Clearly lower labor costs as well as less onerous environmental and other regulatory regimes have contributed to the decisions to relocate production assets or outsource, as have the cost advantages of specialization and the many tax and other incentives commonly provided. Another significant contributing factor, however, has been the growing intolerance of people and communities in the developed world for dirty and disruptive industries close to their neighborhoods.[37]

Whatever the underlying causes for the dispersal of manufacturing operations, the net result has been an exacerbation of the dynamic of consumption: the geographical and political separation of the environmental and social harms, and risks, attendant to production from the actual consumption of the object.[38] The end consumer neither has to suffer the harms nor bear the risks attributable to the production of the object of desire. The local (but far away) harms to air and

---

[37] After going out of their way to woo the company that makes the popular Sriracha hot sauce to locate to their town, Irwindale residents decided that they could not tolerate the odors; see "Sriracha shortage? California holds the hot sauce, and foodies are fuming," Patrik Jonsson, *Christian Science Monitor*, December 13, 2013, at www.csmonitor.com/USA/2013/1213/ .UvESdlb7TlA.email.

[38] For a critique of the limits of some positive trends in consumer practices, see Raymond L. Bryant and Michael K. Goodman, "Consuming Narratives: The Political Ecology of 'Alternative' Consumption," *Transactions of the Institute of British Geographers*, New Series vol. 29, No. 3 (September 2004), pp. 344–66.

water quality, water and land degradation do not come home to the consumer. Given the geographic (and regulatory) distances between the producer, the intermediate producer-consumers and the end consumer, not only are the local negative externalities not borne by the end consumers' society but they are occluded. The end consumer, if he or she thinks about it at all, simply assumes that elsewhere producers must be subject to an appropriate amount of environmental and social regulation and oversight. The end consumer, for whom the act of consumption often produces only a fleeting pleasure and for whom each act of consumption is merely a transitory event, situated between manifold other acts of consumption, completed or anticipated, is usually blissfully unaware of the social and environmental impacts of production and experiences no sense of responsibility or culpability.[39] For most consumers, the primary concern relates to the asking price of the object at the moment it will pass into their hands, and their eager hope is that they can acquire it as cheaply as possible. The idea that they are getting a superb bargain, not only because the price is low but because the price does not reflect the environmental and social externalities created in the object's production, does not cross their mind. That communities in developing countries, who are bearing the local impacts of environmental and social externalities of production, are in effect subsidizing the cost of the object in the consumer's hand is even further from their thoughts. The ongoing practice of easy consumption cannot bear so much weight. Occasionally, a dramatic story of an egregious case of environmental or social harm resulting from production for export rises to the level of international

---

[39] Spectacular catastrophes that receive media attention such as the 2013 collapse of the Bangladesh factory buildings result in some momentary consumer concern and soul searching, and may even trigger action by the brand name companies who fear consumer defection. However, there is little evidence that such concern rise to the level of putting our consumption practices into question. The assumption remains that all that is needed is better regulation and monitoring. See also Steven Greenhouse, "U.S. Retailers Decline to Aid Factory Victims in Bangladesh," *New York Times* November 11, 2013, at www.nytimes.com/2013/11/23/business/international/us-retailers-decline-to-aid-factory-vi/ctims-in-bangladesh.html.

news.[40] The collapse of the poorly constructed factory in Savar, Bangladesh, that led to more than 1,100 deaths is a recent example.[41] Such stories can be spun as failures of the producing state, whose lax regulations or inadequate enforcement is faulted, and whose culturally embedded practices of corruption have yet to be eradicated. Such stories can lead to some degree of mobilization and a call to regulatory reform by activists in developed countries who wield the power of consumption (the power to withhold consumption). But, as is well understood, in the end the only way to address any local deficiencies in workplace and environmental protections requires an increase in the cost of production (for higher wages, safe buildings and equipment and the infrastructure necessary to protect the environment from degradation, including proper waste disposal and air and water treatment facilities). The end consumers of a t-shirt produced in Bangladesh may wish that the Bangladeshis would do the right thing by their people, but when acquiring their next t-shirt they will likely choose the cheaper item (at the same quality point).

The geographic separation of production, intermediate production, and the end consumer also complicates the challenge of attributing the share of natural resource and energy consumption across states. For instance, large-scale agriculture utilizes large quantities of fresh water for irrigation. If the product is grown for export, who should water use be accounted to, the producer or the consumer? When coal is burned to power the plant that supplies electricity to a manufacturing facility in China whose products are intended for export, who should the resulting greenhouse gas emissions be

---

[40] As Rob Nixon argues, the un-dramatic slow violence that is characteristic of much environmental devastation, rarely produces the kind of focused attention that can lead to mobilization in favor of policy changes. The challenge for those who suffer under the impacts of slow violence is to make the violence visible and urgent. See Nixon, *Slow Violence and the Environmentalism of the Poor* (2011).

[41] The Rana Plaza factory collapse in Savar, Bangladesh on April 24, 2013 left more than 1,100 people dead. See Jason Burke, "Bangladesh factory collapse leaves trail of shattered lives," June 6, 2013, *The Guardian* at www.theguardian.com/world/2013/jun/06/bangladesh-factory-building-collapse-community.

attributed to, the producer or the end consumer? There is no easy answer. Rees and others have documented the extent of the ecological footprint of urban areas in the developed world. Their work has dramatized the extent to which the lifestyle of urban dwellers in the developed world depends on the capacity to appropriate the ecosystem services and natural resource base of a much greater land base. The ecological footprint approach reminds developed country consumers of the extent of their privilege while highlighting the fact that the earth cannot supply the resources necessary to offer anything like a comparable lifestyle to the rest of the world's population. Nonetheless, as long as we remain locked into a consumption-driven model of global economic growth, the one policy response that is off limits is the commitment to consume less in absolute terms.

Consumers may be mobilized to choose greener products, fair trade products, or domestically manufactured products. They may be encouraged to spend a little more (if they have the means) to reduce the likelihood that indentured or child labor was used to manufacture their object of desire. They may be willing to join a boycott of a particular product to induce a producer to change their objectionable practices, but their overall level of consumption will remain undiminished. Consumers may transfer their allegiance among products in response to concerns about particular environmental or social harms, but in the process they also feed the experience of their agency, as the power of consumption.

Our twenty-first-century societies have become societies of consumers. Indeed, the last few decades have seen the gradual substitution of the consumer as subject and agent in place of the political citizen as subject and agent. The seed for this transformation was planted by classical economics' adoption of the scarcity postulate. In classical economics, the scarcity postulate, which assumes a perpetual state of scarcity and the existence of competing means, was used to explain choice, and hence to set comparative value.[42] In the absence of scarcity no choice was necessary and nothing had value, for everything would be freely available. Consumers, in this model, were the

---

[42] See discussion at the beginning of Section I.

paradigmatic choice-makers, whose choices (driven by scarcity and competing means) determined the comparative value of things in markets. Economics, as we have seen, was agnostic as to the reasons underlying the preferences of the consumer. The consumer was always right, by virtue of being the one who chooses. As the centrality of consumption to the economy has grown, and as consumption itself has become an all-encompassing fact of daily life, the logic and terminology of the market have inexorably come to pervade all realms of human existence. All choices, in whatever domain, are now understood though the lens of consumption. The citizen-consumer has become the new subject and our agency is the power to choose. Through this transition, the space for the non-commoditized has shrunk. Everything, it appears, can now be expressed in monetary terms, even when we remain convinced that not everything should be subject to exchange for money-value. In our consumer-focused societies, the buyer-seller relationship has become the most familiar relationship, and by extension our sense of the duties and obligations we owe to each other and the state arises most naturally out of the consumer contract.

Meanwhile, human identity is increasingly constructed through the lens of consumption. Indeed, our consumer identity is now given concrete and visible shape through our participation in social media. Whatever the platform, when we create our online social media identity, we are invited to identify our likes and dislikes, and to link ourselves virtually to family, friends and followers. The object of all this self-identifying is to facilitate the production of community around consumption – communities that openly include providers who are themselves reshaped by signals of demand. Further, our online identities are, as is well known, mined for information whether intentionally provided or not, allowing vendors of all sorts to improve their ability to target potential customers.

The transition to the citizen-consumer has further reinforced the disenfranchisement of the poor and their communities. In a world of citizen-consumers, only consuming subjects have import, and the more they consume the more relevance (political clout) they have. From this perspective, those whose level of consumption is negligible, who do not move through the world as consumers, are liable to become invisible. Like land that lies unused or lightly used, humans whose consumption is negligible are viewed, from this perspective, as of no use. It is then possible to identify such people as "surplus people," people whose patterns of consumption do not amount to much. Surplus people can be ignored or displaced if they are in the way.[43] They must be transformed into useful consumers or disappear. In modern societies, then, the most effective strategy to gain political purchase is to re-characterize your communities as communities of consumption or, at the very least, of potential-consumption.

II SUSTAINABLE DEVELOPMENT, FEAR OF SCARCITY, AND BINGE DEVELOPMENT

> Growth has no set limits in terms of population or resource use beyond which lies ecological disaster. Different limits hold for the use of energy, materials, waste, and land ... But ultimate limits there are, and sustainability requires that long before these are reached, the world must ensure equitable access to the constrained resource and reorient technological efforts to relieve the pressure.
>
> (*Our Common Future*, 1987)[44]

By 1987,[45] the accumulation of scientifically reliable knowledge pointing to severe (and potentially catastrophic) local and global

---

[43] For a recent case of invisibility and the "empty" land syndrome see Lorenzo Cotula, *The Great African Land Grab? Agricultural Investments and the Global Food System* (2013) [Hereinafter *Great African Land Grab*], p. 84. For an account of the irrelevance of entire communities in the face of hydroelectric dam development see Arundhati Roy, *The Greater Common Good*.

[44] See World Commission on Environment and Development, *Our Common Future* (1987), p. 45. [Hereinafter *Our Common Future*]

[45] I highlight the year 1987, because that is the date of the publication of the World Commission on Environment and Development's influential report *Our Common Future*, a.k.a. the Brundtland Report. The Commission is widely credited with having popularized the concept of sustainable development and the Report is the source of the most frequently cited definition of sustainable development: "[D]evelopment that meets the needs of the present without compromising the ability of future generations to meet their own needs." Ibid., p. 43.

effects of environmental degradation arising out of human activity had given rise to a general scientific consensus that the world had entered a new era, now often termed the Anthropocene.[46] The accumulating evidence of risk was sufficient to attract the attention of a broad array of policymakers, including those engaged in promoting economic development and others committed to social justice issues. New and conflicting perspectives were brought to bear on the environmental concerns. Caught up in the enthusiasm of post cold-war globalization rhetoric of the 1990s, the environment took on a global dimension. In the crucible of the international policy making machine, environmental issues were refashioned and reframed. The emphasis shifted from the risks posed to the world's critical ecosystems by human productive activity, to the risks posed to continued economic growth by vulnerable ecosystems and finite resources. Warnings about degradation of the environment and over-exploitation of natural resources and sinks, were funneled into pre-existing constructs of North-South relationships, and lent new rhetorical force to old claims of structural and historical inequities, exemplified by the debate over the proposed New International Economic Order.[47] The result was the principle of sustainable development endorsed with great fanfare at the Earth Summit in 1992.[48]

[46] The term Anthropocene describes a new geological epoch, which takes account of the scale of the impact of human activity on the natural world since the industrial revolution, an impact that has effected geologic-scale change. See W. Steffen et al., 'A Global Perspective on the Anthropocene', (October 2011) 334 *Science* pp. 34–5.

[47] Beginning in the mid-seventies developing countries, many of them newly enfranchised, made a concerted attempt to restructure the international economic system. *See* Mohammed Bedjaoui, *Towards a New International Economic Order* (1979).

[48] The United Nations Conference on Environment and Development, UNCED, took place from June 3 to June 14, 1992, in Rio de Janeiro, Brazil. Delegations from 178 countries, heads of state of more than 100 countries, and representatives of more than 1,000 non-governmental organizations attended the meetings. UNCED documents are available at www.ciesin.org/datasets/unced/unced.html.

Sustainable development was and is a contested concept. At a minimum, however, sustainable development requires that at every level of government and decision-making, policies, projects, and plans be consciously and transparently assessed in terms of their likely and potential effects on the three values of environmental protection, economic development, and social equity. Since UNCED, the principle of sustainable development has been embedded in international law. Numberless international treaties assert it as an objective or a guiding principle. International soft law is replete with its presence. It has become a staple not only in the international realm but also at the national and municipal level, and is routinely invoked by corporations and civil society. International courts and arbitration panels have alluded to it and interpreted its implications, as have numberless domestic courts. Indeed, it has been argued that sustainable development is so ubiquitous as to have emerged as a new principle of customary international law.[49] This apparent success, however, belies a decisive double failure of implementation: the failure to staunch the wasteful and ecologically destructive practices of economic production, and the failure to correct the disproportionate impact on the poor and marginalized. In other words, neither the core value of environmental protection, nor that of social equity have been furthered. On the contrary, the environmental crisis has deepened, imposing ever-greater present and future risks on the world's most vulnerable populations.

The causes for this radical disjunction between expressed commitment to sustainable development and meaningful implementation have been much commented upon. There is no question that effective solutions to global and local environmental degradation are stymied

---

[49] See for example Nico Schrijver, *The Evolution of Sustainable Development in International Law: Inception, Meaning and Status* (2008) and Marie-Claire Cordonier Segger and Ashfaq Khalfan, *Sustainable Development Law: Principles, Practices, and Prospects* (2005). See also the Preamble of "ILA New Delhi Declaration of Principles of International Law Relating to Sustainable Development," UN doc. A/57/329, August 31, 2002. For a fascinating elaboration of the principle see Judge Weeramantry's separate opinion in the Gabcikovo-Nagymaros Project (*Hungary* v. *Slovakia*), 1997 *ICJ Reports* (September 25) 96–111.

by classic collective action problems and the slow violence of environmental harms.[50] However, in this section I wish to make a rather different point by focusing on the construct of scarcity and the fear of scarcity. My claim is that from the outset, the concept of sustainable development, with its forceful focus on globalization and equity issues, and its heavy emphasis on biophysical constraints and limits and contained within it the seeds that fed the latent fear of scarcity. Compounded by the anxiety and insecurity that characterized the beginning of the twenty-first century, this gnawing fear of scarcity, I argue, has not only undermined the will to act in furtherance of the agreed objectives of sustainable development, but has contributed to an outbreak of irrational over-consumption and binge development.

From its inception, one of the defining characteristics of the concept of sustainable development has been its global outlook and cosmopolitan orientation. There was a time when the environment, economic development, and social equity were thought to be the peculiar domains of local or national polities.[51] International attention was warranted in these arenas only in limited circumstances. In the case of trans-boundary resources or harms, for instance, or insofar as those states that had achieved high GDPs might be called on to contribute development aid to address underdevelopment or poverty

---

[50] Rob Nixon argues that the failure of politicians and policy makers to respond to and address severe environmental harms and risk is due in part to the fact that however significant, most of the harms of environmental degradation take place in an unspectacular way, diffused over broad geographical spaces and long periods of time, whereas political action and policy responses are generated by the spectacular. See Nixon, *Slow Violence*.

[51] This point is consistent with the argument made by Anghie, Pahuja, and Rist among others that the introduction of the concept of "development" by President Truman in 1944 and its subsequent deployment, must be understood as an attempt by the nations of the industrialized first world to continue to have access to the natural resources of the third world. See Antony Anghie, *Imperialism, Sovereignty and the Making of International Law* (2004) [Hereinafter *Imperialism*]; Sundhya Pahuja, *Decolonising International Law: Development, Economic Growth and the Politics of Universality* (2011) [Hereinafter *Decolonizing International Law*]; and Gilbert Rist, *The History of Development: From Western Origins to Global Faith* (1997). [Hereinafter *History of Development*].

in developing countries. Looking back, however, there is almost a sense of inevitability about the global framing of sustainable development. In the first place, the environment seemed to transcend political boundaries. Ecosystems could be shown to traverse multiple jurisdictions and neither the atmosphere nor the oceans could be physically partitioned. In both cases the harms and risks seemed uncontainable. Ocean acidification, the ozone hole and climate change, could all be constructed as global problems creating shared risks and needing global solutions.[52] The image of a shared biosphere implied that depleting fish stocks, destruction of biodiversity and loss of tropical forests were of common concern. Furthermore, the emergence of the concept of sustainable development coincided with the end of the Cold War, and the wave of optimism about new possibilities for international cooperation. The result was an aspirational call for a new form of global cooperation and solidarity in order, literally, to save the planet.[53] It was no accident that the Brundtland Report's official title was *Our Common Future*, and that so many reports issued since have emphasized the supposedly shared nature of our common interest in achieving sustainable development.[54]

---

[52] For a critique of the idea that risks are "shared" see Klaus M. Meyer-Abich, *Winners and Losers in Climate Change in Global Ecologies*, pp. 69–87. As the IPCC has made clear from the start, vulnerability to climate change risks is not distributed equally. See for example "Contribution of Working Group II to the Fourth Assessment Report of the Intergovernmental Panel on Climate Change," (2007) at https://ipcc.ch/publications_and_data/ar4/wg2/en/contents.html.

[53] The intention to adopt a global frame for sustainable development was apparent from the opening line of *Our Common Future*, which reads: "In the middle of the twentieth century, we saw our planet from space for the first time." *Our Common Future*, p. 1. This romanticized image was widely picked up and during the preparations for UNCED 1992 a failed attempt was made to turn it into a centerpiece of a proposed Earth Charter. For a brief account, see Ileana Porras, "The Rio Declaration: A New Basis for International Cooperation," in Philippe Sands (ed.), *Greening International Law* (1994).

[54] For the argument of globalism as hegemony see Wolfgang Sachs, *Global Ecology and the Shadow of Development in Global Ecology*, pp. 3–21 and p. 17 et seq. For the use of the image of earth as spaceship to emphasize the urgency of survival see Achterhuis, "Scarcity and Sustainability," p. 111.

Behind the globalizing gaze of sustainable development, however, lay a darker narrative: one that told of scarcity. Nature had once been envisaged as the site of limitlessness, and offered to the imagination plenty and abundance. Scarcity at home could always be offset from the plenty that resided elsewhere and was available to appropriation.[55] In its stead, sustainable development spoke of biophysical limits, natural constraints and vulnerable ecosystems. It spoke of needing multiple planets to sustain the growing economy on which depended the overconsumption-based lifestyles to which people in the North had become accustomed and to which many in the South aspired.[56] It was a narrative that emphasized that many of the natural resources on which our economies relied, were not, in fact, inexhaustible; a narrative that confronted us with the fact that even renewable resources, such as freshwater and fish stocks, could be exhausted; and warned that degradation of our land base could reduce our agricultural output, while unmitigated emission of greenhouse gases could lead to climate change and rising water levels. In the prosperous North, scarcity had been understood in economic theory as driver of consumer choice, or in experience as a temporary condition, which could always be resolved by finding a new source for the resource that was lacking. With the advent of the discourse of sustainable development, however, the possibility of a scarcity, which could not be offset, took shape. In the impoverished South, meanwhile, the fear of scarcity

---

[55] Ileana Porras, "Appropriating Nature: Commerce, Property and the Commodification of Nature in the Law of Nations," *Leiden Journal of International Law*, 27:3 (2014), pp. 641–60.

[56] "The single largest demand humanity puts on the biosphere is its carbon footprint, which has increased tenfold since 1961. The Ecological Footprint exceeds the earth's capacity to regenerate by 30%. Alternatively, 1.3 planets would be needed to stay within the planet's carrying capacity. This is another, simplified way of picturing planetary boundaries and ecosystem thresholds. Under a business-as-usual scenario, 2 planets would be required by 2030 to support the world's population. This assumes a continued unequal world with 15% of the population using 50% of the resources. World Wildlife Fund (WWF) estimates that three planets would be needed now if every citizen adopted the UK lifestyle, and five planets if they adopted the average North American lifestyle." UNDESA, *Trends*, p. 5.

became more acute as the avidity of the North for the world's finite resources became a threat.

The new narrative of finite resources, environmental degradation and scarcity within a global context also called forth the specter of large-scale immiseration.[57] Indeed, the world's poor, both present and future, and their essential needs were a central concern of the influential Brundtland Report. Its well-known definition of sustainable development refers twice to "needs," stating that "sustainable development is development that meets the *needs* of the present without compromising the ability of future generations to meet their own *needs*." [58] While the "needs" referred to in the definition appear to encompass all equally, so that each of us is able to assume that *my* needs are as relevant as anyone else's, this reading is belied by the clarification that "needs" should be read as a reference to the "essential needs of the world's poor, to which overriding priority should be given."[59] The world's poor are, of course, a familiar figure in the vast textual universe of UN sponsored reports, resolutions, declarations, treaties, and so forth. Indeed, in the post–World War II economic development era, the world's poor have inhabited the international policy agenda as a subject of consternation and an object of reform.[60] Their plight served to justify a host of increasingly intrusive programs and investment opportunities created by a new international

---

[57] In the SD literature, immiseration is causally connected to consequent social disturbances and ecological refugee flows. On the subject of environmental refugees see Diane C. Bates, "Environmental Refugees? Classifying Human Migrations Caused by Environmental Change," *Population & Environment*, 23:5 (2002), pp. 465–477. For a good summary of the recent challenge to the predictions regarding climate change refugees see Hannah Barnes, How many climate migrants will there be? BBC News September 1, 2013, at www.bbc.com/news/magazine-23899195.

[58] *Our Common Future* (emphasis added).

[59] Ibid. This theme was picked up in the Rio Declaration on Environment and Development, which refers to "the essential task of eradicating poverty as an indispensable requirement for sustainable development," Principle 5.

[60] For a compelling account of the discovery of poverty and the invention of the construct of underdevelopment in the post World War II era see Arturo Escobar, *Encountering Development: The Making and Unmaking of the Third World* (1995).

development industry, whose headquarters included the UN, the IMF and the World Bank.[61] Until the advent of sustainable development, however, the world's poor might be an object of reform, a target of missionary zeal and ideological influence, or pose a challenge to our conscience (and our pocketbook), but they did not pose a threat to our way of life. While the Bretton Woods Institutions led the reform effort, the UN, standing in for the conscience of the international community, periodically insisted that wealthy states had a moral obligation to share some small portion of their abundance with the world's poor, in the form of development aid, but it was understood that this voluntary aid would be coming out of a comfortable surplus.[62]

Sustainable development cast the world's poor in a radically different light. Their needs, always pressing, were now pressing in a finite and constrained material world. According to the endless studies and reports of the experts, it appeared that humanity had already hit, or was about to hit, the biophysical limits of the planet and was at risk of inducing abrupt global environmental changes.[63] Ecosystems

---

[61] For a series of accounts of the function of the Third World and its discovered backwardness and poverty in the emergence of international organizations and the development project, see Antony Anghie, "Colonialism and the Birth of International Institutions: The Mandate System of the Law of Nations," in *Imperialism*, p. 115 et seq.; Pahuja, *Decolonizing International Law*, and Balakrishnan Rajagopal, *International Law From Below: Development, Social Movements and Third World Resistance* (2003).

[62] The duty to cooperate to promote economic and social progress and development is recognized in Chapter IX on International Economic and Social Co-operation of the UN Charter, which is the basis for the UN's action in the field, including most recently the Millennium Development Goal 1 to eradicate extreme poverty (MDG 1). For a lively account of the history of the West's efforts to help the world's poor see William Easterly, *The White Man's Burden: Why the West's Efforts to Aid the Rest Have Done So Much Ill and So Little Good* (2006). Overseas Development Aid (ODA) commitment targets of 0.7 % of GDP, first agreed to in 1970 and repeatedly reaffirmed since, have been met by only a handful of countries. See www.unmillenniumproject.org/press/07.htm.

[63] The concept of "planetary boundaries" has recently been introduced to highlight that we cannot know the point at which the limits will have been exceeded with precision. "Planetary boundaries define ... the boundaries of

could not provide as much as humans demanded of them and they could not absorb as much waste as humans were producing, while still remaining healthy and productive, and pressing them too far might lead to catastrophic results. It was clear that something had to give. In the world imaged by sustainable development there was no abundance, no surplus, only scarcity. In a world of scarcity everyone suddenly had to be envisaged as a competitor for the finite goods in a world at risk. If the world's poor had a priority claim to a share of the world's natural resources, the pie would be reduced, and less would be left for the rest of us. To make things worse, according to the sustainable development experts, worldwide environmental degradation was already contributing to greater immiseration in the global South. The absolute number of the destitute was growing, and with them, their needs.

The Brundtland Report definition of sustainable development alludes to future generations whose needs must to be taken into account when making policy choices in the present. The Commission could have stated instead that sustainable development objectives required that decision-makers take a long-term view, rather than a short-term view. The rhetorical choice of "future generations" to give concrete form to an otherwise abstract future sought to emphasize a duty of stewardship and may have seemed to offer greater moral suasion. But the Report's imagined future generations became a standard reference in the sustainable development literature, and accordingly their needs became omnipresent and insistent.[64] Having

the 'planetary playing field' for humanity if we want to be sure of avoiding major human-induced environmental change of a global scale." See J. Rockstrom et al., "Planetary Boundaries: Exploring the Safe Operating Space for Humanity," *Ecology & Society* 14(2) 32 (2009).

[64] The conjunction of sustainable development's globalizing gaze and its emphasis on the needs of future generations was captured in the sentiment expressed by Helen Clark, Administrator of the UNDP: "In June 2012 world Leaders will gather in Rio de Janeiro to seek a new consensus on global action to safeguard the future of the planet and the right of future generations everywhere to live healthy and fulfilling lives. This is the great development challenge of the 21st century . . . We have a collective responsibility towards the least privileged among us today and in the future around the world—and a

given concrete reality to the future in the form of future generations, the Report and its progeny made their essential needs equally concrete. The future was now readily visualized as containing endless generations of demanding, hungry, consuming competitors for increasingly limited natural resources.[65] Population projections showing an expected rise of the world population by two and a half billion people by the year 2050, including a doubling of the population in the forty-nine poorest countries, simply compounded the fears.[66] Under these conditions, the Brundtland Report's insistence on the overriding priority of meeting the essential needs of the world's poor, present and future, took on an alarming note.

moral imperative to ensure that the present is not the enemy of the future." Foreword, "Sustainability and Equity: A Better Future for All," UNDP Human Development Report 2011, pp. iv–v.

[65] The UN has focused on population issues since at least 1969 when it established the UN Population Fund, temporally coinciding with the emergence of the Limits to Growth movement. The third population conference, the Cairo Population and Development Conference, was held in 1994, just two years after UNCED. The theme of the conference was "Interrelationships between Population, Sustained Economic Growth and Sustainable Development." Population discussions have a tendency to become focused on poverty. It is the disproportionate growth of the world's poor that causes anxiety. The Cairo Conference was no exception. Apart from a few rote references to the need to address unsustainable patterns of consumption, the program was aimed at the world's poor. The objectives were sustained economic growth and sustainable development. The future generations of the world's poor and their needs are manifest: "The number of people living in absolute poverty has increased in many countries. Around the world many of the basic resources on which future generations will depend for their survival and well-being are being depleted." "Programme of Action of the International Conference on Population and Development 1994," Preamble 1.2.

[66] According to UNDESA the 2012 worldwide population of 7.1 billion will increase by almost a billion to 8.1 billion by 2025 and climb to 9.6 billion by 2050, with most of the growth occurring in developing regions. While, in this period, population in developed regions is projected to remain relatively stable, the 49 least developed countries will experience a doubling of their population from about 900 million in 2013 to 1.8 billion in 2050. "UNDESA World Population Prospects: The 2012 Revision."

With its insistence on biophysical limits and constraints, and with its underlying anxiety about population pressures, sustainable development arguably fits well within the neo-Malthusian tradition exemplified by the Limits to Growth movement of the early seventies.[67] Indeed, in certain respects, sustainable development might have been suspected of carrying forward the legacy of the Limits to Growth movement. Yet, proponents of sustainable development and the post-UNCED policy agenda expressly and repeatedly rejected this association. Denial of the association was manifest already in the Brundtland Report. Taking an explicit stand against the controversial conclusions of the Limits to Growth movement and eager to distinguish itself from its alarmist forbears, the Commission made the bold contrary statement that: "growth has no set limits in terms of population or resource use beyond which lies ecological disaster."[68] The limitations, such as they were, were "imposed by the state of technology and social organization on the environment's ability to meet present and future needs."[69] In other words, according to the Brundtland Report, properly understood, sustainable development does not put future economic growth into question. Even a rising global population in the Commission's view is not an object of concern. The expansive promise of sustainable development was that with proper management we could still have it all: environmental protection, social equity, and sustained economic growth.

[67] See D. H. Meadows et al., *The Limits to Growth: A Report for the Club of Rome's Project on the Predicament of Mankind* (1972). The team of MIT analysts who produced this report applied new computer modeling techniques to study the interactions of five subsystems of the global economic system, namely: population, food production, industrial production, pollution, and consumption of non-renewable natural resources. Their conclusion was that continued growth would likely lead to various forms of planetary collapse in the twenty-first century. Their theories and conclusions were deemed unsupported and alarmist by many, but proved influential among a small group of ecological economists and scientists. See for example Herman E. Daly, "The Steady-State Economy," in Herman E. Daly and Kenneth N. Townsend (eds.), *Valuing the Earth: Economics, Ecology, Ethics* (1993), pp. 325–63.

[68] *Our Common Future*, p. 45.   [69] Ibid., p. 43.

The concept of sustainable development has been much criticized in environmental circles for its embrace of economic growth, even as it stressed the material reality of biophysical limits. Yet it was precisely this ability to hold the two in tension that enabled the transformation of sustainable development from concept to ubiquitous principle and policy agenda. Sustainable development proposed an optimistic ideology. To the prosperous, it promised sustained economic growth rather than contraction; to those who lacked, it offered hope of continuing development and a better future. Sustainable development assumed the emergence of a global ethic of efficiency (not wasting or squandering), along with an ethic of solidarity, but was careful never to hint at the need for any form of equitable redistribution or allocation of a limited asset base. Rather, the solution sustainable development offered to the challenge of biophysical limits and constraints was good management of resources on behalf of present and future generations to secure "our common future."[70] The tools proposed were market mechanisms and science and technological innovation. Indeed, such faith was placed in the human entrepreneurial spirit that proponents of sustainable development went so far as to encourage the view that the apparent risks of environmental degradation and natural resource depletion should be taken as a challenge and an opportunity to develop whole new industries (and grow the economy).[71]

With its optimistic message that planetary management is not only desirable but within reach, and the assurance that, despite undeniable

---

[70] The idea that either nature or the planet can be managed has been strongly criticized see generally *Global Ecology*. For the argument that the management of nature entails its capitalization and treatment as a commodity see Arturo Escobar, *Constructing Nature in Liberation Ecologies*, pp. 46–68 and 49. The project to manage the planet may well need to be added to the long list of hubristic human schemes that are bound to fail; see James C. Scott, *Seeing Like a State: How Certain Schemes to Improve the Human Condition Have Failed* (1998).

[71] "Americans [should] understand that green is not about cutting back. It's about creating a new cornucopia of abundance for the next generation by inventing a whole new industry." Thomas L. Friedman, "The Power of Green," April 15, 2007, *New York Times Magazine* www.nytimes.com/2007/04/15/magazine/15green.t.html?_r=0&pagewanted=all.

biophysical limits, sustained economic growth and a better quality of life for both present and future generations are achievable, sustainable development veers into a form of utopianism. Perhaps this helps explain why it has failed to convince. For at the same time that the concept and principle of sustainable development are accepted into the mainstream of policy pronouncements and commitments,[72] the evidence suggests that few are persuaded by this optimistic vision. In part, the problem may be that, even at its least demanding, sustainable development's promise still depends on the generalized adoption of an aggressive program of new market mechanisms and scientific and technological innovations, and these require a hefty and risky investment. The price tag is experienced as present reality. By contrast, the rosy outlook promised by sustainable development simply feels too uncertain. We are not able to believe in it, even if for the sake of convenience we pretend to do so. That so much of the narrative of sustainable development, with its references to markets, efficiency and techno-science, is told in the dry register of expert speak, has made it difficult for it to capture either the heart or the imagination of the public. The commonplace notion that "we value only what we measure" may have a certain degree of resonance, but this kind of value neither inspires nor motivates. On the other hand, the darker side of the story told by sustainable development has connected powerfully to our latent fears and anxieties.

Modernity and the science of economics have conditioned us to believe that we live in a state of perpetual scarcity; we are primed to believe there is not enough. Until recently, however, in the prosperous parts of the world at least, we confronted scarcity as consumers.

---

[72] For a recent example of the mainstreaming of sustainable development's aspirations see the G20's *Seoul Development Consensus for Shared Growth* (2010) which emphasizes the need to attend to and promote economic development of developing countries, including low income countries, in order to achieve the G20's objective of "strong, sustainable, inclusive and resilient growth." According to the G20's statement, the "shared growth" framework is borne of the recognition that "for the world to enjoy continuing levels of prosperity it must find new drivers of aggregate demand and more enduring sources of global growth." See G20, *Seoul Development Consensus for Shared Growth* (2010) p. 1.

We accepted the fact that we could not have it all, that we had to choose, but we were comforted by the sense that there was nonetheless plenty to be had, and that later, another different choice would be available. For the less prosperous, the choices were more constrained and the sense of scarcity more palpable, but still, the assumption was that with greater means more could be had. Sustainable development sought to reassure us that with proper management there would be plenty for all, but it could not help but convey the more powerful message that absent proper management there would inevitably be scarcity. Sustainable development's utopian optimism could not mask the underlying and frightening reality of natural resource depletion and environmental degradation. When Thomas Malthus published his theory about population, the coming scarcity and the inevitable famine, in 1798, the world's population was by today's standards insignificant.[73] Yet, Malthus hit a chord that continues to resonate today, as the underlying anxieties about running out, and the fierce competition for scarce resources, have never really been put to rest. Most of us, I would argue, carry a little neo-Malthus in our hearts and must work hard not to let our fears dominate our choices.[74] In the context of sustainable development, it has gotten harder to resist our fears. Sustainable development not only reminds us of the biophysical limits and constraint we face, should we fail to manage the planet, but insists that the essential needs of the world's poor, present and future, must be given priority. The realization that this sector of the global population is projected to grow significantly in absolute numbers simply adds to the anxiety. If their needs are the priority, what about *us*, what will *I* be expected to give up? Potential competition from the world's poor produces

[73] Thomas Malthus, *First Essay on Population* (1798). Estimates for the global population in 1800 range from 813–1,125 million www.census.gov/population/international/data/worldpop/table_history.php.

[74] Immigration reform discourses are often peppered with neo-Malthusian strains. Mainstream environmental groups, such as the Sierra Club, have at times become infected with the condition. Entire communities have chosen to erect regulatory and physical fences to prevent imagined invasions from the desiring hordes.

anxiety, but of even greater concern to our latent little neo-Malthus are the much-applauded successes of the so-called emerging economies and their growing middle classes. The emerging economies, China, India, Brazil, and South Africa, together contain a major portion of the world population. As GDP increases, this significant sector of the global population, whose relative consumption was once negligible, is now expected to demand an ever-greater share of the world's limited natural resources. Already as their incomes have risen, their expectations about quality of life have grown, and in a world where consumption is the most common measure of quality, they have already begun to eat further up the food chain, installed air conditioning and central heating, and acquired cars, electronics, and other consumer goods, all of which unavoidably place additional pressures on our shared planet's ecosystems. Where the essential needs of the world's poor might have been experienced as a future threat, the demands of the world's no longer quite so poor is experienced as direct competition. Meanwhile, from the perspective of the global South, the evidence of the continuing disproportionate demands placed by the North's lifestyles on the world's remaining natural resources and its ecosystems, reinforces the anxiety of not-enough.

Under the new dispensation, sustainable development's globalizing gaze and its insistence on a common concern and the shared nature of the world's natural resources, once reassuring and expansive when it meant we had access to it all, turns into a worrisome term of contraction when it means others also have access to it all. In this context, the frequent allusions to equity in sustainable development also feed the fear. Deep down we share a suspicion that if everyone really had equal access (and some have a possible priority claim) then someone is going to be left with not-enough.[75] The much-debated sustainable development principle of common but differentiated

[75] According to the Stern Review, by 2050 global average per capita emissions of CO_2 will need to be around 2 tons; see "Stern Review: Key elements of a global deal on climate change," (2008), p. 5, and http://eprints.lse.ac.uk/19617/1/Key_Elements_of_a_Global_Deal-Final_version(2)_with_additional_edits_post_launch.pdf.

responsibilities has served to accentuate this fear.[76] From the perspective of the North, the reminder of the disproportionate historical and ongoing contribution industrial societies have made to ecological problems and their consequent responsibility to address them, portends a future of scarcity as they are now expected to make do with a smaller slice of the pie.[77] From the perspective of the South, it is a reminder that because so much has been taken already, there is too little left to provide for their growing expectations.

The discourse of sustainable development has brought the fear of scarcity into the everyday. When a community (accustomed to abundance) is confronted today with an actual experience of shortage or constraint, such as for instance a reduction in the amount of fresh water available for existing uses due to drought, the community's response is strongly colored by a generalized fear of scarcity. The evidence of drought and depleted reservoirs, the knowledge that there is less available abundance, produce an outsize feeling of insecurity. The fact that the community may have to reconsider both its short-term and long-term usage priorities, that non-critical uses may have to be severely restricted or prohibited, and that other uses may need to be better monitored and possibly reduced, are experienced not as necessary adjustments but as existential threats to lifestyle. Even if the

[76] The principle of common but differentiated responsibilities holds that all states have a common responsibility to protect the environment, but because of different social, economic situations, and due to the different pressure their societies have placed on the environment, the share of responsibility they should bear in pursuit of the common objective of sustainable development is different. See Climate Change Convention Article 3, Rio Declaration Principle 7, and New Delhi Declaration Principle 3. The principle remains controversial as demonstrated by the latest round of negotiations in preparation for the next round of climate change emissions cuts targets and commitments (COP 18 Warsaw).

[77] Official sustainable development policy statements coming out of UN are generally careful not to take this approach, yet the general sustainable literature is peppered with statements that suggest the need for belt tightening. "It is . . . time that the wealthy contemplate consuming less in order to free up ecological space for the poor." W.E. Rees, "Globalization, Trade and Migration: Undermining Sustainability," *Ecological Economics*, vol. 59 (2006), 220–5, p. 224.

community's present levels of use reflect superfluity, waste or squander, it views these uses as critical to lifestyle and identity, and therefore deems them an entitlement. The reaction to the existential threat of scarcity is the desire to compensate for the loss by appropriating more water from elsewhere.[78] Thus, we see that the experience of not-enough (even if there is underlying waste and squander) generates a fear of scarcity and insecurity that justifies grabbing to protect existing lifestyles. This dynamic can be seen at work not only in the case of water grabs (water security), but also in land grabs[79] (food security) and energy grabs[80] (energy security).

As the discourse of sustainable development has penetrated ever further into the fabric of society, every experience, hint or threat of shortage, limit or constraint, is now inevitably read through this dark lens. Pervasive scarcity, once the province of economists' imaginations, has become actualized. In the world of scarcity painted by sustainable development, every allusion to equity, every reference to the growing world population, every mention of the mounting demands of a rising middle class, every allusion to disproportionate historical appropriation of natural resources or contributions to environmental degradation, every reminder of unsustainable patterns and levels of consumption has further fed the fear of scarcity by placing us in a world of fierce competition. Thus, while the official response of both public and private actors to the call for sustainable development

---

[78] See Daniel B. Wood, "California drought: Why state's big cities aren't in crisis mode," February 25, 2014, at www.csmonitor.com/USA/2014/0225/California-drought-Why-state-s-big-cities-aren-t-in-crisis-mode-video; see also Michael Wines, "West's Drought and Growth Intensify Conflict Over Water Rights," March 17, 2014, at www.nytimes.com/2014/03/17/us/wests-drought-and-growth-intensify-conflict-over-water-rights.html?action=click&contentCollection=U.S.&region=Footer&module=MoreInSection&pgtype=article.

[79] For the rush to secure access to agricultural lands in Africa see *Great African Land Grab?*

[80] A number of international conflicts concern competing claims of sovereignty over small islands, not because the islands themselves offer anything of value, but because of the attendant claims for territorial seas and the rights to exploit mineral resources based on the LOS's Exclusive Economic Zone.

has been a generalized commitment to its objectives, in practice, the response to the augmented fear of scarcity, brought on by the dark narrative of sustainable development, has been not careful management of resources, but glut, waste, and squander. In the face of certain scarcity and fierce competition, we forge ahead and use up whatever we are able to appropriate. After twenty-five years of sustainable development we have binge development and over-consumption.

I use the term binge development in an effort to capture a number of distinctive characteristics of much economic development around the world today. Binge development is development that is at root irrational, often has a performative intention, and can best be described as excessive, wasteful, and careless. It is in other words development as a form of hyperconsumption. Binge development, as I am using the term, refers specifically to post-sustainable-development economic activity. Before the advent of the era of sustainable development, some instances of economic activity might have shared many of the characteristics of binge development, but such projects would not have been irrational in the same sense. For the particular form of irrationality shared by binge development is tied to sustainable development. Binge development is irrational in at least two ways. First, it is an irrational reaction to the fear of scarcity and competition embedded in the calls to sustainable development. In fear of running out, in fear of not-enough, rather than marshal natural resources and avoid the unnecessary degradation of ecosystems, binge development seems to revel in excess and full-blown waste. Second, it is irrational because in the post-sustainable-development era, the stated objective of economic development is to improve the quality of life for the many and provide for the future, whereas binge development is wasteful of natural and human resources. Viewed from a narrow, short-term economic perspective, the individual choices of investors or developers to engage in such projects might be deemed rational if their sole stated objective was the profit motive. There are, undoubtedly, small fortunes to be made in binge development. But today very few development projects fail to make claims about how their proposed project will promote some sustainable development objective. Whether or not such projects might be deemed rational from the short-term perspective of the investors or developers, the irrationality I allude to rather is the collective irrationality of communities and states that enable, promote, and even encourage binge development.

Beyond the claim of its irrationality, however, my central proposition is that binge development is development transmuted into an act of consumption. As such it shares in the logic of hyperconsumption. In a world of scarcity and competition we want more, and we want it now. But, since pleasure is produced in the interplay of lack, desire, and satisfaction-of-desire, we are less concerned with whether things will last, for we want to be able to desire more later too. By and large just as consumption is oriented to the production of the ephemeral, to that which must be replaced, binge development builds for the short term. Furthermore, binge development is a form of public performance. It is showy, calling attention to itself and its own excessiveness. It is development designed to promote mimetic desire and further acts of binge development. But it is also performative, proud of its own excess and full-blown waste. In its excessiveness it produces the impression of frenzy. Unconcerned with the future, binge development unabashedly squanders and wastes natural resources and is careless of the human harms it produces along the way. Binge development simulates development, but it is essentially non-productive. Despite its often-spectacular character, binge development is ineffective as development at the local level because its excess and waste are careless of the indispensable biophysical and ecological foundations of its own success and because it is poorly designed to achieve the objective of improving the quality of life of the local communities.

The concept of sustainable development assumes, and we like to believe, that most human beings and their communities are governed by a set of norms that dictate that waste, excess, degradation of our or others' environment, and the imposition of unnecessary risks on others are somehow reprehensible – and that if we just knew about it, if we had information about the negative impacts of our choices, we would do something about it. Our individual and collective behaviors and choices, however, suggest that these norms, if they exist at all, are relatively weak. Humans, it appears, may be brought to assent to these and other related norms. Working at cross-purposes to these disciplining norms, however, is a seemingly irrepressible human urge to expend and waste with abandon. The joy of wasting may be short lived but it is intense while it lasts. Binging, over-consuming to the point of purging, may be an extreme case; the moment at which the irrationality of excess becomes visible as harmful and self-destructive. Nonetheless, individually, when given a chance, most of us over-consume and get some pleasure out of it, even if later there is regret. We are accosted by conflicting norms and messages. One, which tells us we should care about not abusing nature, not spoiling the earth for others (or ourselves), and that we should want there to be enough for others, especially when we are, in theory, sated. Another, louder message, is that our value, importance and status individually and collectively, depends on how much we are seen to consume. Our desire bends towards consumption, our pleasure tends us to excess. Meantime, in an era of sustainable development imperatives, besieged by fear of scarcity, we convince ourselves that we are entitled to whatever we can grab for ourselves, and that if others were given the chance, they would do it too. In the midst of the anxieties generated the by the security crisis and the economic crisis, the dark narrative of sustainable development has triggered an unacknowledged but deep fear of scarcity, producing both tunnel vision and distraction, resulting in binge development.

III SCARCITY AND THE SHAPING OF INTERNATIONAL LAW

Sustainable development, as concept and principle, is the progeny of the fecund new world of international law and institutions. As noted by the International Law Commission (ILC) and others,[81] the new world of international law and institutions provides multiple overlapping venues for the production of international law and its interpretation. It is a world no longer inhabited and controlled solely by a

---

[81] On the fragmentation of international law see Report of the Study Group of the Int'l Law Comm'n, 58th Sess., May 1–June 9, July 3–August 11, 2006, UN Doc. A/CN.4/L.682 (April 13, 2006); on the globalization of jurisdiction see Paul Schiff Berman, "The Globalization of Jurisdiction," *U. Penn. L. Rev.* (2002).

limited number of sovereign states, but rather one managed by an expanding community of international organizations, who are in effect responsible for the production of large amounts of international law and vast amounts of international policy.[82] It is a world open as never before to the participation and contributions of non-governmental organizations, including business and industry groups.[83] And it is a world where sub-national actors, are seeking to play a role, apart from the sovereign state.[84]

The success of sustainable development, its penetration into every domain of international, domestic, civic, and business life and activity, can largely be attributed to the concept's emergence at a moment when this expansive new world of international law and institutions was taking shape. At the same time, arguably, the concept of sustainable development may have served as one of the conduits though which the international came to extend its tendrils everywhere. Given sustainable development's origin in the international realm, and given the broad access the international has gained down to the fabric of the local, it would seem reasonable to conclude that international law and institutions are well positioned to take the lead in guiding the world towards implementation. In this section, I seek to question this easy assumption by highlighting one important respect in which international law seems poorly situated to promote the implementation of sustainable development.

My argument turns on scarcity, and the intimate relationship between international law and scarcity. In brief, my argument is that from its inception in the sixteenth century international law has had an overriding affinity for international commerce. Under the guise of the doctrine of the providential function of commerce,[85] international

---

[82] See Jose Alvarez, "International Organizations: Then and Now," *100 Am. J. Int'l L.* 324 (2006).

[83] See Steve Charnovitz, "Nongovernmental Organizations and International Law," *100 Am. J. Int'l L.* (2006).

[84] See Ileana Porras, "The City and International Law: In Pursuit of Sustainable Development," *36 Fordham Urb. L.J.* 537 (2009).

[85] For a discussion of the doctrine of the providential function of commerce see Ileana Porras, "Constructing International Law in the East Indian Seas: Property, Sovereignty, Commerce and War in Hugo Grotius' *De Iure*

law used the trope of scarcity to justify international commerce and the appropriation of distant lands. Modernism's later construction of a perpetual state of scarcity was thus easily accommodated in the international realm. Over time, even as international law doctrines and practices evolved, scarcity continued to serve as a readily available justification for law and practice. At various times the trope of scarcity has been used in international law to justify: opening up unreceptive foreign lands to international commerce; the acquisition of distant lands and their natural resources on the basis that the locals did not put them to sufficiently productive use; colonialism because backwards people were incapable of supplying their own or others' needs; the mandate system to ensure the sustained supply of natural resources critical to the continued development of industrial nations; and the international development project necessary to guide developing nations towards levels of productivity sufficient to raise their own people out of poverty. I do not propose, in this chapter, to address in detail the various uses to which international law has put scarcity. Rather, in the rest of this section I will focus primarily on the function of scarcity in international law as it relates to international commerce, for it is here that scarcity began to make its mark. International law from the beginning has served as the handmaiden of international trade. Simply put, today's global volumes of trade would not have been possible absent the enabling role of international law and institutions. My contention is that through its commerce-enabling role, international law has become deeply invested in the logic of scarcity and consumption. Because it is structurally oriented towards enabling trade and promoting consumption-based economic growth, international law is hobbled when confronted with the problem of implementing sustainable development.

In the mid-sixteenth century, when Francisco de Vitoria articulated his theories regarding the legal basis of international relations

---

Praedae—The Law of Prize and Booty, or 'On How to Distinguish Merchants from Pirates,'" *31 Brooklyn J. Int'l L.* (2006), pp. 741, 761 et seq. See also Ileana Porras, "Appropriating Nature: Commerce, Property and the Commodification of Nature in the Law of Nations" (forthcoming *Leiden J. of Intl L.*).

between Spaniards (Christians) and New World Indians (Barbarians), he chose to assume that the purpose of the Spaniard's travel to these distant lands was to engage in commerce.[86] At one stroke, Spanish adventurers and conquistadors were transformed into merchants. To Vitoria, it was self-evident that those who put out to sea on long and risky voyages did so in pursuit of trading opportunities. As merchants, according to Vitoria, they carried with them a natural right to engage in trade and a right to travel freely (in search of trading opportunities).[87] In counterpart, the Indians, recognized as humans and therefore subject to natural law, had a duty of hospitality, which meant they had no right to interfere with Spanish merchants' pursuit of trading opportunities.[88] According to Vitoria, when the Indians failed in their duty of hospitality and interfered with the Spaniard's right to engage in commerce, they inflicted an injury in natural law, sufficient to justify war.[89] I have addressed the structure and details of Vitoria's argument elsewhere.[90] For the purposes of my argument here, suffice it to say that according to Vitoria, it was in their quality as merchants seeking trading opportunities that the Spaniards first suffered injury from the Indians, an injury that in natural law and the law of nations justified war and conquest of Indian lands.

When Vitoria elected to characterize the Spaniards in the New World as merchants pursuing trading opportunities, he was occluding the other well-known motivations that drove early modern Europeans to engage in long distance sea travel: fame and fortune were to be achieved through some combination of adventure, appropriation of lands through military conquest or discovery, and plunder, the appropriation of goods and valuables through raids, piracy, pillage, booty, and prize taking. More modestly, European fishermen sought out

---

[86] F. Vitoria, "On the American Indians," in A. Pagden & J. Lawrance (eds.) *Francisco de Vitoria, Political Writings* (1991), pp. 231–292 [Hereinafter *DE INDIS*].

[87] Ibid.   [88] Ibid.   [89] Ibid.

[90] See Porras, *Constructing International Law*; see also Ileana Porras, "Liberal Cosmopolitanism or Cosmopolitan Liberalism? Notes from International Law," in Mortimer Sellers (ed.), *Parochialism, Cosmopolitanism, and the Foundations of International Law* (Cambridge University Press, 2011). [Hereinafter Porras, *Cosmopolitan Liberalism*].

richer fishing grounds further afield as competition exhausted nearby
stocks. Trading opportunities, in the sense of consensual and mutually advantageous acts of barter and exchange, might have been
considered among the possible objectives, but it was by no means
the sole or primary driver. Long-distance sea travel was an expensive
and risky proposition. Many ships were lost at sea. The sunk-costs
involved in equipping such expeditions were significant, while the
profits were at best speculative. Investors, who tied up and risked
their capital in such ventures, did so in the hope of spectacular
returns. Conquest, pillage, plunder and the taking of prize and booty
by force were the most direct means to such profits. Still, by the early
sixteenth century, as becomes clear in Vitoria's texts, such profitable
activities had to be morally and legally justified. Absent an existing
state of war or an injury received, you could not lawfully set out on a
mission of conquest or in pursuit of prize or booty. Engaging in
traditional forms of barter and exchange may have been the last thing
on the minds of either the Spanish adventurers or their investors, but
trade was a lawful activity, which according to Vitoria needed no
further justification as it was endorsed by natural law.

But why did merchants engage in international commerce? In the
early modern period, before economists had fully theorized scarcity or
dwelt on the question of the wealth of nations, international commerce was understood to be a means of acquiring goods that were not
readily available at home, and the means of disposing of goods of
which there was a domestic surplus. Attitudes about international
commerce inherited from Late Antiquity ranged from disapproval to
enthusiastic endorsement.[91] Disapproval stemmed from a number
of concerns, including: that engaging in foreign commerce led to

---

[91] See Jacob Viner, *The Role of Divine Providence in the Social Order: An Essay in
Intellectual History* (1972) pp. 32 et seq. [Hereinafter Viner, *Role of Providence*].
I take Late Antiquity to be the historical source of the providentialist doctrine.
While there are earlier Greek sources for the providentialist perspective, such
as Plato and Euripides, it seems fairly clear that as Viner posits the vehicle for
the introduction of providentialist view of commerce into early modern
Europe, and in a particular into international law was through Libanius in the
fourth century CE.

morally questionable conduct; that it risked lives and fortunes in pursuit of profits to be gained from unnecessary luxury goods; and that it meant dealing with foreigners (and therefore entailed the risk of contamination by foreign ideas). Those who disapproved of foreign commerce endorsed the value of self-sufficiency, insisting that to depend on others for necessities was a sign of weakness. The promoters of international trade borrowed from a different strand of thought, which viewed international trade as an instance of divine providence. Under this view, providential design had distributed different goods to different peoples and places around the world in order to ensure that men had need of one another and cause to go in search of one another. The ultimate object of providence was to bring a divided mankind to friendship with one another; friendship would result from the reciprocal fulfillment of each other's needs. Commerce in this view was mutually beneficial and necessary, whereas the pursuit of self-sufficiency could be read as contrary to the divine plan. It was this positive attitude to international commerce as providential design that Vitoria imported into international law, and which was thenceforth carried forward by international law theorists as varied as Hugo Grotius and Emmerich de Vattel, until it reached its apogee in Immanuel Kant's essay on Perpetual Peace.[92]

The doctrine of the providential design of international commerce, invoked by Vitoria and others, fit effortlessly with the common description of commerce as a mutually beneficial activity in which each party provided the other's shortage from their own surplus. The providentialist overlay, however, re-articulated international commerce in two important ways. First, it provided divine sanction. Commerce was no longer to be understood as simply an activity engaged in for private profit. Merchants were doing God's work and natural law supported this work. Second, the divine plan required scarcity, for scarcity was the occasion that would drive merchants in search of goods (and through reciprocity lead to amity between peoples). The obverse was that for

---

[92] Immanuel Kant, "Perpetual Peace: A Philosophical Sketch," in *Political Writings* 93 (1795; Hans Reiss ed., 2nd ed. 1991). For a discussion of the theme of the providential function of commerce in Kant, see Porras, *Cosmopolitan Liberalism*.

every scarcity, the divine plan had prepared a plenty elsewhere. The merchant's job was to find it and bring it home.

The providential view of commerce, in other words, not only lifted commerce and merchants to a newly elevated plane, but provided a divine basis for the proposition that for every scarcity there was a corresponding plenty. That was the design. Consequently, a people with a scarcity could confidently assume that *their* corresponding plenty was out there, in the form of another people's surplus, and that it was their duty to actively go in search of it, for this was what providence had intended.[93] Further, the providentialist understanding of commerce supported the belief that once the plenty corresponding to their scarcity had been located, they had an entitlement to acquire it. Those who held the plenty could not legitimately deny those with scarcity from acquiring the surplus, for the surplus had been providentially granted to the one for the benefit of the other. Under this view, scarcity was the providentially purposed engine that drove merchants in search of plenty. Providence had not intended that any scarcity be permanent, but had placed the manner of its fulfillment within reach. Merchants engaged in international commerce were to be understood not merely as profit seeking private actors, but as the agents of providence serving the public good.[94]

The full-blown providentialist design perspective of commerce largely disappeared from view in international law in the nineteenth century, yet traces of the doctrine persisted in a number of important ways. First, in the conventional wisdom that international commerce

---

[93] See Viner, *Role of Providence*, discussing the optimistic strain of providential design thinking.

[94] Hugo Grotius, writing as the Dutch miracle unfolds, develops the idea of the ennobled merchant most fully. He describes the Dutch favorably, as a nation of virtuous merchants, and argues that interference with Dutch merchants is tantamount to an injury to the nation itself. He does not deny that merchants are motivated by the pursuit of profits. The hope for profits and the acquisition of riches was for Grotius a legitimate and necessary incentive, for, in his view, private actors could not otherwise be expected to take the necessary investment risks. Long before Adam Smith, Grotius theorized that the pursuit of private interest redounded to the public good. See Porras, *Constructing International Law*, pp. 756–61 and 783–6.

contributes to international peace as opposed to war; second, in
international law's commitment to promoting and facilitating international commerce; third, in international law's support for the presumption that wherever natural resources are located, they should be
made available to those who wish to acquire them; and fourth, in
international law's continuing contribution to the commodification of
nature. Perhaps the most lasting legacy of the providentialist view,
however, is that in ennobling international seaborne commerce and
the merchants engaged in it, it gave seemingly unassailable cover to
violent and coercive practices that departed radically from the theoretical image of pure commerce propounded by the doctrine. International law did not demand that the practices of those engaged in
international commerce conform to the ideal of consensual, mutually
beneficial, reciprocal exchange of goods between equals. In practice,
as the authors who contributed to international law were well aware,
beyond the confines of Europe, what passed for international commerce, was little more than plunder, exploitation or expropriation.
European trade with the Americas, consisted of a one-way flow of
gold and silver from the New World to the Old, and the flow of slave
labor from Africa to the Americas. In Asia, early attempts by
Europeans to create markets for their domestic wares were unsuccessful. Until they were able to take control over their Asian hosts and
their natural resources, Europeans in search of luxuries such as
spices, tea, silk and porcelain, resorted to shipping bullion to Asia to
pay for them. With few exceptions, European settlements and colonies
in all three continents quickly became the primary trading partners for
Europeans in an international commerce that consisted primarily of a
flow of natural resources, agricultural products, furs and manufactured goods to Europe.[95] The return flows such as they were, consisted only modestly of European sourced goods. Instead, Europeans
served as middlemen, transporting the resources and goods extracted

---

[95] The most significant exceptions were China, which was able to retain effective
domestic control over its international commerce until the mid-nineteenth
century, and a number of sovereignties within the Indian subcontinent, which
remained for a period beyond the control of the East India Company and its
successor the British Empire.

or acquired elsewhere, including slaves, tea, sugar, spices, tobacco, molasses, rum, and fabrics. Competition among Europeans seeking to control trade routes, markets, sources and production abroad was the cause of violence, oppression, conflicts and war. Reciprocity, exchange and mutual advantage with distant peoples were not as profitable as appropriation and control of the terms of trade. As wealth in Europe grew to unprecedented levels, faith in the ideal of pure trade as contributing to peaceful relations among separated peoples continued to inhabit international law and served to mask the ugly reality.

The various elements of the providentialist doctrine of trade are embedded in the genetic structure of international law. Some have mutated. Not all of them are expressed at the same time, but remain available, ready to be turned on when the conditions are right. At the beginning of the twenty-first century, the faith seems undiminished. Today's international law and institutions hold firm to the belief that international trade is the harbinger of amicable relations among nations and international peace. In this way, international law can justify its central role in enabling and facilitating an ever more expansive and voluminous global international trade regime, a regime that actively seeks to incorporate those still outside its ambit into a single marketplace. If trade is a good thing,[96] then it follows that the more trade the better, and since trade volumes depend on consumption, the more consumption the better. International law and institutions have thus willingly contributed to the objective of stimulating demand for goods around the world. International commerce has traversed the intervening centuries with its providentialist aura intact, and this aura has made it difficult to challenge either the practices it has covered, or the assumptions that undergird it. In a time of fear and anxiety, at a time when sustainable development has fed the fear of scarcity, international law is unable to put into question its own history and deep structures. Instead, it draws once again on its providentialist roots and insists that there is always a corresponding plenty for scarcity, and that what is needed is more trade and more consumption (albeit, perhaps, more sustainable trade and more sustainable consumption).

---

[96] There is an etymological connection between the two senses of "good," a connection also found in the French and Spanish equivalent "bien."

This brief review of the providentialist doctrine of commerce in international law is not intended to be a comprehensive account of the complex relationship between sustainable development and international law. Its purpose rather, is to highlight the active role that scarcity has played in international law from its origin in sixteenth-century Europe to today. Scarcity in the providentialist doctrine was the engine of trade, in that it was scarcity that drove men to sea in search of plenty. But scarcity in the providentialist design also stood as promise, for every scarcity called forth a corresponding plenty, to which active merchants would have access. Neither international lawyers, nor those who achieved wealth from international trade felt the need to theorize either scarcity or plenty. If something could be acquired, by whatever means, and placed into commerce then it was by virtue of that fact alone transformed into the plenty corresponding to a scarcity somewhere. No more was needed.

In this way, international law, structured by a universalizing logic and inflected by a progress narrative, became deeply implicated in the construction of our present trade-dependent, resource-extractive, energy-intensive, consumption-led global economic model. Though international law and institutions have been the venues for the elaboration of the principle of sustainable development and have played an important role in its diffusion there is a clear sense in which they have failed to spur the transition to implementation. Meanwhile, as discussed in Section II, despite a lack of action, the rhetorical insistence of international law and institutions on the principle of sustainable development has fed a global fear of scarcity that has, in turn, contributed to binge development and hyper-consumption around the globe. Nonetheless, as a number of critical legal scholars associated with Third World Approaches to International Law (TWAIL) have reminded us recently, international law offers, almost despite itself, a fertile space for contestation and mobilization.[97] Thus, despite the obvious limitations of international law, if our objective is to

---

[97] For a nuanced account of the attempts of the Global South to use international law to achieve a more equal global order, see Sundhya Pahuja, *Decolonising International Law: Development, Economic Growth and the Politics of Universality* (2011).

collaborate with those who pursue social justice and those who are committed to the protection of the natural environment, it is then our task to identify the opportunities that reside in international law that may feed the hope that is a prelude to change, and ultimately to a radical reorientation.

IV CONCLUSION

In this chapter, I have made the argument that the general and global adoption of the principle of sustainable development has not only not led to any meaningful progress in terms of the values of social justice and environmental protection, but that it has triggered a wave of development as hyper-consumption, irrational, performative, wasteful and excessive, which I have termed binge development. Binge development, I argue, is the response to a deep-seated fear of scarcity. Scarcity lies at the heart of my analysis and connects the three parts of my argument. In Section I, I provide a wide-ranging exploration of the construct of scarcity, need and consumption. Here, I seek to emphasize that human beings' unique capacity to generate new needs and thus experience new scarcities lies at the heart of restless human creativity, and that consumerism merely taps into and takes advantage of the structure whereby the fulfillment of desire creates a potent but evanescent joy, which in turn awakens a desire for a new experience of fulfillment in an endless cycle. Finally, making reference to some recent research, I suggest that while scarcity as a concept is undoubtedly a social construct, nonetheless the experience and fear of scarcity carries a powerful charge at the biophysiological level, producing a destabilizing combination of tunnel vision and distraction that can lead to irrational behavior. In Section II, I turn to the concept of sustainable development. The concept of sustainable development, as sketched out by the Brundtland Commission in 1987, and endorsed by the international community at UNCED in 1992, has been much critiqued for its commitment to economic growth. Indeed, the proponents of sustainable development sought to distinguish their construct from the much-maligned Limits to Growth movement of the seventies. While raising concerns of an unfolding environmental crisis, the promise of sustainable development was that with a combination of better management of resources, use of market tools, and technological and scientific innovation, the world could have it all; economic growth for all was not only desirable but achievable. This optimistic view, however, was not convincing. The discourse of sustainable development contained a darker narrative strand that proved more compelling. With its emphasis on natural constraints and biophysical limits, and with its persistent references the essential needs of the world's poor and its insistence on equity, the discourse of sustainable development inevitably fed the fear of scarcity and triggered a descent into binge development. The concept of sustainable development was born in and transmitted through the new world of international law and institutions. In Section III, I argue that international law is, nonetheless, poorly suited to the challenge of spurring implementation of policies and practices that encourage sustainable development because it is so deeply implicated in the construction of the present model of export-intensive, trade-based, consumption-led economic growth. The seeds of its implication, I argue, lie in its origin in the sixteenth century and the adoption of the doctrine of the providential design function of commerce. Elements of the providentialist design doctrine carried in the twenty-first century include the assumption that international commerce creates the necessary conditions for friendship, and the belief that for every scarcity there is a plenty that must be found.

If the insistent call to sustainable development, with its important reminders of ecological limits and the demands of social justice, have fed the fear of scarcity and triggered binge development, what are we to do? Throwing up our hands and throwing in our lot with the binge developers may well provide significant, if momentary, pleasure for those able to indulge the spree, but that way lies folly: it clearly cannot serve as a viable long-term strategy. Renouncing our needs and demanding great sacrifices also seems untenable. As Shakespeare's Lear reminds us, reduced to bare existence man's life is "cheap as beasts':" This way too, lies folly. In 1987, sustainable development seemed to offer a middle way. But, it has failed.

I do not have a plan. I offer no more than fragments, suggestions about the way forward that might be cobbled together in an eventual strategy:

- The call to sustainable development has fed the fear of scarcity, while failing to mobilize decision-makers to attend to either the environmental or the social justice impacts of their choices. It may therefore be time to set aside the concept of sustainable development, and to replace it with a concept that emphasizes environmental justice.
- We must attend to and reevaluate the construct of scarcity, which in turn requires a redefinition of needs and wants.
- We should probably stop making reference to the world's poor and their essential needs. This abstraction dehumanizes the individuals, families and communities it might refer to, and portrays them unidimensionally through their wants.
- We must definitely do away with all references to future generations and their needs. The utility of conjuring up these emotionally charged potentialities, to make a claim of obligation on us regarding our present choices, is far outweighed by the fear and anxiety they generate with their unreasonable an open-ended demands. Much better to return to the traditional requirement that we consider the long-term consequences of our decisions.
- However irrational it appears, we need to recognize the human desire to expend and waste in a performative manner and make space for it. This urge cannot be repressed, but it may be possible to cabin it off by channeling it into periodic rituals.
- International law can never be fully dissociated from its commitment to international commerce. At the same time, international law offers an aspirational space of hope. The question is how elements of the providentialist doctrine of commerce might be used to good account. Perhaps, the answer lies in making it true to itself. The ideal of pure trade has until now functioned to mask the ugly realities. Can the ideal be used to challenge and discipline some of the ways in which the practice fails to conform to the ideal.
- The providentialist account implies that to every scarcity there is a corresponding plenty. When re-evaluating our construct of scarcity we will need to consider how it will fit into this narrative. It is not just that we need a gradation of relative scarcities in accordance with their closeness to basic needs. The fact that a thing can be acquired should no longer be taken to imply that it is a plenty for

which there must be a scarcity out there. The fact that a thing can be acquired, or that land can be put to more efficient production, does not mean that it should be. Whether or not it should be, will require an evaluation of claims of scarcity in light of the uses to which the plenty is to be put.

- Somehow we will need to wrench citizenship away from consumer identity. The movement towards alternative and green consumption offers some real opportunities for change, but consumption pursued as political strategy will take us in the wrong direction. Certainly it is important that we become more conscious of our acts of consumption so that they become real choices rather than mere rote or unconscious expenditure. But attentive consumption will be a good thing only if it does not reinforce the conviction that our political action passes through our pocketbook and acts of consumption.

- Alternative consumption may drive positive trends such as fair trade, organic farming, and fair labor standards, but we must be attentive to the assumptions that underlie the producer-consumer relationship, especially when production is located in a developing country while the product is destined for western consumption. Too often the trade and practices it promotes mirror the traditional structures of exchange established already in the colonial period where foreign companies imposed not only quality and product characteristics, but determined the acceptable conditions of production. There is a danger that this will be perceived as a continuation of the civilizing mission.

- Alternative consumption should be used as an invitation to reflect on the dynamic of modern consumption, which separates the environmental/social harms attendant to production from the actual consumption. While alternative consumption may be fine as a partial strategy of political intervention there is a danger that it merely assuages the consumer's anxiety without producing much change in the production/consumption dynamic. It does not break the cycle of needing more and in fact may encourage some consumers to increase consumption.

- Despite the evident temptation, we should to the extent possible avoid the terminology of security and insecurity. Allusions to food security, energy security, or ecological security tend to remind us of our vulnerability and create anxiety, feed our fear of scarcity and lead to grabbing. We never think we need so much as when we are in fear of not enough.

- Finally, the biggest challenge will be to find a way of confronting scarcity without fear. If scarcity is a social construct, then it can be modified if not transformed. The problem is that our twenty-first-century construct has been shaped not just by modernity and the modern economy's already urgent insistence to create consumer demand, but by neo-liberalism's vision of the world as a global market place inhabited by actual or potential hyper-consumers blessed with insatiable desire. In order to cease fearing scarcity we will need to train ourselves away from our learned consumption-driven tendency to believe we need more. Always more.

2 INTERNATIONAL LAW AS A WAR AGAINST NATURE?

Reflections on the Ambivalence
of International Environmental Law

Karin Mickelson

INTRODUCTION: ON RE-READING *CIVILIZATION AND ITS DISCONTENTS*

Having been asked to contribute to a collection entitled *International Law and its Discontents*, I found it impossible to resist the temptation to turn back to Freud. I recall encountering *Civilization and its Discontents* during my undergraduate studies, and dismissing it with a sense of complacent certainty that it was of historical interest only.[1] Coming back to it more than thirty years later, Freud's insights seem fresher, and their implications more chilling. Perhaps this is simply a variation of the old joke that our parents know very little when we are adolescents, and then undergo an astonishing metamorphosis into wisdom as we ourselves age, but it is worth considering whether something more is at work. It may be that Freud's attempt to apply the insights of psychoanalysis to social theory resonates now because so many of us find it increasingly difficult to understand what we see as an irrational denial of the dependence of human society on the natural systems that sustain us, and the rest of life on this planet. Looking back on more than two decades of lost opportunities with regard to climate change, and many more decades of partially successful or

---

[1] Sigmund Freud, *Civilization and its Discontents*, James Strachey (ed. and trans.), (New York: W.W. Norton, 1989).

failed attempts to come to terms with other environmental harms associated with industrialization, how do we account for the fact that we keep falling short of the mark?

In this essay, I take Freud's insistence on the profound ambivalence that exists at the heart of human civilization as a starting point from which to explore the ambivalence that might be said to structure our relationship with the natural world.[2] In *The Future of an Illusion*, Freud asserted that "the principal task of civilization, its actual *raison d'être*, is to defend us against nature."[3] It could be argued that the essence of modern environmentalism is a rejection of this view and its replacement with a depiction of nature as that which must be defended against civilization (or humans more generally). Environmental law, whether in its domestic or international form, is supposed to play an equalizing role, placing limits on the exploitation of nature while allowing for the supposedly rational pursuit of economic development. However, many have come to question whether the mainstream understanding of economic growth and prosperity is fundamentally inconsistent with environmental sustainability. Given that this understanding is deeply embedded in the structures and principles of international law – including international environmental law –could one argue that international law constitutes an elaborate façade that justifies a war against nature?

In seeking to explore this question, I have framed this essay as a set of reflections. I use the term "reflections," deliberately, to highlight the sense of what (and how) we see when we look at the world around

---

[2] In using this as a starting point rather than a focal point, I am not engaging directly with the rich and fascinating body of literature that explores the interface between psychoanalysis or psychology and the environment. For a concise discussion of some of the major themes, see Renee Lertzman, "Psychoanalysis, culture, society and our biotic relations: Introducing an ongoing theme on environment and sustainability," *Psychoanalysis, Culture and Society*, 15:2 (2010), p. 113. For an evocative example, see Shierry Weber Nicholsen, *The Love of Nature and the End of the World: The Unspoken Dimensions of Environmental Concern* (Cambridge: MIT Press, 2003).

[3] Sigmund Freud, *The Future of an Illusion*, W. D. Robson-Scott (trans.), James Strachey (ed.), (Garden City: Anchor Books, 1964), p. 20.

us.[4] In the next section, I begin by assembling a series of images depicting the current relationship between humans and the environment: pictures, as it were, from the frontlines of a war against nature and against those who are sometimes referred to as "ecosystem people," the peoples and communities who depend upon and largely live within the constraints of particular ecosystems.[5] In the following two sections, I consider, first, whether there is a pattern into which the seemingly inexplicable images fit and further, how a shift in perspective might require us to see a different pattern. I conclude by considering whether there might be a different way of creating patterns that could enable us to make sense of the contradictions and perhaps even find a way of beginning to reconcile them.

I REFLECTIONS IN A HALL OF MIRRORS: PICTURES FROM THE FRONTLINES OF A WAR AGAINST NATURE?

August 26, 2013: Speech by Joe Oliver, Canada's Minister of Natural Resources to the Energy and Mines Ministers Conference, Yellowknife, Northwest Territories[6]

[W]e are hearing objections from those who see resource development and responsible environmental stewardship as an either/or zero-sum game. Let me be clear, I am not talking about the many Canadians, including our Aboriginal peoples, who have legitimate concerns about environmental safety and are open to a fact- and science-based discussion.

---

[4] Perhaps it goes without saying that these observations represent a particular point of view, albeit one that benefits from the insights derived from over twenty years of teaching and research in the field of international environmental law.

[5] Ramachandra Guha, How *Much Should a Person Consume?: Environmentalism in India and the United States* (Berkeley: University of California Press, 2006), p. 233.

[6] Natural Resources Canada, online: www.nrcan.gc.ca/media-room/speeches/2013/7311.

My objection is to those who oppose virtually every form of resource development, whose opinions are not based on facts and whose vision is simply too limited.

My friends, Canada was not built by naysayers. It was built by women and men who dared greatly. Took on big challenges. And applied their ingenuity to overcome them ...

"Nation-building" is not confined to our history, an echo from our past. It is our obligation to the future. And every generation must honour that obligation.

Many portions of Joe Oliver's keynote speech at the 70th annual meeting of federal and provincial ministers with responsibilities in the areas of mines and energy would have made complete sense to the ministers who gathered at the first annual meeting in 1953. Others would have resonated with politicians of a much earlier time, for whom a call to "nation-building" was a part of ordinary political discourse. Why is Oliver speaking in these terms?

The speech comes at a time when the Canadian government appears to be enthusiastically pursuing any and all possibilities for resource extractive industries. Oliver mentions the possibility of "hundreds of major resource projects, worth $650 billion" that could be undertaken in the coming decade, and enthusiastically listing some of the highlights:

From hydroelectricity in Manitoba and Newfoundland and Labrador; to new mining projects in Nova Scotia, New Brunswick, Northern Quebec and the Ring of Fire in Ontario; to rare-earth elements in the Northwest Territories, iron ore in Nunavut, gold mines in the Yukon, uranium mines in Saskatchewan, the oil sands in Alberta and liquefied natural gas in BC – few countries in the world are bringing on resource projects of this scale or at this pace.

This plethora of development prospects is something to be celebrated, in Oliver's view, and he is insistent on the need to embrace the challenge that they represent:

If we are going to seize the opportunities we need to act now – develop our resources, build the infrastructure, diversify our markets and lay the foundations for the future. So we have a choice: to proceed or procrastinate. We can roll up our sleeves or wring our hands. *We can decide to get this done or we can dither – and watch the opportunities pass to others.* (emphasis added)

So here we come to what appears to be the crux of the matter, the reason that Oliver may well have chosen, later in his speech, to invoke the powerful (and loaded) language of history and nation-building. In a nutshell, he is exhorting his listeners to beware of the ditherers, of those who would "wring their hands" and agonize over the choice of whether or not to develop these resources. To be fair, Oliver does not crudely equate ditherers with environmentalists. In the passage quoted at the beginning of this section, Oliver insists that he is "not talking about … [those] who have legitimate concerns about environmental safety and are open to a fact- and science-based discussion." Instead, he seems to suggest that the ditherers are those "naysayers" "whose opinions are not based on facts and whose vision is simply too limited." There is no acknowledgement that there could be legitimate differences of opinion about the wisdom and need to pursue resource extraction on such a broad scale, and that those opinions could have a solid scientific, and even economic, basis. And while Oliver discusses the importance of ensuring the environmental safety of resource projects, stating that the goal is "world-class environmental protection," the possibility that some of these projects might not be consistent with that goal does not even seem to be worth mentioning.

Even more disturbing are the allusions Oliver makes to indigenous peoples in this regard. His speech opens with an expression of appreciation for Canada's North, characterizing it as the "perfect setting" for the meeting "because of its history in both pursuing economic opportunity and respecting the environment." Towards the end of the speech, he highlights the economic and employment opportunities that many of these projects will open up for indigenous communities. In contrast, Oliver states, "where development is deferred, communities suffer from loss of opportunity." In a particularly troubling reference that reveals a certain disregard of the history that Oliver seems determined to centre, he specifically mentions the Mackenzie Valley Pipeline Inquiry, during which the indigenous peoples of the North rose up in opposition to the proposed pipeline:

The Mackenzie gas project represented a tremendous opportunity for Aboriginal partners. But the regulatory review took almost a decade to complete. By the time it was done, the opportunity had passed – an irretrievable loss for an entire generation.

Again, there is no room for doubt, or for genuinely different perspectives. Within the framework Oliver presents, you are either moving with the times or sitting on the sidelines, watching those opportunities pass you by.

July 12, 2012: FAO Fisheries and Aquaculture Department, The State of World's Fisheries and Aquaculture 2012

The proportion of non-fully exploited stocks has decreased gradually since 1974 when the first FAO assessment was completed. In contrast, the percentage of overexploited stocks has increased, especially in the late 1970s and 1980s, from 10 percent in 1974 to 26 percent in 1989 . . . About 29.9 percent of stocks are overexploited, producing lower yields than their biological and ecological potential and in need of strict management plans to restore their full and sustainable productivity . . . The remaining 12.7 percent of stocks were non-fully exploited in 2009, and these are under relatively low fishing pressure and have some potential to increase their production although they often do not have a high production potential and require proper management plans to ensure that any increase in the exploitation rate does not result in further overfishing . . .

The declining global marine catch over the last few years together with the increased percentage of overexploited fish stocks and the decreased proportion of non-fully exploited species around the world convey the strong message that the state of world marine fisheries is worsening and has had a negative impact on fishery production.[7]

Reading the most recent *State of World Fisheries and Aquaculture* report, with its facts and statistics conveyed in brisk, technical language, one starts to feel a sense of having descended down a rabbit hole.

[7] Food and Agriculture Organization Fisheries and Aquaculture Department, *The State of World Fisheries and Aquaculture 2012* (Rome: FAO, 2012), pp. 11–12. Online: www.fao.org/docrep/016/i2727e/i2727e00.htm.

When each of the series of numbers regarding fish stocks mentioned earlier is considered in isolation, things may not actually appear as dismal as one might expect, given the news about decline or even collapse of many fish stocks over the last few decades. There might even seem to be room for cautious optimism. Less than 30 percent of fish stocks are overexploited, after all; almost 13 percent are actually *under-*exploited, offering the possibility of further, albeit carefully managed, production. This means, of course, that 57 percent of stocks are fully exploited, in the sense that they "produce catches that are very close to their maximum sustainable production and have no room for further expansion and require effective management to avoid decline."[8]

It is when the numbers are combined that the picture starts to be brought into focus. Almost 90 percent of fish stocks are either close to or past the limit for maximum sustainable production. The proportion of overexploited stocks has tripled since 1974, now accounting for almost a third of fish stocks worldwide. While this is acknowledged to be a "worrisome global situation,"[9] the Report points to progress being made in some areas, mentioning the United States, Australia, and New Zealand in particular, and noting that in the case of the United States, "67 percent of all stocks are now being sustainably harvested, while only 17 percent are still overexploited."[10] What is not mentioned, as pointed out by fisheries scientist Daniel Pauly, is that these examples of progress "are the same few countries (notably the United States and Australia) as in the last assessment, their 'virtuous' behaviour apparently having found few imitators."[11] What also goes unsaid is that the examples mentioned are all developed countries, with substantial resources at their disposal, which might have been expected to have made far more significant progress toward achieving sustainable fisheries.

These alarming statistics need to read against the backdrop of decades of attempts to develop legal responses to fisheries at the national, regional, and global level. The recognition of an "exclusive economic zone" in the *United Nations Convention on the Law of the Sea*

<hr/>

[8] Ibid., p. 11.   [9] Ibid., p. 13.   [10] Ibid.
[11] Quoted in "fishnewseu.com," July 10, 2012, online: www.fishnewseu.com/index.php?option=com_content&view=article&id=8544:sofia-report-must-inspire-action&catid=46:world&Itemid=56.

(UNCLOS)[12] was intended at least in part to reinforce the ability of coastal states to conserve marine resources, and UNCLOS also imposed a duty on states to cooperate on conservation measures regarding fish stocks beyond the limits of coastal state jurisdiction.[13] A perception of the limitations of the UNCLOS framework, particularly with regard to high seas fisheries, led to the negotiation of the 1995 *Agreement for the Implementation of the Provisions of the [UNCLOS], Relating to the Conservation and Management of Straddling Fish Stocks and Highly Migratory Fish Stocks.*[14] Scientists, [15] environmental NGOs and other civil society groups have laboured to raise public awareness and concern regarding fisheries in general, as well as specific problem areas such as deep-seabed trawling. There have been attempts to use soft law instruments such as UN General Assembly resolutions to push the legal framework further.[16] Nevertheless, there appears to be little appetite for genuinely robust regulatory responses.

Meanwhile, as noted elsewhere in the *State of the World's Fisheries* report, global fish consumption continues to rise, part of an overall increase in per capita food consumption.[17]

---

[12] *United Nations Convention on the Law of the Sea*, Montego Bay, December 10, 1982, in force November 16, 1994, 1833 UNTS 3, Art. 87.

[13] UNCLOS imposes a duty on states to seek to agree on conservation measures with regard to straddling fish stocks, defined as stocks that occur "within the [EEZ] of two or more coastal states" or "both within the [EEZ] and in an area beyond or adjacent to it," (Art. 63). With highly migratory fish species such as tuna, states are required to cooperate to ensure conservation and optimum utilization of such stocks both within and beyond the EEZ (Art. 64).

[14] *Agreement for the Implementation of the Provisions of the United Nations Convention on the Law of the Sea of 10 December 1982 relating to the Conservation and Management of Straddling Fish Stocks and Highly Migratory Fish Stocks,* New York, August 4, 1995, in force December 11, 2001, 2167 UNTS 3.

[15] See for example Elliott A. Norse et al., "Sustainability of deep-sea fisheries," *Marine Policy*, 36:2 (2012), pp. 307–20.

[16] See for example Deep Sea Conservation Coalition, "Unfinished business: a review of the implementation of the provisions of United Nations General Assembly resolutions 61/105 and 64/72, related to the management of bottom fisheries in areas beyond national jurisdiction," online: www.savethehighseas.org/publicdocs/DSCC_review11.pdf.

[17] FAO, *State of World Fisheries*, p. 87.

> September 10, 2013: Minority Rights Group International press release, "U.S. energy company must suspend oil exploration until government of Belize obtains free, prior and informed consent of Toledo's Maya and Garifuna peoples, says new report"[18]

> In 1994, without consulting Toledo Maya or Garifuna people, the government [of Belize] converted almost 42,000 acres of their ancestral territory into government land, the Sarstoon-Temash National Park (STNP). The government then opened the STNP to oil exploration by U.S. Capital Energy Belize, Ltd, a wholly owned Belizean subsidiary of American company U.S. Capital Energy, Inc.

> The legality of these actions has been challenged by both national and international bodies.... These bodies concluded that the Belize government must recognize Maya collective land ownership in Toledo and obtain the free, prior and informed consent of Maya communities before awarding concessions.[19] The government of Belize has refused to comply with these decisions, however, and recently awarded U.S. Capital a permit to begin drilling in Toledo.

The press release excerpted earlier is a recent one, but one must step back in time to understand the full extent of the challenges facing the Maya and Garifuna peoples of the Toledo District of Belize. One could go as far back as a history of colonial dispossession, or focus on the more recent story of social marginalization within postcolonial Belize. At the very least, one would have to go back to 1994, the year in which a new national park was created in Toledo District without prior consultation with local communities, or perhaps just to 1997, three years later, when the communities actually learned that the park had been created. Despite their concerns about both the process and the outcome, "communities have worked in good faith with the government to conserve the park,"[20] according to the Minority Rights

---

[18] Online: www.minorityrights.org/12052/press-releases/us-energy-company-must-suspend-oil-exploration-until-government-of-belize-obtains-free-prior-and-informed-consent-of-toledos-maya-and-garifuna-peoples-says-new-report.html.

[19] See text accompanying note 22 in this chapter.

[20] Chelsea Purvis, "'Suddenly we have no more power': Oil drilling on Maya and Garifuna land in Belize," *Minority Rights Group International Briefing*, September 2013, p. 3.

Group, entering into a co-management arrangement that was abruptly – and unilaterally –terminated by the Forestry Department in July 2013.

Meanwhile, the government seems to have taken pride in its move to grant a protected status for Sarstoon-Temash. This was signalled when, in 2005, Belize designated Sarstoon Temash as its second "wetland of international importance" under the *Convention on Wetlands of International Importance especially as Waterfowl Habitat* (Ramsar Convention), to which Belize had become a party in 1998.[21] The description of Sarstoon Temash on the Ramsar Convention website even acknowledges indigenous and minority interests, albeit in a somewhat muted fashion, stating that "[t]he buffer zone of the park is home to the indigenous Kekchi Maya and Garifuna people, both of which attach high cultural importance to parts of the site ..."[22] Nonetheless, there have been ongoing struggles between local communities and the government about the granting of logging and oil concessions, leading to the series of legal challenges in both domestic and international fora mentioned earlier. On September 2, 2013, Prime Minister Dean Barrow indicated that any court rulings could only relate to lands owned by the communities in question, stating that as far as he is concerned, "the court decision does not include the national park at all."[23] A few days later, the Maya Leaders Alliance (MLA) reacted to the Prime Minister's statement with concern, pointing out that the government has "chosen to ignore the invitation of Maya leaders to resume negotiations about how best to implement Maya land rights that have now been upheld three times by the courts and by human rights bodies of the Organization of

---

[21] *Convention on Wetlands of International Importance Especially as Waterfowl Habitat, Ramsar*, February 2, 1971, in force December 21, 1975, 996 UNTS 245. Article 2(4) requires parties to designate at least one wetland as such upon signature, ratification, or accession to the Convention.

[22] Online: www.ramsar.org/cda/en/ramsar-pubs-annolist-annotated-ramsar-16673/main/ramsar/1–30–168%5E16673_4000_0__.

[23] Channel 5 Belize, "Barrow says ruling on communal land does not include Sarstoon-Temash National Park", September 2, 2013, online: http://edition .channel5belize.com/archives/89938.

American States and the United Nations."[24] While the MLA had decided to appeal some aspects of the latest Court of Appeal decision to the Caribbean Court of Justice, it stated, "Even as we appeal, we would prefer to resolve these issues through dialogue with our government on the premise that our land rights exist."[25]

II FROM HALL OF MIRRORS TO KALEIDOSCOPE: SEEING PATTERNS

kaleidoscope, n.

a. An optical instrument, consisting of from two to four reflecting surfaces placed in a tube, at one end of which is a small compartment containing pieces of coloured glass: on looking through the tube, numerous reflections of these are seen, producing brightly-coloured symmetrical figures, which may be constantly altered by rotation of the instrument.

b. *fig.* A constantly changing group of bright colours or coloured objects; anything which exhibits a succession of shifting phases.[26]

The previous section revealed disturbing images that seem fundamentally at odds with many of our assumptions about the current state of environmental awareness. In this section, I would invite the reader to leave the hall of mirrors and instead take up a kaleidoscope, in order to see underlying patterns that can help us make sense of these seemingly bizarre and inconsistent impressions. To do this requires that we step back in time, to the end of the Second World War and the emerging consensus about the postwar world.

A From Postwar Consensus to Development Ideology

Against the backdrop of an interwar period characterized by global depression, mass unemployment and social dislocation, as well as the

---

[24] Quoted in Adele Ramos, "Sarstoon-Temash National Park in 'Ancestral Lands' – Maya Leaders", September 6, 2013, online: http://amandala.com.bz/news/sarstoon-temash-national-park-ancestral-lands-maya-leaders/.

[25] Ibid.   [26] "Kaleidoscope," Oxford English Dictionary.

devastation caused by the war itself, the architects of the postwar economic order had to reconcile a number of competing policy objectives. A rejection of "beggar-thy-neighbour" policies that were seen as having exacerbated the economic turmoil of the inter-war period, coupled with the need to respond to domestic concerns about employment and social welfare, led to an agreement, in which American and British policy makers played a central role, on a multi-lateral system "that would attempt to reconcile openness and trade expansion with the commitments of national governments to full employment and economic stabilization."[27] Institutions such as the International Bank for Reconstruction and Development, International Monetary Fund, and International Trade Organization were intended to play a role in the economic sphere comparable to that of the United Nations with regard to the maintenance of international peace and security, part of an overall vision of global well-being to which its proponents were deeply committed. Despite any underlying differences of opinion regarding the relative merits of free trade versus national controls over tariffs and other trade barriers, there appears to have been little dissension about the fundamental means by which economic prosperity for all was to be achieved. The preamble to the original General Agreement on Tariffs and Trade, concluded in 1947 and intended to operate on an interim basis pending establishment of the International Trade Organization refers to the contracting parties' recognition:

> that their relations in the field of trade and economic endeavour should be conducted with a view to raising standards of living, ensuring full employment and a large and steadily growing volume of real income and effective demand, developing the full use of the resources of the world and expanding the production and exchange of goods.

The Final Act of the United Nations Conference on Trade and Employment, which had adopted the *Havana Charter for an International Trade*

---

[27] G. John Ikenberry, "The Political Origins of Bretton Woods," in Michael D. Bordo and Barry Eichengreen (eds.), *A Retrospective on the Bretton Woods System: Lessons for International Monetary Reform* (Chicago: University of Chicago Press, 1993), p. 155.

Organization, was more direct, referring to the Economic and Social
Council of the United Nations having called the Conference "for the
purpose of promoting the expansion of the production, exchange
and consumption of goods."[28] The United States, in particular,
embraced the vision of consumption as integral to both economic
and political well-being. Lizabeth Cohen has described this as the
notion of a "consumers' republic": "a complex shared commitment
on the part of policymakers, business and labor leaders, and civic
groups to put mass consumption at the center of their plans for a
prosperous postwar America."[29] The expansion of mass consumption, according to Cohen, was seen as critical not only to the reconstruction of the U.S. economy but also to the reaffirmation of its
democratic values.[30] It also came to be perceived as a fundamental
aspect of the model the United States was to offer the world. As
President Dwight Eisenhower noted in a 1960 speech:

> Around the world, one of the most widely known features of the
> United States today is its unprecedented wealth. But much less
> understood abroad is the great spread, throughout the peoples
> of our nation, of the benefits of the American system. Other
> peoples find it hard to believe that an American working man can
> own his own comfortable home and a car and send his children
> to well-equipped elementary and high schools and to colleges
> as well. They fail to realize that he is not the downtrodden,
> impoverished vassal of whom Karl Marx wrote. He is a
> self-sustaining, thriving individual, living in dignity and in
> freedom.[31]

[28] Final Act of the United Nations Conference on Trade and Employment,
Havana, March 24, 1948, UN Doc. E/Conf. 2/78, online: www.wto.org/
english/docs_e/legal_e/havana_e.pdf, 5.
[29] Lizabeth Cohen, *A Consumers' Republic: The Politics of Mass Consumption in
Postwar America* (New York: Vintage Books, 2004), p. 11.
[30] Ibid.
[31] Dwight D. Eisenhower, Address in Detroit at the National Automobile Show
Industry Dinner, October 17, 1960. Online by Gerhard Peters and John
T. Wooley, *The America Presidency Project.* www.presidency.ucsb.edu/ws/?
pid=11982. A portion of this speech is also quoted in Cohen, Ibid.,
p. 125.

The relatively narrow understanding of economic growth, prosperity and well-being that emerged from this postwar consensus not only came to be reflected, but arguably received its purest and most definitive form in the understanding of development that was formulated in the halls of international financial institutions. The newly decolonized states of Africa and Asia, along with the African, Asian and Latin American states which had either achieved independence earlier or had, at least formally, managed to evade colonial control, were swept up in a vision of development as the pinnacle of human progress. And that pinnacle was itself defined in terms of consumption at a high level and on a broad scale. W. W. Rostow's influential categorization of the "stages of economic growth," for example, began with "traditional society," moved through "the condition for take-off," to "the drive to maturity," and culminated in "the age of high mass consumption."[32] It is noteworthy, however, that Rostow, writing in 1954, postulated that some so-called "mature" societies were "close to the point where the pursuit of food, shelter, clothing, as well as durable consumers goods and public and private services, may no longer dominate their lives. A new and revolutionary set of choices is being confronted, or is a mere generation or so over the horizon."[33]

One might have expected that an emerging awareness of the environment might have provided just such a "revolutionary set of choices." This raises an important question: how did understandings of development and economic well-being manage to remain unchanged in their essential orientation when confronted with concerns about environmental degradation and resource depletion?

B Containing the Challenge From Environmentalism

Challenges to mainstream understandings of economic growth and development have, of course, been articulated ever since the

---

[32] W. W. Rostow, "The Stages of Economic Growth," in David E. Novack and Robert Lekachman (eds.), *Development and Society: The Dynamics of Economic Change* (New York: St. Martin's Press, 1964) p. 41.

[33] Ibid., p. 54.

beginnings of the Industrial Revolution. Many of them came from land-based communities who remained unconvinced that the promises of future prosperity were sufficient to compensate for the disruption and dislocation that were all too easily perceived, while others emerged from the protests of workers who paid the price of industrialization through their exposure to hazardous workplace conditions.[34] In their resistance it is possible to detect many concerns that would later come to be seen as falling under a broad understanding of "environmental" issues, although these were often closely linked with human well-being. Beginning in the 1960s, however, concern for the environment in and of itself came to be an important rallying point for social protest. The environmental movement wove together a number of different strands from both earlier and contemporary social movements, but created something that was new and distinctive. In so doing, it created something that had the potential to be – and was sometimes perceived as being – a radical challenge to the status quo. However, relatively few environmentalists insisted that a fundamental reordering of society was required in order to address environmental challenges, and most were careful to distance themselves from the more radical elements within the movement. This proved to have its advantages when a narrower and more politically acceptable version of environmentalism was incorporated into the policy mainstream, but it also limited the movement's transformative potential.

On the international stage, an environmentalism that had largely defined itself in terms of its opposition to pollution and resource extraction confronted the need to articulate a version of environmental law and policy that would incorporate the concerns of developing countries. The lead-up to the United Nations Conference on the Human Environment, held in Stockholm in 1972, involved a difficult

---

[34] There is an increasingly rich body of literature that has helped expand our understanding of the history of environmental engagement and activism. For a classic example, see Ramachandra Guha and Juan Martinez-Alier, *Varieties of Environmentalism: Essays North and South* (London: Earthscan, 2000). For a recent example focusing on the United States, see Chad Montrie, *A People's History of Environmentalism in the United States* (London: Continuum, 2011).

process of consensus-building that sometimes seemed doomed to failure, leading to an outcome that reflected a linkage between environmental and developmental concerns. This linkage grew more visible in the 1980s, in the work of the World Commission on Environment and Development (known as the Brundtland Commission in recognition of its chair, Gro Harlem Brundtland of Norway), and was reflected in the name of the major multilateral gathering held twenty years after the Stockholm Conference in Rio de Janeiro, the 1992 United Nations Conference on Environment and Development.

According to Steven Bernstein, reports such as that of the Brundtland Commission "turned the corner on environmental thinking that had put it in direct opposition to classical economic views of growth and development."[35] Bernstein terms this the "compromise of liberal environmentalism," which he describes as follows:

> Liberal environmentalism accepts the liberalization of trade and finance as consistent with, and even necessary for, international environmental protection. It also promotes market and other economic mechanisms (such as tradeable pollution permit schemes or the privatization of commons) over "command and control" methods (standards, bans, quotas, and so on) as the preferred method of environmental management. The concept of sustainable development, while it legitimated this shift in norms, now masks this compromise that characterizes international environmental governance.[36]

While Bernstein's critique of international environmental law and policy's liberal orientation is rather sweeping, he makes an important point about the perceived "compatibility of growth and environmental protection."[37] There may very well have been good strategic reasons for pursuing a moderate agenda that could be assured of a wider degree of political support. However, by setting these parameters on the terms of debate, some tough questions about the genuine compatibility of economic and environmental concerns remained not only unanswered, but frequently unasked.

[35] Steven F. Bernstein, *The Compromise of Liberal Environmentalism* (New York: Columbia University Press, 2001), p. 73.
[36] Ibid., p. 7.   [37] Ibid., p. 73.

III A TURN OF THE KALEIDOSCOPE: SEEING THE HUMAN DIMENSION OF ENVIRONMENTAL DEGRADATION

Our metaphorical kaleidoscope has, I hope, helped bring a sense of order to the chaotic series of images with which this paper opened. Placed against the backdrop of a dominant understanding of economic well-being that has prioritized mass consumption, it is easier to understand, if not to accept, why in the twenty-first century a Canadian Minister of Natural Resources would speak of nation-building in terms of resource extraction, a park in Belize would be open to drilling in disregard of the interests of indigenous and minority peoples, and the international community would sit by and watch global fish stocks teeter past the edge of sustainability. But I chose this metaphor with more than mere symmetry in mind. Kaleidoscopes fascinate not so much because of the patterns they reveal as the change in pattern which a simple turn permits us to see. And I would suggest that a turn of our kaleidoscope is essential. Consider just one example drawn from the images presented earlier. The Maya and Garifuna peoples, among the many concerns that they have raised regarding the Belizean government's decision to allow U.S. Capital to drill in Toledo, have protested against the company's efforts to promote support for oil drilling among residents and local leaders, characterizing these efforts as an interference with their right to free, prior and informed consent. In interviews conducted by the Minority Rights Group, "employment was the most important reason that community members listed for supporting U.S. Capital."[38] The MRG argues persuasively that unrealistic promises of long-term employment interfere with the community's autonomous decision-making power, but apart from mentioning that such promises have particular traction in "deeply impoverished, underserved communities," does not elaborate on this point. The fact that employment would be such an appealing prospect, however, complicates what might otherwise be a straightforward "economy versus environment" scenario (with indigenous and minority peoples firmly on the side of the environment, as is so often assumed to be the case). This is, in

---

[38] Minority Rights Group International, (see note 18), p. 5.

fact, a different aspect of the same picture, impossible to ignore when it is revealed by a slight shift in perspective.

A The Need for Critical Perspectives

For this reason (among others), it is essential to engage with viewpoints that reveal the human and social dimensions of environmental degradation, and to integrate those considerations both when diagnosing the problem and when prescribing a response. The dual aspect is crucial; a failure on either end is likely to lead to narrow and skewed understandings of the challenges facing us, as well as the ways in which we might meet those challenges. While there are a wide range of useful and important critiques of dominant understandings of both environmentalism and international law, there are some that can be particularly helpful in encouraging a shift in perspective.

Murray Bookchin's work, for example, continues to stand as a beacon of trenchant critique more than fifty years after the publication of his first book-length analysis of environmental ills, *Our Synthetic Environment*.[39] Bookchin is second to none in terms of offering a scathing assessment of the failure of liberal environmentalism, which he describes as "a balm for soothing the bad consciences of rapacious industrialists who engage in a tasteless ballet with environmental lobbyists, lawyers, and public officials,"[40] resulting in a series of "trade-offs" and "compromises" that have failed to restrain environmental degradation. Bookchin insists that this is due at least in part to liberal environmentalism's failure to come to terms with the tension inherent in mainstream economic thinking:

> [L]iberal environmentalism suffers from a consistent refusal to see that a capitalistic society based on competition and growth for its own sake must ultimately devour the natural world ... An economy that is structured around the maxim, "Grow or Die,"

[39] Lewis Herber, *Our Synthetic Environment* (New York: Knopf, 1962). Bookchin also used this pseudonym to publish an article entitled "The Problem of Chemicals in Food," *Contemporary Issues*, 3:12 (1952), which is regarded as his first foray into ecological critique.

[40] Murray Bookchin, *Remaking Society: Pathways to a Green Future* (Boston: South End Press, 1990), p.14.

must necessarily pit itself against the natural world and leave ecological ruin in its wake as it works its way through the biosphere.[41]

However, Bookchin is equally (if not more) critical of environmentalists who overlook or ignore the social dimensions of environmental harm, and characterize humans as the problem:

> If "people" as a *species* are responsible for environmental dislocations, these dislocations cease to be the result of *social* dislocations. A mythic "Humanity" is created – irrespective of whether we are talking about oppressed ethnic minorities, women, Third World people, or people in the First World – in which everyone is brought into complicity with powerful corporate elites in producing environmental dislocations. In this way, the social roots of environmental problems are shrewdly obscured. A new kind of biological "original sin" is created in which a vague group of animals called "Humanity" is turned into a destructive force that threatens the survival of the living world.[42]

In Bookchin's view, what is required instead is a "social ecology" that draws conceptual and practical connections between social hierarchy and environmental harm. And those connections are precisely those emphasized by social movements that have coalesced around demands for environmental justice.[43] These movements share the conviction that many communities are more the victims than the perpetrators of environmental degradation; that a disproportionate burden of environmental harm has fallen on those who are already marginalized by racial, class and gender inequality. But while

---

[41] Ibid., p. 15.   [42] Ibid., pp. 9–10.

[43] For anthologies that highlights many of the key aspects of movements for environmental justice, see Robert D. Bullard (ed.), *The Quest for Environmental Justice: Human Rights and the Politics of Pollution* (San Francisco: Sierra Club Books, 2005); Sylvia Hood Washington, Paul C. Rosier and Heather Goodall (eds.), *Echoes from the Poisoned Well: Global Memories of Environmental Injustice* (Lanham, MD: Lexington Books, 2006). For an analysis from the viewpoint of international environmental law, see Carmen G. Gonzalez, "Environmental Justice and International Environmental Law", in Shawkat Alam et al. (eds.), *Routledge Handbook of International Environmental Law* (London: Routledge, 2012).

reminding mainstream environmentalism that it should pay attention to the ways in which environmental burdens are unequally distributed, environmental justice has also insisted that demands for decent housing and safe working conditions must also be seen as part of the environmental platform, every bit as significant as the demand for clean air and water and wilderness conservation.[44]

From within the field of international law itself, TWAIL (Third World Approaches to International Law) scholarship emphasizes the need to engage with the perspectives and concerns of Third World peoples, and highlights the way in which dominant understandings of the field, like dominant understandings of environmentalism, have tended to assume and impose certain values as universal that are actually the product of a particular set of perspectives imposed through the exercise of political, economic, and disciplinary power. Usha Natarajan notes that TWAIL engagement may "help counteract the dominant international environmental law narrative of the Third World as seeking only poverty alleviation and uninterested in environmental protection," pointing out that "[t]he narrative obfuscates the lack of environmental consciousness in wealthy societies and ignores the progress that many Third World communities have made on sustainability issues."[45] With regard to environmental protection, TWAIL demands that we engage with the perspectives of marginalized communities, but it also points to the need to pay attention to history, to previous attempts to articulate alternatives to mainstream understandings of environmental protection and its relationship to development and the ways in which they seem to have fallen on deaf ears.

Consider, as one notable example, the "Cocoyoc Declaration" adopted by the participants at a joint UNEP/UNCTAD Symposium

---

[44] Similarly, concepts of "environmental space" and "ecological debt" have been developed as alternative ways of framing and understanding environmental degradation. See Karin Mickelson, "Leading Towards a Level Playing Field, Repaying Ecological Debt, or Making Environmental Space: Three Stories about International Environmental Cooperation," *Osgoode Hall Law Journal* 43 (2005), p. 137.

[45] Usha Natarajan, "TWAIL and the Environment: The State of Nature, the Nature of the State, and the Arab Spring," *Oregon Review of International Law*, 14 (2012), p. 189.

on Resource Use, Environment, and Development Strategies held in
Cocoyoc, Mexico, in 1974.[46] The Declaration calls for a new system
that could meet fundamental human needs for all without exceeding
the carrying capacity of the planet.[47] It highlights the continuing
effects of colonialism in the skewed distribution of resources,[48] and
goes further to proclaim that "pre-emption by the rich of a disproportionate share of key resources conflicts directly with the longer-term
interests of the poor."[49] Insisting that the fundamental problem facing
the international community is not a lack of resources but "maldistri-
bution and misuse" of existing resources, the Declaration asserts that
"mankind's predicament is rooted primarily in economic and social
structures and behavior within and between countries."[50] Market
mechanisms cannot be relied upon to address these issues. The
Declaration calls instead for a redefinition of the purpose of development, to focus on human beings and their needs, of which basic needs
are a necessary component. It also emphasizes the "diversity of development," taking into account the ways in which historical, cultural,
and other factors may shift developmental priorities in different directions. In so doing, the Declaration is absolutely clear as to what is
being abandoned:

> We reject the unilinear view which sees development essentially
> and inevitably as the effort to imitate the historical model of the
> countries that for various reasons happen to be rich today. For this
> reason, we reject the concept of "gaps" in development. The goal
> is not to "catch up," but to ensure the quality of life for all with a
> productive base compatible with the needs of future
> generations.[51]

In keeping with this attention to national circumstances, the Declaration also emphasizes national self-reliance, specifically rejecting
the notion that this should be equated with autarky, and pointing
instead to the need for "international cooperation for collective self-
reliance."[52]

---

[46] "The Cocoyoc Declaration: A call for the reform of the international
economic order," *Bulletin of the Atomic Scientists*, 31:3 (1975), p. 6.
[47] Ibid., p. 6.   [48] Ibid., pp. 6–7.   [49] Ibid., p. 7.   [50] Ibid., p. 6.
[51] Ibid., p. 8.   [52] Ibid., p. 9.

The Cocoyoc Declaration is often cited as a turning point in the rethinking of orthodox development theory,[53] in particular for its emphasis on participatory development. Read against the backdrop of the critical approaches to environmentalism and international law discussed previously, it reminds us that while mainstream or dominant understandings of economic growth and prosperity may well be fundamentally at odds with what would be required to establish ecological equilibrium, we need to be wary of blanket condemnations that lose sight of legitimate aspirations that are held by so many of the world's peoples. The reality is that the problems identified in 1974 remain, forty years later; many continue to live in unimaginably difficult conditions, and inequality persists and has worsened. While we have seen progress on some of the Millennium Development goals, one wonders whether this reflects their relatively modest scope rather than a ramping up of the commitment to poverty alleviation. Furthermore, progress is not uniform across all the goals; it appears to be particularly slow with regard to those with a specific gender dimension, for example, and even where gains in gender equality have been made, the needs of some of the most vulnerable women, including indigenous and minority women, lag behind.

B Guarding Against Double Standards

However, this is not the only turn that our kaleidoscope needs to make. Another aspect that needs to be kept in mind is the double standard of condemning the rush to develop and consume on the part of many states (and citizens) of the developing world. In recent years, China, India, and other large developing countries have increasingly come to be perceived as the international community's *nouveau riche.* There is a pronounced tendency to tut-tut at their ill-mannered insistence on conspicuous consumption. Examples of this attitude abound. A review in the *New York Times* of "Red Obsession," a 2013 documentary about the Chinese elite's passion for fine red wines, notes that the

---

[53] See for example Keith Pezzoli, "Sustainable Development: A Transdisciplinary Overview of the Literature," *Journal of Environmental Planning and Management,* 40:5 (1997), 549–74, p. 551.

movie "raises legitimate concerns about the cultural and economic implications of status-minded overconsumption."[54] An entry in the Worldwatch Institute's "China Watch" discussing luxury spending in China refers to a senior Worldwatch editor as pointing out that "[a]lthough the average Chinese still consumes far less than the average North American or European, as the global demand for goods and services skyrockets, this could have serious implications for the planet's natural resource base."[55] At one level, these statements are simply factual assessments of the indisputable dangers involved in the replication of the Northern (and specifically North American) model of consumption across the globe: the "bomb under the world," as it was once described in the title of a documentary by Canadian journalist Gwynne Dyer that presented the potential effects of consumerism spreading across the planet.[56] At a deeper level, however, they reflect a lack of awareness of both the historical resonance of these types of assertions and the hypocrisy that might be said to infuse them.

When we look at China and India and see doom lurking, are we wilfully blind to the extent to the ways in which an "Asian menace" or images of being overcome by a mass of people of darker-hued skin tones have haunted "the West" in the past? Matthew Connelly, who has explored these concerns in the troubled history of population control policy, notes that at an influential "Conference on Population Problems" held in 1952, "the most sensitive and contentious debates ... concerned whether 'industrial development should be withheld' from poor, agrarian countries like India."[57] In fact,

---

[54] Nicole Herrington, "Red Obsession," *New York Times*, September 6, 2013, p. C15. While this does not refer specifically to Chinese overconsumption, nothing in the review indicates that overconsumption in the North is a concern.

[55] Worldwatch Institute, China Watch, "Luxury Spending: China's Affluent Entering 'Enjoy Now' Phase of Consumption," online: www.worldwatch.org/luxury-spending-chinas-affluent-entering-enjoy-now-phase-consumption.

[56] "The Bomb Under the World," Part 1 of "The Human Race," National Film of Canada and Green Lion Productions, 1994.

[57] Matthew Connelly, *Fatal Misconception: The Struggle to Control World Population* (Cambridge: Harvard University Press, 2008), p. 157.

according to Connelly, India appears to have been a particularly significant concern. Connelly quotes from the transcript in which one of the conference participants stated:

> What is there about India that makes this situation so acute?
> [I] think unconsciously we are scared, and I think we have a right to be. In other words, that is where the ferment is taking place. That is where the pressure is the greatest.[58]

A sense of historical perspective might perhaps be excused, but the censure of the "rush to develop" also reflects an inability (or unwillingness) to come to terms with the extent to which the model of consumption which has been so enthusiastically embraced by many in the developing world that has been fostered by economic and social elites within the global North. The emphasis on trade and consumption, as already discussed, was one of the hallmarks of the post-war consensus on economic prosperity. And quite apart from the imposition of these models on at the state-to-state level, one must also acknowledge an equally pervasive, and perhaps even more effective, influence. For decades, through movies, television shows, and advertising, people around the world have been bombarded with images of a "good life" that requires – indeed, that is *defined* by – consumption on a scale that is unprecedented in human history.

Perhaps most disturbing, however, is the hypocrisy of assuming that consumption will or should be curtailed in the global South while taking for granted (whether explicitly or implicitly) that Northern standards of consumption will continue. It would be problematic enough if these were simply pious variations on the theme of the enduring nature of poverty, but this is only part of the problem. Overconsumption, whether amongst large portions of the population of the global North or amongst a proportionally smaller but equally enthusiastic percentage of citizens of the global South may well *require* underconsumption by vast numbers of people. It is a pattern of consumption that assumes and necessitates a lack of consumption, given that its replication across the globe would make environmental collapse an all too real possibility.

---

[58] Ibid., p. 158.

Meanwhile, it is worth asking: how many in the North are reducing their own consumption in far-reaching ways that actually have the possibility of reducing this imbalance? Eliminating meat from their diet, or reducing it to the occasional special event? Reducing their carbon footprint by limiting air travel to the extent absolutely necessary? While a small number of individuals are beginning to make a shift in this direction, and that number may in fact be growing, for the majority, overconsumption remains the norm.

A simple thought experiment might help illustrate this point. Suppose that we were to translate this debate onto the domestic stage. Would we accept any arguments that posited the continuation of vast social and economic inequality not only alongside the lavish lifestyles of an elite class (which one could argue we are witnessing today all around the world), but in fact precisely *in order* to maintain those lifestyles? Could there be any doubt that any such argument would be little more than a screen for self-interest and hypocrisy? And would even the most cynical among us accept its logic? The answer to all these questions is clear. What that means is that we do not have the luxury of an "either/or" solution to the tension between meeting human needs and aspirations and maintaining (or reestablishing) the natural systems upon which we and other species depend. Resolving this tension, then, remains the central – and inescapable – challenge for international environmental law.

IV CONCLUSION: FROM KALEIDOSCOPE TO FRACTAL?

It seems fitting, in drawing these reflections to a close, to come back to Freud and his own concluding remarks in *Civilization and its Discontents*. Writing in 1929 with considerable prescience, he noted:

> Men have gained control over the forces of nature to such an extent that with their help they would have no difficulty in exterminating one another to the last man. They know this, and hence comes a large part of their current unrest, their unhappiness and their mood of anxiety.[59]

---

[59] Freud, *Civilization and its Discontents*, p. 112.

Despite what many have perceived as a bleak assessment of humanity's prospects in the book as a whole, Freud seems to have been unwilling to end on a despairing note. He went on to express the expectation that "eternal Eros," the life instinct, would reassert himself, adding in 1931: "But who can foresee with what success and with what result?"[60]

We may not share the sense that a powerful instinctive force might act to restore some kind of equilibrium, but Freud's characterization of the point that human society had reached in the early part of the twentieth century is all the more compelling at the present time, as we face an array of environmental challenges that appear overwhelming in their magnitude and scope. It is clear that a fundamental shift is required – so fundamental, in fact, that many view it as impossibility. The current state of affairs is often treated as a kind of runaway train – certainly beyond our control individually, a view with which it is difficult to take issue, but also (and much more problematically) as being beyond the reach of even collective action. This is a kind of learned helplessness that all too often can become an excuse for inaction or even its reverse. After all, if things are moving inexorably towards the precipice, why not simply sit back and enjoy the ride? As Ileana Porras has suggested, it is worth considering whether a fear of overreaching ecological constraints contributes to what she terms "binge development": "exclusively present-oriented, clearly excessive, unconstrained by any sense of limits and blissfully unconcerned with future repercussions ... We know there are consequences; we know it is not sustainable; yet we continue to consume in a manner that is out of control and irresponsible: as though there were no tomorrow."[61]

It is essential to bear in mind, however, that economic models do not exist in a Platonic ether, beyond the purview of mere mortals. The dominant model of economic prosperity is not an ideal that has informed human thinking about progress and well-being throughout

---

[60] Ibid.

[61] Ileana Porras, "Panama City Reflections: Growing the City in the Time of Sustainable Development," *Tennessee Journal of Law and Policy*, 14:2 (2008), p. 394.

human history. It is the product of a particular time and place, a set of assumptions and choices that can and should be challenged. In criticizing liberal environmentalism's inability or unwillingness to offer meaningful alternatives to the status quo, Bookchin argues:

> [W]hat renders the liberal approach so hopelessly ineffectual is the fact that it takes the present social order for granted, like the air we breathe and the water we drink. All of [its] "compromises" and "trade-offs" rest on the paralyzing belief that a market society, privately owned property, and the present-day bureaucratic nation-state cannot be changed in any basic sense. Thus, it is the prevailing order that sets the terms of any "compromise" or trade-off," just like the rules of a chess game and the grid of a chess board determine in advance what the players can do—not the dictates of reason and morality.[62]

If what is required is a refusal to take the current dominant model and its assumptions for granted, is the solution the replacement of the prevailing paradigm with a new pattern, a new and better way to arrange our many overlapping and competing interests, both human and non-human? In this essay I have used the metaphor of a kaleidoscope to reveal an overarching pattern that can help us understand what appears to be an irrational "war against nature," but I have also argued that we cannot overlook different aspects of the pattern that are far more difficult to reject out of hand. Perhaps what we need rather than a new pattern is a new way of understanding patterns, along the lines of a fractal through which order emerges organically out of what might initially appear to be chaos, the sort of design that can be perceived in crystals or ferns.

Such an approach might be perceived in the alternative understandings of human well-being that have begun to emerge in countries like Bolivia and Ecuador, where the idea of "Buen Vivir" or "Vivir Bien" (literally "to live well," but often translated as "the good life") have come to inform the discourse of both governments and social movements.[63] The concept is often contrasted with the idea of a

---

[62] Bookchin, *Remaking Society*, p. 15.

[63] Although the government of Evo Morales in Bolivia is often identified with these ideas, it has been criticized for merely paying lip service to them. For a

"better life," which is characterized as "individualistic, separate from others and even at the expense of others."[64] While drawing on Quechua, Aymara, and other indigenous traditions that perceive the non-human world as equally deserving of value and respect, this is not seen as a return to past traditions so much as a way of bringing those traditions into dialogue with other perspectives as well as the needs of the present. As Eduardo Gudynas explains, "Buen Vivir offers a common ground where critical perspectives on development, originated from different ontologies, meet and interact ... But [it] is also a politically oriented platform, as its actors pushes for alternatives to development."[65]

Humans, then, are not omnivorous pests, akin to bacteria that multiply in a Petri dish. In communities like these, all over the world, they are creating new ways of interacting with the natural world, or reclaiming old ways that offer insights and values that the dominant model has lost sight of, or coming up with innovative fusions of the two. Amidst the horrors that we confront in what appears to be a never-ending war against nature, we should never lose sight of the beauty of those images, and of the patterns that may emerge to join them.

highly critical account from a leading Aymara intellectual, see Simón Yampara Huarachi, "Cosmovivencia Andina. Vivir y convivir en armonía integral," *Bolivian Studies Journal/Revista de Estudios Bolivianos*, 18 (2011), 1–22, pp. 3–5.

[64] Julieta Paredes, "Plan de las Mujeres: marco conceptual y metodogía para el Buen Vivir," *Bolivian Studies Journal/Revista de Estudios Bolivianos*, 15–17 (2008–10), 191–210, p. 195. The translation is mine.

[65] Eduardo Gudynas, "Buen Vivir: Today's tomorrow," *Development*, 54:4 (2011), 441–7, p. 447.

PART II Gender

3 DECODING CRISIS IN INTERNATIONAL LAW: A QUEER FEMINIST PERSPECTIVE

Dianne Otto

INTRODUCTION

International law has aptly been called a "discipline of crisis"[1] – although I rather like the idea that it could be a "crisis of discipline" (as I inadvertently described it in a recent footnote).[2] For better or worse (and I will argue that it is usually for worse), many of international law's most productive formative moments have been in response to calamitous occurrences understood to be crises, and efforts by scholars to map the development of the law, through the lens of those "incidents" or "events" that count as crises, abound.[3] While emergency law-making was a regular feature of colonial governance,[4] the productivity of crisis for international law intensified in the aftermath of 9/11, which suspended the international community in a more or less permanent state of catastrophe. Since then, crises, both real and imagined, are no longer confined to (post) colonial, military, and

---

[1] Hilary Charlesworth, "International Law: A Discipline of Crisis," (2002) *Modern Law Review*, 377, p. 65.

[2] Dianne Otto, "Celebrating Complexity," *Proceedings of the 106th Annual Meeting of the American Society of International Law* (2012), p. 169, footnote 5, wrongly citing Charlesworth above.

[3] See, for example, Fleur Johns, Richard Joyce and Sundhya Pahuja (eds.), *Events: The Force of International Law* (Oxford: Routledge, 2011); Michael Riesman and A. Willard (eds.), *International Incidents: the law that counts in world politics* (Princeton: Princeton University Press, 1988).

[4] Nasser Hussain, *The Jurisprudence of Emergency: The Rule of Law under Colonialism* (University of Michigan Press, 2003).

financial emergencies – although these have not been in short supply. They have been declared with respect to issues of the everyday, such as the environment, immigration, poverty, health, and scarcities of food and water. The spreading atmosphere of crisis has enabled technologies of "crisis governance" to assume ascendancy, including the increased acceptability of executive law-making[5] and reliance on economic, technocratic, and military experts to solve global problems.[6] Crisis governance has fostered neoliberal expansionism by legitimating the adoption of short-term, quick-fix responses that ignore the larger historical context of causation and individualize responsibility, dismissing analytical and critical perspectives, shutting out democratic participation and deliberation in the name of urgency, and depicting everyday structural inequalities and injustices as given.[7]

In thinking critically about our discipline of crisis, I am assisted by Italian philosopher Giorgio Agamben who, drawing on the work of Carl Schmitt and Walter Benjamin, argues that the fiction of the emergency has a long history of creating new spaces for law's production and reproduction, enabling law to extend its empire, reconfiguring the relationship between the state and its subjects and further colonizing "life itself" by taking possession of the human sphere of activity that we know as "politics."[8] While Agamben sees this process as inexorable, I do not (or at least I hope it is not). But if life and politics are to be reclaimed from the grip of crisis-law, which all too

---

[5] Detlav Vagts, "Editorial Comments, Hegemonic International Law," *American Journal of International Law*, 95 (2001), p. 843; Jose Alvarez, "Hegemonic International Law Revisited," *American Journal of International Law*, 97 (2003), p. 873.

[6] Sally Engle Merry, "Measuring the World: Indicators, Human Rights and Global Governance," paper for Wenner Gren/School of Advanced research conference, "Corporate Lives: New Perspectives on the Social Life of the Corporate Form," January 6, 2009 (copy on file with author). See also Kevin E. Davis, Angelina Fishes, Benedict Kingsbury and Sally Engle Merry (eds.), *Governance by Indicators: Global Power through Quantification and Rankings* (Oxford University Press, 2012).

[7] Charlesworth, "International Law."

[8] Giorgio Agamben, *State of Exception*, K. Attrell (trans.), (University of Chicago Press, 2005), pp. 11–12.

often becomes permanent and can even intensify its hold, as so often happens in the postcolonial context,[9] it is important to understand what makes a crisis so amenable to the spread of unaccountable executive power and the demise of politics. As seen since 9/11, explosions of crisis-law can make many practices, long thought to be unjustifiable, widely accepted. Crisis has provided the means of garnering new public support for racialized policing and security agencies acting outside the law, for blatant disregard of long-standing norms of human rights and fundamental freedoms, and for military and economic interventions that shore up the inequitable global order. The question that ultimately interests me is whether it is possible to turn the momentum of a crisis to more progressive ends. My focus in this chapter is on the insights that queer and feminist theory and activism offer in partial response to these questions.

I THE TECHNOLOGIES OF SEXUAL AND GENDER PANICS

One of the recurring features of the anatomy of crisis governance and the law it produces, not discussed by Agamben but impossible to miss from a queer feminist perspective, is the proliferation of sexual and gender "panics." Such panics play an important role in crisis governance by helping to divert attention from larger injustices perpetrated in the name of the emergency, while also enabling the adoption of ever more personally invasive laws and regulations that states would otherwise not be able to justify. As Gayle Rubin, sex-radical feminist anthropologist, observed over two decades ago in relation to sexual panics, "sexual acts are burdened with an excess of significance," making them available to "function as signifiers for personal and social apprehensions to which they have no intrinsic connection."[10]

---

[9] Hussain, *The Jurisprudence of Emergency* , pp. 137–40.
[10] Gayle Rubin, "Thinking Sex: Notes for a Radical Theory of the Politics of Sexuality," in Carole S. Vance (ed.), *Pleasure and Danger: Exploring Female Sexuality* (1984), p. 297.

The mystification of sexuality, at least in western societies, she said, makes sex a productive site for the generation of "rage, anxiety, and sheer terror" which, in turn, enables the state to enact new laws and regulations that extend its control even more deeply into our intimate lives.[11]

Anxieties associated with gender transgressions – when people do not perform their gender identities in keeping with mainstream social norms – are also often implicated in sexual panics as, for example, with the issue of sex work/prostitution. Panics about sex work are productive because they draw on anxieties about sexuality, associated with its commodification, as well as expectations about gender, associated with women's domestic focus and dependency. As I will argue, gender panics can also work independently of sexuality, in a similar way to the sexual panic described by Rubin, by creating a climate of fear that enables the proliferation of law that reaches more deeply into our personal lives and helps to deflect attention from those everyday injustices that work in the interests of the state and the privileged few.[12] The generation of fear by sexual and gender panics fosters compliant populations who are more ready to accept – even welcome – an increase in executive law-making and militarized policing. In the context of international law, examples of such panics, in the service of crisis governance, abound.

Those directly responsible for the 9/11 atrocities were themselves cast as sexually dubious by reports in the west of their apparent preference for masculine company while on earth and their hopes for reward in the form of eternal access to virgins in the afterlife.[13] The intonation of sexual perversity assisted the project of denigrating Islam and dehumanizing the perpetrators, casting them in the (more) alarming register of hysterical fanatics, rather than that of (less alarming) international criminals. This undertone of erotic

[11] Ibid.
[12] Susan Marks, "Human Rights and the Bottom Billion," *European Human Rights Law Review*, 1 (2009), p. 37.
[13] Anna M. Agathangelou, "Power, Borders, Security, Wealth: Lessons of Violence and desire from September 11," *International Studies Quarterly*, 48 (2004), p. 530.

depravity helped US President Bush to declare the advent of a "new kind of war,"[14] a manoeuvre that simultaneously released him from the need to comply with the existing law and signalled the necessity of new law to deal with the emergency. Indeed, the crisis of 9/11 has been a bonanza for international law. I want to discuss two other examples of sexual panics, which have served as triggers for explosions of law that restrict individual rights and freedoms while also averting attention from systemic injustices of western economic and military domination: panics about the trafficking of women and girls into prostitution and peacekeeping sexual exploitation and abuse.

Sexual panics about the cross-border trafficking of women and girls to work in the sex industry have been a recurring feature of the development of international law. International agreements, ostensibly aimed at curbing the international trade in "white" women, were first adopted in the early twentieth century.[15] While the scare of large numbers of vulnerable European women being deceived or forced into satisfying the sexual appetites of foreign (racialized) men has been shown to lack a factual basis (most women involved made choices based on their economic circumstances),[16] the treaties based

---

[14] The *New York Times*, September 16, 2001, reporting on President Bush's radio address to the nation on September 15, 2001.

[15] *International Agreement for the Suppression of the White Slave Traffic*, Paris, May 18, 1904, entered into force July 18, 1905, 1 LNTS 83; *International Convention for the Suppression of White Slave Traffic*, Paris, May 4, 1910, 211 Consol TS 45; 1912 Gr Brit TS No. 20; *International Convention for the Suppression of the Traffic in Women and Children*, Geneva, September 30, 1921, 9 LNTS 415; *International Convention for the Suppression of the Traffic in Women of Full Age*, Geneva, October 11, 1933, in force August 24, 1934, 150 LNTS 431. For discussion see Jo Doezema, "Loose Women or Lost Women? The Re-Emergence of the Myth of White Slavery in Contemporary Discourses of Trafficking in Women," *Gender Issues*, 18 (2000), p. 30, who notes that the term "white slavery" was first used in 1839 in an anti-Semitic context where Jewish men were seen as responsible for trafficking European women.

[16] Elizabeth Bernstein, "Militarized Humanitarianism Meets Carceral Feminism: The Politics of Sex, Rights, and Freedom in Contemporary Anti-Trafficking Campaigns," *Signs: Journal of Women in Culture and Society*, 36 (2010), p. 50.

on this mythology of panic proved to be an effective means of justifying harsher immigration controls and more punitive and discriminatory border policing.[17]

Another spike in anti-trafficking crusades has occurred over
the last decade and a half, driven largely by the United States in the
context of post–9/11 nervousness about security and undocumented
(potentially terrorist) migration.[18] As a result, there has been another
surge in international and domestic anti-trafficking laws.[19] Like the
earlier campaigns, the contemporary crusades rely heavily on iconic
narratives of innocent and helpless women, unable to exercise free
will, needing to be rescued from the clutches of traffickers, and even
sometimes their own families, who exploit their sexual vulnerability.[20]
The anxiety induced by these images, intensified by efforts to equate
sex trafficking with modern-day slavery, has enabled governments,
supported by the international community, to adopt draconian laws
that impose harsh criminal penalties on supposed traffickers as well as
their purported victims. These measures, like the early anti-trafficking
treaties, completely deny women's agency by making the question
of their consent to migration, and/or working in the sex industry,
irrelevant, even in this post-colonial age of universal human rights.[21]
The idea that women are not capable of autonomous sexual decision-
making, or cannot be trusted in this regard, is made possible by

[17] Jo Doezema, "Loose Women or Lost Women? The Re-Emergence of the
Myth of White Slavery in Contemporary Discourses on Trafficking in
Women," *Gender Issues*, 23 (Winter 2000), pp. 43–4.

[18] Janie Chuang, "The United States as Global Sheriff: Using Unilateral
Sanctions to Combat Human Trafficking," *Michigan Journal of International
Law*, 27 (2005–2006), p. 437. See further *Trafficking Victims Protection Act
2000*, 22 U.S.C. ss 7107–10 (2000) and subsequent amendments.

[19] Protocol to Prevent, Suppress and Punish Trafficking in Persons, Especially
Women and Children, Supplementing the UN Convention Against
Transnational Organized Crime, G.A. Res. 55/25, 2237 U.N.T.S. 319,
November 15, 2000.

[20] Jayashri Srikantiah, "Perfect Victims and Real Survivors: The Iconic Victim in
Domestic Human Trafficking Laws," *Buffalo University Law Review*, 87
(2007), pp. 191–5.

[21] Janie A. Chuang, "Exploitation Creep and the Unmaking of Human
Trafficking Law," pp. 29–37 (copy on file with author).

conservative masculinist tropes of both gender and sexuality. These laws have, in turn, justified states allocating substantially increased financial and administrative resources to border surveillance, security police and detention facilities, all cloaked in a "mantle of righteous-ness"[22] that claims to be protecting defenceless women and children. In fact, these efforts have made matters worse for many women who are treated as victims of trafficking, despite seeing themselves as economic migrants.

Global neoliberal governance is served by the panic about sex trafficking in a number of ways. By deflecting attention from other forms of human trafficking and other forms of exploitative labour, although significantly more prevalent, the panic almost normalizes them by contrast. It also locates the source of harm in wicked individuals, rather than in the structural conditions of inequality, poverty and destitution that motivate people to migrate, often at great personal risk, in order to secure their livelihoods and a better future for their children. Individualizing the blame depoliticizes the issue of exploitative labour and serves to absolve states and corporate actors, who reap the benefits of unfair and abusive labour practices, from responsibility. Human rights advocates have tried to counter the dominance of the crime control paradigm, legitimated by the sexual panic, by advocating for the human rights of trafficking victims. But their efforts have been limited to promoting the rights of victims *after* they have been trafficked, partly in response to highly aggressive criminal justice measures and partly because of internal disagreement over prostitution reform.[23] The disproportionate focus on sex trafficking has also made it much more difficult for those human rights advocates seeking to address the structural inequalities that drive all forms of human trafficking, because they have to work against the power of a panic to define the field.

A second example of a sexual panic in the service of global crisis governance is the response to the problem of sexual exploitation and

---

[22] Karen E. Bravo, "Exploring the Analogy: Modern Trafficking in Humans and the Trans-Atlantic Slave Trade," *Boston University International Law Journal*, 25 (2007), p. 207.

[23] Chuang, "Exploitation Creep," pp. 49–50.

abuse in UN peacekeeping missions. We are led to believe the problem to be endemic, as with sex trafficking. Sexual violence and exploitation by peacekeepers has been documented in Angola, Bosnia and Herzegovina, Cambodia, Democratic Republic of the Congo (DRC), East Timor, Liberia, Mozambique, Kosovo, Sierra Leone, and Somalia.[24] In Liberia, Guinea, and Sierra Leone, a pattern of peacekeeping personnel trading sex for in exchange for humanitarian commodities and services was found to be "chronic and entrenched,"[25] while in the DRC, the problem of sexual exploit-ation and abuse of local Congolese women and girls was found to be "serious and ongoing."[26] Yet, on close reading, the reports of sexual mistreatment, and the various official responses to them, make no effort to distinguish between sex that is exploitative or abusive, and sex that is not. Repeatedly, no substantive or consequential distinc-tions are made between consensual sexual relationships and sex work, on the one hand, and sexual offences like rape, forced prosti-tution, and sex trafficking on the other. A typical explanation for this slippage is as follows:

> There have been abuses involving peacekeepers and local women. The most commonly reported ones are those associated with prostitution ... Although some peacekeepers have established more permanent intimate connections with local women, such relationships can rarely be considered purely voluntary, tinged as they are by the necessities of hunger and the need for housing or jobs.[27]

[24] Elisabeth Rehn and Ellen Johnson Sirleaf, *Women, War and Peace: The Independent Experts' Assessment on the Impact of Armed Conflict on Women and Women's Role in Peace-building* (New York: United Nations Development Fund for Women, 2002), p. 70.

[25] UNHCR and Save the Children UK, *Sexual Violence and Exploitation: The Experience of Refugee Children in Liberia, Guinea and Sierra Leone*, report of assessment mission carried out from 22 October to 30 November 2001, January 2002, p. 9.

[26] Office of Internal Oversight Services, *Investigation by the OIOS into allegations of sexual exploitation and abuse in the UN Organization Mission in the Democratic Republic of the Congo*, A/59/661, 59th Sess., January 5, 2005, para. 39.

[27] Rehn and Sirleaf, *Women, War and Peace*, p. 71.

The result is that diverse sexual activities are conflated by an atmosphere of crisis and a culture of "sexual negativity"[28] into a single problematic of sexual injury or harm, and the response is protective rather than rights-based.[29]

Fuelled by the alarm that was generated, the UN Secretary General's Bulletin, adopted in 2003 to address the problem, takes the extreme position of banning virtually all sex between peacekeeping personnel and host populations.[30] This astounding over-inclusiveness would not have been possible without the power of panic. Some implementation policies in specific peacekeeping missions go even further than the letter of the Bulletin, prohibiting all forms of "fraternization" (everyday interactions) between off-duty peacekeepers and local populations,[31] reviving colonial hierarchies of race, sexuality, and gender. The Bulletin's promotion of protective representations of women, and its conflation of women and children, set back the projects of women's and children's rights and give a renewed legitimacy to conservative hierarchies of gender and sexuality in post-conflict societies.[32] In reality, the zero tolerance of sex has pushed the sexual economies of peacekeeping missions underground, preventing

---

[28] Rubin, "Thinking Sex," p. 278, uses this term to describe the prevalence of the idea that sex is a "dangerous, destructive, negative force," unless performed pursuant to a narrow set of socially approved "excuses," such as "marriage, reproduction and love." She limits her observations to "Western cultures," and blames "most Christian traditions" for originating the idea. However, it is clear that sexual negativity characterizes many non-Western traditions as well, although it is manifested through historically and culturally specific social practices.

[29] Dianne Otto, "The Sexual Tensions of UN Peace Support Operations: A plea for 'sexual positivity'," *Finnish Yearbook of International Law*, 28 (2007), p. 33.

[30] Secretary-General's Bulletin, *Special measures for protection from sexual exploitation and abuse*, ST/SGB/2003/13, October 9, 2003. The only exceptions are when the people involved are married, or have been given permission by the Head of Mission to engage in a sexual relationship.

[31] Thalif Dean, "'No Go' Zones to prevent Sexual Abuse by UN Peacekeepers," International Press Service, April 14, 2005.

[32] For further development of this idea, see Dianne Otto, "Making sense of zero tolerance policies in peacekeeping sexual economies," in Vanessa Munro and

organisation around health and employment conditions and making the survival of the victims it claims to protect even more precarious.

The hyperbole about sexual exploitation and abuse, and all the regulatory and surveillance activity that it has generated, stands in striking contrast to the silence about the scandalous shortage of humanitarian resources in peacekeeping missions. It is poverty which largely drives peacekeeping sexual economies, and the problem is exacerbated by the imposition (without democratic consent) of free market economic policies in post-conflict societies, in the name of neoliberal globalization, which benefit only a privileged few. These matters threaten to tarnish the UN's reputation much more fundamentally than a sex scandal.[33] Thus, the outrage about sex displaces outrage at the global inequalities in wealth that are reflected in peacekeeping missions – the lack of employment opportunities in post-conflict societies; the insufficient clean water and food rations available to international aid agencies to meet human needs in a world of plenty; and the despair of humanitarian workers who feel they are unable to make a difference.[34] In the dire poverty of postconflict societies, manufacturing a sexual panic serves to (mis)recognize the primary harm as sexual, rather than economic, and its solution is understood in terms of apprehending and punishing individual perpetrators rather than addressing the systemic conditions of poverty and deprivation. Attention is deflected from the responsibilities of international community, including its neoliberal economic institutions, to address poverty in post-conflict societies. Also unacknowledged are the obligations of states to cooperate internationally to ensure that everyone enjoys economic and social rights[35] and promote development that is equitable and sustainable.[36] As Alice Miller

Carl F. Stychin (eds.), *Sexuality and the Law: Feminist Engagements* (Routledge-Cavendish, 2007), p. 259.

[33] Otto, "Sexual Tensions."

[34] Barbara Harrell-Bond, "Can Humanitarian Work with Refugees by Humane?," *Human Rights Quarterly*, 24 (2002), p. 51.

[35] International Covenant on Economic, Social and Cultural Rights (1966), art. 2(1).

[36] Declaration on the Right to Development, GA Res. 41/128, December 4, 1986.

wryly observes, "sexual exploitation" is the only form of exploitation that appears to be generating policy responses.[37]

In the foregoing examples, anxiety about performances of gender takes a back seat to those stirred by sexual practices outside the institution of heterosexual marriage. However, I now turn to a number of instances where gender is the primary signifier that, like sexuality, can be attributed an "excess of significance," enabling alarm to be manufactured around non-conformity with authorized gender roles, as a technique of crisis governance. In the aftermath of 9/11, anxiety about veiled women, whose performances of gender do not conform to western models of "enlightened" gender expression, was soon whipped into frenzy by headline news stories,[38] including a national radio address by US First Lady Laura W. Bush.[39] The gender panic helped to justify the continuing muscularity of the military occupation of Afghanistan as a means of rescuing Muslim women from the barbarism of their culture, in the face of waning popular support for the occupation in the West. The panic also drew attention away from the repressive new laws and techniques of crisis governance that were rapidly emerging, including the Security Council's (executive) requirement that all UN member states adopt a far-reaching and detailed set of anti-terrorism measures, that seriously eroded personal rights and freedoms and granted extensive new powers to security organizations.[40] Meanwhile, in Afghanistan, the situation for women worsened considerably, compounded by a backlash against women's rights fuelled by the failure to work with local women and men to translate universal norms into local vernacular.[41]

---

[37] Alice M. Miller, "Sexuality, Violence Against Women, and Human Rights," *Health and Human Rights*, 7 (2004), pp. 31–2.

[38] Ratna Kapur, "Un-Veiling Women's Rights in the 'War on Terrorism'," *Duke Journal of Gender Law and Policy* 9 (2002), p. 211.

[39] Laura Bush, "Radio Address to the Nation," November 17, 2001.

[40] Security Council Resolution 1373, UN Doc. S/RES/1373, September 28, 2001.

[41] Sari Kouvo, "Taking Women Seriously? Conflict, State-Building and Gender in Afghanistan," in Sari Kouvo and Zoe Pearson (eds.), *Feminist Perspectives on Contemporary International Law: Between Resistance and Compliance?* (Onati/Hart, 2011), p. 175.

Single mothers have also provided grist to the mill of gender panics, particularly in the context of changes to social security programmes in the wake of the global economic crisis. The punishing regime of austerity measures introduced in Europe relies, at least in part, on the panic of the single (read bad) welfare-dependent mother looting the public purse.[42] Successfully trialled earlier in the United States,[43] shifting the blame for crisis, and its burden, onto poor and often racialized women who do not fit the middle-class stereotype of responsible womanhood, is an effective diversionary technique that draws attention away from the responsibility of states and the corporate beneficiaries of punishing neoliberal economic policies. The panic about lone mothers, and their uncontrolled sexuality, makes the neoliberal shift from social security as entitlement to social security as individual responsibility, more socially palatable. It follows then, as Agamben anticipates, that the shift justified in the name of crisis becomes the norm. Yet, as we know, reduced social protections do not provide a solution to economic crises and are likely to make the situation worse by reducing the flexibility and resilience needed to survive economic uncertainty.[44]

My last example of gender panics that have served the interests of crisis governance is the casting of feminist and queer human rights advocacy and activism as terrorism. The 2009 Report of the UN Special Rapporteur on the promotion and protection of human rights while countering terrorism, which analyzed counter-terrorism from a gender perspective, drew attention to the regularity with which women's human rights defenders are accused of being members of

---

[42] Emily Grabham and Jenny Smith, "From social security to individual responsibility (Part Two): Writing off poor women's work in the Welfare Reform Act 2009," *Journal of Social Welfare and Family Law*, 32 (2010), p. 81.

[43] Nancy Fraser and Linda Gordon, "A Genealogy of Dependency: Tracing a Keyword of the U.S. Welfare State," *Signs: Journal of Women in Culture and Society*, 19:2 (1994), p. 309.

[44] Statement to the General Assembly by Ariranga G. Pillay, Chairperson of the CESCR, 67th Session (October 23, 2012); Ariranga G. Pillay, Letter on behalf of the Committee on Economic Social and Cultural Rights to all States Parties to the ICESCR on the protection of rights in the context of economic and financial crisis, May 16, 2012.

terrorist groups, and consequently arrested and persecuted in the name of countering terror,[45] including in the Philippines, Sri Lanka, and Sierra Leone.[46] In the Special Rapporteur's analysis, this illustrated the danger of overly broad definitions of terrorism, which is characteristic of emergency law and a problem for many reasons. From my perspective, the demonizing of feminists as gender deviants is yet another example of a gender panic that works to justify intensification of the state's disciplinary laws and institutions and to divert attention from systemic economic and social injustices. My reading is borne out by the incarceration of members of the feminist punk rock band Pussy Riot, whose questioning of Russian democracy, homophobia, and gender conformity was described in panicked terms by the judge at their trial as "shatter[ing] the constitutional foundations of the state."[47] The alarm associated with Pussy Riot has clearly justified the introduction of repressive new laws in Russia, some of which threaten the "foreign" funding of women's crisis centres, cast as a menace under the broad arc of the panic of gender deviancy.[48] Meanwhile, the terror of state and corporate brutality, the concentration of wealth in very few privileged hands, and the flagrant disregard of constitutional and democratic rights appears to be unchallengeable.

The heavy reliance of crisis governance on the technique of the panic – whether based on sexual and/or gendered (or racial) anxieties – is clear. Such panics project "rage, anxiety, and sheer

---

[45] Report of the Special Rapporteur on the promotion and protection of human rights and fundamental freedoms while countering terrorism, A/64/211, 3 August 2009, para. 27.

[46] Megan Cossey, "Female Asian Activists Feel Singled Out for Attack," Women's E-News, December 4, 2006, http://womensenews.org/story/equalitywomen%E2%80%99s-rights/061204/female-asian-activists-feel-singled-out-attack.

[47] Janet Elise Johnson and Aino Saarinen, "Twenty-First-Century Feminisms under Repression: Gender Regime Change and the Women's Crisis Center Movement in Russia," *Signs: Journal of Women in Culture and Society*, 38:3 (2013), p. 562.

[48] Ibid. The new law requires NGOs receiving foreign funding to register as "foreign agents."

terror," as observed by Rubin, onto the bodies of those perceived to be deviant because they do not conform to dominant heteronormative and masculinist social prescriptions. Ratna Kapur describes these easy targets for panic as "sexual subalterns," who, in the Indian context of her analysis include sex workers, beauty queens, and migrant women, all of whom make economic choices that give them life outside family supervision.[49] The panic shifts attention and outrage away from the exercise of unaccountable and hegemonic power in the name of crisis. In the process, the disciplinary hierarchies of dualistic gender and hetero-sexuality, which help to make populations compliant and governable, are reinforced.

Homophobia and misogyny, often working hand in hand as with the response to Pussy Riot, make it possible for governments and international institutions to introduce reforms that, in the absence of a panic, would have been impossible. In the United States, the panic of "domestic trafficking" has made possible federal legislation that subjects pimps (traffickers) to ninety-nine year prison sentences, puts sex workers at risk of apprehension by law enforcement in order to secure their testimony, and puts their clients at risk of arrest and vehicle seizure.[50] Sexual and gender panics fuel the sense of emergency, enabling the technicians of crisis governance to adopt emergency laws that are never rescinded, like the so-called austerity measures adopted in the wake of the global financial crisis and, I fear, the zero tolerance of sex outside marriage in post-peacekeeping governance. These panics help to remap the legal and political landscape and invigorate a more hegemonic social and economic order, which is less constrained by political deliberation, less open to contestation and critique, more amenable to corporate capitalism and more hostile to "life" in its full sense of human empowerment, dignity, equality, self-determination, and freedom. Succinctly outlining the benefits for the broader neoliberal project that flow from recasting the panic of sex trafficking into one of modern-day slavery, Elizabeth Bernstein explains that the

---

[49] Ratna Kapur, "The Tragedy of Victimization Rhetoric," in *Erotic Justice: Law and the New Politics of Postcolonialism* (Glasshouse, 2005) pp. 129–31.

[50] Elizabeth Bernstein, "The Sexual Politics of the 'New Abolitionism'," *Differences: A Journal of Feminist Cultural Studies*, 18 (2007), p. 143.

language of "slavery" employed by diverse evangelical and feminist groups in the U.S. who share international abolitionist ambitions,

> effectively locates all social harm *outside of* the institutions of corporate capitalism and the state apparatus ... [reconfiguring] the masculinist institutions of big business, the state, and the police ... as allies and saviours, rather than enemies, of unskilled migrants workers, and the responsibility for slavery is shifted from structural factors and dominant institutions onto individual, deviant [often brown] men.[51]

Crisis governance, assisted by sexual and gender panics, inaugurates a more repressive paradigm for the management of life, wherein the structures of privilege are protected and strengthened by ignoring structural injustices, individualizing responsibility and vigorously silencing dissent.

II THE POSSIBILITY OF RESISTANCE

Crises, while clearly productive for law, produce a deeper crisis for progressive thinking, making feminist and queer activism and ways of life more dangerous. Not only does the crisis paradigm provide a pretext for criminalizing dissidence and banning critique, as in the Pussy Riot example. It also offers a means to strengthen disciplinary ideologies and the exercise of biopolitical power through bodies, as in the peacekeeping sex example. Some feminist and queer ideas have even been drawn into the service of crisis governance. For instance, the strand of feminism (radical or subordination feminism) that understands (hetero)sex as the locus of women's subordination and dismisses sexual "freedom" as a means of extending male privilege and power, resonates with the anti-trafficking and anti-peacekeeping-sex panics unleashed by crisis, and has helped to legitimate them.[52] Similarly, some currents of gay and lesbian activism have supported

[51] Ibid., p. 144.
[52] See further, Janet Halley, Prabha Kotiswaran, Hila Shamir, and Chantal Thomas, "From the International to the Local in Feminist Legal Responses to Rape, Prostitution/Sex Work, and Sex Trafficking: Four Studies in

"pink-washing" by the United States, the United Kingdom, Israel and other states, by drawing xenophobic comparisons between the sexual freedoms (superiority) of the west and the unfreedoms of many non-western (uncivilised) traditions, aligning particularly with Islamophobia in the present crisis-driven conjuncture of international politics.[53] Indeed, crises have proved to be a dangerous time for all forms of critical and progressive thought and action, which are subjected to co-option and vilification, which we have seen extend to charges of treason in the context of the crisis of international terror. Clearly, then, crisis governance threatens international law's emancipatory potential (assuming it exists) by dramatically reducing the space for political contestation and critique.[54] I turn now to the question of whether it might nevertheless be possible to resist gender and sexual panics and turn the moment of crisis to more progressive, counter-neoliberal ends.

A crisis, whether real or imagined, always creates opportunities that did not exist before, as Milton Friedman, economic rationalist and notorious proponent of disaster capitalism has observed:

> Only a crisis – actual or perceived – produces real change. When that crisis occurs, the actions that are taken depend on the ideas that are lying around. That, I believe, is our basic function: to develop alternatives to existing policies, to keep them alive and available until the politically impossible becomes the politically inevitable.[55]

Although these opportunities seem particularly amenable to capture by neoliberal forces, there surely is also the possibility of turning them to progressive ends. Indeed, Aboriginal activist and scholar Marcia

Contemporary Governance Feminism," *Harvard Journal of Law and Gender*, 29 (2006), p. 335.

[53] Jasbir Puar, *Terrorist Assemblages: Homonationalism in Queer Times* (Duke University Press, 2007); Sarah Schulman, *Israel/Palestine and the Queer International* (Duke University Press, 2012).

[54] Dianne Otto, "Remapping Crisis through a Feminist Lens," in Sari Kouvo and Zoe Pearson (eds.), *Feminist Perspectives on Contemporary International Law: Between Resistance and Compliance?* (Onati/Hart, 2011), p. 75.

[55] Milton Friedman, *Capitalism and Freedom: 40th Anniversary Edition* (University of Chicago Press, 2002), p. xiv. See also Naomi Klein, *The Shock Doctrine: The Rise of Disaster Capitalism* (Penguin/Allen Lane, 2007).

Langton made precisely this point, in relation to the Australian government's emergency intervention into Aboriginal communities in
the Northern Territory on the basis of hurriedly adopted legislation
in 2007.[56] To enact its lengthy and complex emergency legislation,
the government relied on a report which found child sexual abuse in
remote Aboriginal communities to be serious, widespread and often
unreported.[57] While a robust response to the report's findings was
entirely warranted, the government fostered a panic, which enabled it
to impose unprecedented control over Aboriginal land and resources,
without any prior consultation with those affected, and suspend the
normal prohibition of discrimination on the basis of race from application to the new legislation.[58] As Irene Watson had earlier observed,
neo-colonial protectionism, in the guise of saving Aboriginal women
and children, fundamentally undermines the possibility of indigenous
self-determination.[59] Yet despite all this, Langton urged that there
was always the possibility of using the increased attention to Aboriginal disadvantage and the new resources provided in the emergency,
to the advantage of Aboriginal communities. Whether and in what
form this advantage will eventuate, we have yet to see.

A powerful counter-crisis strategy is to question the certainties of
the crisis paradigm and explore possibilities for disrupting the neoliberal agendas that are being served. One example of disruption is the
collaborative endeavour by human rights and labour advocates to shift
the focus of anti-trafficking efforts from their preoccupation with sex
trafficking, and the highly moralistic criminal justice approach that it
sponsors, into a framework of labour exploitation.[60] Chuang argues

---

[56] Marcia Langton, "Trapped in the Aboriginal Reality Show," *Griffith Review: Reimagining Australia* (2008), p. 145.

[57] *Ampe Akelyernemane Meke Mekarle "Little Children Are Sacred,"* Report of the Northern Territory Board of Inquiry into the Protection of Aboriginal Children from Sexual Abuse, 2007 www.nt.gov.au/dcm/inquirysaac/pdf/bipacsa_final_report.pdf.

[58] *Northern Territory National Emergency Response Act 2007 (Cth)*, s. 132.

[59] Irene Watson, "Illusionists and Hunters: Being Aboriginal in this Space," *Australian Feminist Law Journal*, 22 (2005), p. 15.

[60] Hila Shamir, "A Labour Paradigm for Human Trafficking," *UCLA Law Review*, 60 (2012), p. 2.

that this shift would move the debate about prostitution "to its rightful place on the periphery," and bring to the fore the question of the responsibility of states and corporations for maintaining conditions of poverty, conflict and disadvantage that make forced labour and human trafficking, in their many forms, so prevalent.[61] Such a strategy would also remove the dynamic of panic from the picture, enabling responses that build on and strengthen the existing framework and institutions of international labour and human rights law, which aim to eradicate all forms of labour exploitation, not just those at the extremities. In contrast to crisis governance, a human rights and labour approach would seek to address the problem of structural inequalities, rely on critical and analytic thinking for its development, and promote the participation of employers and employees, including those most disadvantaged by the current arrangements, in collective efforts to find solutions. It would provide a platform for challenging the exploitative labour practices encouraged and normalized by neoliberal economics.

Another strategy of disruption would be to resist the panic itself, and thereby disable the sense of urgency that is used to justify executive decision-making and emergency law. The activism of gay men and sex workers, in the context of the HIV-AIDS pandemic, is a case of successful diffusion of a sexual panic, which led to a dramatic change in the World Health Organization's paternalistic and utilitarian approach to public health crises. The initial public health response to HIV/AIDS, in the early 1980s, was defined by a sense of urgency which meant that the public health message was dominated by the idea of danger, rather than providing clear information about prevention.[62] Eventually, in response to demands from many of those directly affected, the importance of respecting the human rights of HIV-infected people became, for the first time, an integral part of a global health strategy to address and control an epidemic.[63] Further,

[61] Chuang, "Exploitation Creep," pp. 49–52.

[62] Jonathan Mann and Daniel Tarantola, "Responding to HIV/AIDS: A Historical Perspective," *Health and Human Rights: An International Quarterly Journal*, 2:4 (1998), p. 5.

[63] Sofia Gruskin, Janathan Mann and Daniel Tarantola, "Past, Present, and Future: AIDS and Human Rights," Editorial, *Health and Human Rights: An*

this trajectory away from crisis and into considered analysis and reflection led, in due course, to the recognition that structural inequality and marginalization are root causes of vulnerability to the epidemic; that discrimination and human rights violations did not arise only as the effects of HIV-infection, but preceded it.[64] This recognition necessitated responses that decriminalized sex work and homosexuality, demystified sexuality by promoting sex education and safe sex practices, empowered women in sexual decision-making, including within marriage, and addressed the social determinants of vulnerability.[65] These outcomes are a spectacular departure from the fear-mongering, criminalizing, individualizing, and repressive techniques of crisis governance.

To turn the opportunities created by crisis to progressive ends, we need to promote a "crisis of discipline" by disrupting the certainties of emergency law and executive power – following the example of Pussy Riot, whose name brazenly brings the discipline of femininity into crisis, as explained by one member:

> ["Pussy Riot" refers to when] a female sex organ, which is supposed to be receiving and shapeless, suddenly starts a radical rebellion against the cultural order, which tries to constantly define it and show its appropriate place.[66]

International lawyers, too, have been cast as "receiving and shapeless" – or compliant, at least – as when Oscar Schachter described us as an "invisible college" (referring to the relationship between government lawyers and the academy)[67] and Phillip Alston portrayed us

---

International Quarterly Journal, 2:4 (1998), p. 1; Teresita Marie P. Bagasao, "Moving Forward through Community Response: Lessons Learned from HIV Prevention in Asia and the Pacific," *Health and Human Rights: An International Quarterly Journal* 3:1 (1998), p. 8.

[64] Gruskin et al., "Past, Present and Future."

[65] Helen Jackson, "Societal Determinants of Women's Vulnerability to HIV Infection in Southern Africa," *Health and Human Rights: An International Quarterly Journal*, 2:4 (1998), p. 9.

[66] Henry Langston, "Meeting Pussy Riot" (undated) Vice Beta www.vice.com/read/A-Russian-Pussy-Riot.

[67] Oscar Schachter, "The Invisible College of International Lawyers," *Northwestern University Law Review* (1977), p. 217.

as myopic "handmaidens" of free market globalization.[68] Like Pussy Riot, we international lawyers also need to start a radical rebellion against the cultural order of the discipline of international law, which has proved to be so well-suited to normalizing crisis governance and its attendant silencing of critical politics concerned with addressing sexual and gender unfreedom, and economic and social injustice. There are already traces of past movements of discontent in the law, left by rebellions against colonialism and racism[69] and struggles against women's inequality and heteronormativity,[70] which provide footholds for another uprising – a rebellion that contests the discipline's logic of crisis thinking, revitalises participatory emancipatory politics, and refuses to countenance the instrumentalization of gender and sexual non-conformity as the grounds for panic.

III CONCLUSION

Marxist international lawyer China Miéville, author of many compelling futurist fantasy novels, including *Un Lun Dun* for young adults,[71] has argued that looking to the existing law as a means of progressive change is to deny its "imperial actuality"[72] and risk "legitimising ... the very structure of international law that critical theory has so devastatingly undermined."[73] There is some truth in his claim that the chaotic, crisis-driven, inequitable, world in which we live "is the

---

[68] Philip Alston, "The Myopia of the Handmaidens: International Lawyers and Globalization," *European Journal of International Law*, 3 (1997), p. 435.

[69] Sundhya Pahuja, "The Postcoloniality of International Law," *Harvard International Law Journal*, 46 (2005), p. 459.

[70] Dianne Otto, "Power and Danger: Feminist Engagement with International Law through the UN Security Council," *Australian Feminist Law Journal*, 32 (2010), p. 97.

[71] China Miéville, *Un Lun Dun* (Macmillan, 2007).

[72] China Miéville, *Between Equal Rights: A Marxist Theory of International Law* (London: Pluto Press, 2005), p. 300.

[73] Ibid., p. 299.

rule of law."[74] However, I do not think that international law's imperial capture, or co-option, of progressive ideas is ever total. Like Miéville's fantasy city of Un Lun Dun, which is the flip-side of the London we all know, where many of London's unwanted people (like bus conductors), broken objects and smog end up hidden from the view of the mainstream, international law also has its own parallel universes, where other ways of thinking about the law and its possibilities are thriving. One place that I experience this shadow world is in the corridors and bars of the annual meeting of the American Society of International Law, where queers, feminists, and others who engage critically with international law seek each other out to discuss tactics. On one occasion I even encountered China Miéville there.

What we need is "un-crisis" thinking – the flip side of crisis thinking – if we are to find liberatory solutions to international problems by using international law. Like Miéville's "un gun" (which, needless to say, does not use typical ammunition), which he creates to fight the "evil" Smog that creeps into the brains of UnLunDuners and has addictive and malicious powers (rather like crisis thinking), un-crisis thinking means thinking outside the narrow confines of the box of crisis logic. It is the kind of thinking that we need in order to ensure that, on the one hand, we are not seduced into compliance by the institutional embrace of some feminist and queer ideas and, on the other hand, that we do not undervalue the "critical instability"[75] created by the footholds that have already been carved into the law. The increased danger that crisis presents to radical ideas necessitates different strategies of resistance, including increased alertness to the possibility that feminist and queer ideas may be turned to the service of crisis governance, efforts to resist and counter sexual and gender panics, and tactics for disrupting the neoliberal agendas they serve.

---

[74] China Miéville, "The commodity-form theory of international law," in Susan Marks (ed.), *International Law on the Left: Re-examining Marxist Legacies* (Cambridge University Press: 2008), p. 132.
[75] Sundhya Pahuja, *Decolonising International Law: Development, Economic Growth, and the Politics of Universality* (Cambridge University Press, 2011), p. 255.

However, law alone is never enough. Essential to exploiting the possibilities of international law's progressive dynamic is the important relationship between politics (life) and law. Political engagement will keep our attention focussed on the deeply entrenched structures of inequality and help to refuse the technologies of crisis governance. A focus on structural inequalities will also help to contest the inordinate reliance on the Security Council and other forms of executive government, to promote feminist and queer change. This necessitates devoting at least as much energy to supporting un-crisis activism "outside" the mainstream institutions of law and politics as to carving out spaces on the "inside."

I can remember sitting in a lecture theatre as a 39-year-old law student, thinking how lucky I was to finally have the opportunity to reflect on the crisis-driven work that I had previously been engaged in, as an activist and as a community development worker with homeless young people and domestic violence survivors, and the role that law played in its perpetuation. And here I am, over twenty years later, still thinking about how crisis so often produces more law to entrench quick-fix responses that avoid addressing the structural causes of injustice, and about what could be done to change that – it is both exhilarating and exhausting. The institutionalization of feminist and queer ideas will always extract a price of compromise and dilution; but it can be mitigated by engaged political contestation by movements of sexual subalterns, as well as human rights advocates, in coalition with others, demanding otherwise. Politics, in all its richness and life-sustaining complexity, must be part of every feminist and queer strategy in law.

4 THE INCREDIBLE SHRINKING WOMEN

Barbara Stark

INTRODUCTION

Unlike most national law systems, international law is not a unified, integrated system. Rather, it consists of multiple systems, or regimes, such as international women's rights and international trade law, each of which has its own rules, tribunals, institutions, bureaucracies, doctrines, theories, and actors. Since the end of World War II, when the UN Charter and the Universal Declaration of Human Rights were drafted and the United Nations and the Bretton Woods institutions were established, international law has dramatically expanded and diversified, generating even more systems. These systems exist independently of one another; coordination among them varies.

In 2006, the International Law Commission issued a Report on the Fragmentation of International Law ("ILC Report").[1] As set out in the ILC Report, fragmentation refers to several related phenomena, including:

> [T]he emergence of specialized and relatively autonomous rules or rule-complexes, legal institutions and spheres of legal practice.

Many of the ideas set out in this chapter were first explored in a longer article, "International Law From the Bottom Up: Fragmentation and Transformation," *U. Pa. J. Int'l L.*, 34 (2013), pp. 687–734 (2013).

[1] Martti Koskenniemi, Chairman Study Group, "Fragmentation of International Law: Difficulties Arising From the Diversification and Expansion of International Law," A/CN.4/L.682, April 13, 2006, p. 8. See generally, Isabelle Buffard et al. (eds.), *International Law Between Universalism and Fragmentation* (2008) (Festschrift in honor of Gerhard Hafner, who initiated the study of fragmentation by the ILC in 2000).

> What once appeared governed by "general international law" has
> become a field of operation for such specialist systems as "trade
> law," "human rights law," "environmental law" . . . and even such
> exotic and highly specialized knowledges as "investment law" or
> "international refugee law" etc. – each possessing their own
> principles and institutions.[2]

According to the ILC Report, international law is losing coherence,
certainty, and predictability because it lacks dependable mechanisms
for reconciling inconsistencies. In addition, as Anne-Marie Slaughter
explains,[3] fragmentation has spawned globalized networks of specialists –
including judges, lawyers, bankers, and drug dealers. Oscar Schachter's
"invisible college of international lawyers" has been replaced by autonomous specialized networks, often oblivious to each other.

This chapter examines the effects of fragmentation on two distinct
regimes – globalization and women's human rights – in light of the
Great Recession, which has had more impact on more people worldwide than any crisis since the Great Depression. Part I of this chapter
explains how international law makes globalization possible, and
how globalization spread the United States' financial crisis to the rest
of the world. International law makes globalization possible through
multiple international regimes governing trade, investment, contracts, standards of weight and measures, and dispute resolution.
Without international law, globalization would collapse.[4]

The fragmentation of international law facilitates globalization.
There are few effective mechanisms for reconciling inconsistent
human rights, labor, and environmental standards among states. In
developed states, these standards are incorporated in domestic law
and enforced by robust national or regional legal systems. There are
violations, of course, but compliance is the norm. It is a scandal when
sex slaves are discovered in New Jersey or a barge loaded with toxic
waste is photographed leaving a European port.

In developing states, where weak domestic legal systems cannot
support human rights, labor or environmental standards, these

[2] ILC Report.   [3] See, Anne-Marie Slaughter, *The New World Order* (2005).
[4] Philip Alson, "The Myopia of the Handmaidens: International Lawyers and
Globalization," *EJIL*, 3 (1997), p. 435.

standards are rarely enforced. For investors and multinational corporations ("MNCs"), the fragmentation of international law is a benefit. It promises greater profits than a unified international legal system. Enforceable human rights, labor, and environmental standards would increase labor and compliance costs.

Part II explains how this dynamic is inverted for poor women in developing states. For these women, the *absence* of enforceable human rights, labor, and environmental standards – combined with the regimes facilitating globalization set out in Part I – has been devastating. This part draws on a recently published study by the Harvard School of Public Health. Noting that changes in average height have long been relied upon as an indicator of a group's standard of living, this study describes the decline and stagnation in average heights among women in fifty-four poor and middle-income countries.[5] These women are not only shorter than their mothers, they are shorter than their *grandmothers*. For these women, the world is "not getting to be a better place ... For them, it's getting worse."[6] This part also explains why efforts to overcome the costs of fragmentation by "mainstreaming" gender are unhelpful in this context.

Part III explains why international financial and economic reforms are more promising. Such reforms, including the regulation of investment banks and the close of tax havens, might have prevented the last major crises and, experts warn, are necessary to prevent the next. Absent such reforms (opposed by a $700 trillion dollar derivatives industry, among other behemoths), *more* fragmentation, rather than less, may well be more constructive, at least for the shrinking women.

---

[5] S. V. Subramanian, Emre Özaltin and Jocelyn E. Finlay, "Height of Nations: A Socioeconomic Analysis of Cohort Differences and Patterns Among Women in 54 Low- to Middle-Income Countries," *Plos One* 6(4): e18962.doi:10.1371/journal.pone.0018962 (2011). See also Donald G. McNeil, Jr., "Very Poor Women are Smaller, As Are Their Chances at a Better Life," *New York Times*, April 26, 2011, p. D6. A different, more comprehensive, study describes the ways in which technological progress has "supersized" those in the affluent West. Robert W. Fogel et al., *The Changing Body: Health, Nutrition, and Human Development in the Western World Since 1700* (2011).

[6] McNeil, "Very Poor Women Are Smaller".

I THE GLOBAL CRISES

The Great Recession, triggered by the United States, has been globalized with grim consequences, especially for women in developing
states. This part explains how high risk gambles on Wall Street
affected them. The financial and economic crises continue for many.
Even where they are officially over, their consequences continue to
play out. In a few states, and in some sectors, men have been hit
harder than women.[7] But overall, even when men may have lost more
wealth and income than women (having had so much more to lose),
women have slipped lower on any standard of well-being, and are
likely to take longer to recover.

A Crises and "Development"

The recession is officially over in the United States, and the outlook in
Europe seems to be improving. The turmoil in the Middle East has
been good for tourism in Spain, Portugal, Italy, and Greece, as
tourists from Russia, Britain, and the Nordic states avoid Egypt.[8]
Even as developed markets recover, however, emerging markets
falter.[9] As Krugman pointed out in August, 2013:

> India's rupee and Brazil's real are plunging, along with
> Indonesia's rupiah, the South African rand, the Turkish lira, and
> more. The flood of money into emerging markets – which briefly
> drove Brazil's currency up by almost 40 percent, a rise that has
> now been completely reversed – was yet another in the long list of
> financial bubbles over the past generation.[10]

There were 124 global financial crises between 1970 and 2008.[11] The
United States and the IMF pressured the stricken developing states to
"tighten their belts," and impose discipline on their markets. They

---

[7] See Hanna Rosin, "The End of Men," *The Atlantic* (July/Aug, 2010), pp. 56–8.
[8] Raphail Minder, "Tourists Wary of Turmoil in the Middle East Are a Boon to
Southern Europe," *New York Times*, September 2, 2013, p. B3.
[9] Paul Krugman, "This Age of Bubbles," *New York Times*, August 23, 2013,
p. A27.
[10] Ibid.   [11] Joseph Stiglitz, *Freefall* (2010).

were instructed to respond with procyclical measures, that is measures that reinforced the recession, such as slashing safety nets, adopting structural adjustment programs, and raising interest rates.

As Stiglitz notes, the United States took a very different approach in 2008: "To pull America out of the hole, the country engaged in massive increases in spending and massive deficits, even as interest rates were brought down to zero. Banks were bailed out left and right."[12] These countercyclical measures reduced the impact of the crises here, just as the procyclical measures imposed on developing states exacerbated the crises there. Forcing the developing states to adopt procyclical measures protected the banks that had loaned them money, at the expense of their people.

As economist Bob Sutcliffe explains, the development story is captured in the metaphor of a journey – nation states start from roughly the same place, but at different times.[13] Thus, the developing states are today where Europe was in the fourteenth century. For Sutcliffe, "The form of travel is characterized by the transfer of labour from low-productivity agriculture to higher-productivity industry and modern services."[14] But everyone ends up at the same place, with high consumption matching high productivity. Economic progress brings electricity, toilets, education, urbanization, medical services, longer lives, democracy, and human rights – in short, modernization.

This notion of development has given rise to three major critiques. Each challenges one of its underlying premises. First, the "polarization critique" argues that everyone does not end up in the same place. Rather, Europe developed, and as a result, nations polarized into developed and underdeveloped states. This was set and unalterable by the end of the nineteenth century. As Sutcliffe puts it, "Underdevelopment is, like Dorian Gray's portrait, development's alter ego."[15] The underdeveloped states

---

[12] Ibid., p. 222.

[13] See Bob Sutcliffe, "The Place of Development in Theories of Imperialism and Globalization," in Ronald Munck and Denis O'Hearn (eds.) *Critical Development Theory: Contributions to a New Paradigm* (1999), p. 135.

[14] Ibid., p. 135.   [15] Ibid., p. 136 (emphasis omitted).

can never catch up, in part because of all the trash – from environmental damage to corrupt regimes – the developed states have left in their wake.

Second, the "attainability critique" is grounded in the realization that it is physically impossible for the whole world to reach the same destination, to enjoy the level of consumption enjoyed by those in the West. Rather, because of greenhouse gases, contaminants, and non-renewable resources, "development ... cannot be generalized ... without causing an apocalypse."[16]

Third, a broad range of "desirability critiques" suggests that not everyone wants a high-consumption, Western lifestyle. These critiques are diverse, ranging from those who seek spiritual, rather than material fulfillment, to those living off the land or off the grid, to those who seek a different *kind* of material fulfillment. What these critiques have in common is their rejection of high consumption/high productivity. They see "[rich developed states] full of needy, oppressed and unfulfilled people."[17] Even if it were possible for the entire world to live like Americans, many would rather not. Some critics argue, further, that development continues the destructive processes of colonialism, eviscerating local cultures.[18]

The core principles of the Washington Consensus, that is, "fiscal discipline," along with "good economic goverance and trade liberalization," were affirmed by the G8 as recently as 2009.[19]

---

[16] Ibid., p. 137; Jared Diamond, *Collapse: How Societies Choose to Fail or Succeed* (2005), p. 498.

[17] Sutcliffe, "The Place of Development," p. 138.

[18] See for example Jane Jenson and Boaventura de Sousa Santos, "Case Studies and Common Trends in Globalization: Introduction," in Jane Jenson and Boaventura de Sousa Santos (eds.), *Globalizing Institutions: Case Studies in Regulations and Innovation* (2000), p. 11 (defining globalization as "the process by which a given local condition or entity succeeds in ... extending its reach over the globe and, in by doing so, develops the capacity to designate a rival social condition or entity as local").

[19] World Economic Forum, Death of the Washington Consensus?, January 29, 2009, www.weforum.org/en/knowledge/Events/2009/KN_SESS_SUMM_26943?url=/ en/knowledge/Events/2009/KN_SESS_SUMM_26943.

The IMF was revamped following the April 2009 meeting of G20 leaders in London to address the "collapsing world economy."[20] Its resources were tripled to $750 billion and it was authorized to issue an additional $250 billion on its own.[21] The focus, however, has been on rescue packages for Hungary, Iceland, Latvia, and other developed states.[22] The developing states are not its current priority.[23] Even if they were, IMF resources amount to merely 3 percent of the world's current account payments, in contrast to the more than 50 percent it controlled when it was established in 1944.[24]

In April 2014 the IMF announced that inequality was part of its mandate. This represented a major shift.[25] The IMF now supports some controls on cross-border capital flows and even for some states, fiscal stimulus.[26] While the new rhetoric is welcome, whether it will translate into new policy is an open question.

B Free Trade

Free trade is a major component of the Washington Consensus, and it was a major reason the crises spread so quickly. It has been argued that, like "development," free trade benefits developed states at the expense of developing states.[27] Trade liberalization does not make everyone better off. Rather, as Stiglitz points out, even when

---

[20] Peter Gumbel, "International Monetary Fund 2.0.," *Time*, April 20, 2009.
[21] Ibid.   [22] Ibid.
[23] As one blogger suggests, this might require a transformation within the IMF, of "values" (the "DNA, the assumption, default solutions, and logic of its staff") as well as institutional norms, arguably requiring a thorough house-cleaning, including "that they hire a load of feminists." "IMF 2.0 or same-old, same old-has the Fund really changed its tune?" www.oxfamblogs.org/fp2p/ ?=254.
[24] Gumbel, "International Monetary Fund 2.0.," p. 3.
[25] Eduardo Porter, "In New Tack, IMF Aims at Income Inequality," *New York Times*, April 8, 2014. The IMF now supports some controls on cross-border capital flows and even for some states, fiscal stimulus.
[26] Ibid.
[27] James Gathii has noted that regional trade agreements are following suit. James Thuo Gathii, "The Neoliberal Turn in Regional Trade Agreements," 86 *Wash. L. Rev.* 86 (2011), p. 421.

it makes "the country as a whole better off, it results in some groups being worse off."[28]

The rules for world trade are established through periodic negotiations or "rounds" of talks among the members of the WTO, whose agendas are set by the wealthy industrialized states. The Uruguay Round, for instance, promised a "Grand Bargain" in which the LDCs would accept new rules on intellectual property, investments and services in exchange for a reduction of agricultural subsidies and textiles quotas in the industrialized states.[29] In fact, however, the industrialized states benefited from the Grand Bargain, but sub-Saharan Africa lost $1.2 billion.[30] Industrialized countries made no concessions on agricultural subsidies and left textile quotas in place for ten years. The United States opened its markets to African cotton producers in 2005,[31] but the United States does not import cotton. Cotton subsidies make it the world's largest cotton *exporter* and effectively make competition by the developing states impossible.[32]

Eleanor Fox argues that the elimination of subsidies by the WTO Member States would be the single most effective and far-reaching measure to improve human welfare in the developing world. As she explains:

> The human costs of unfair trade are immense. If Africa, East Asia, South Asia, and Latin America were each to increase their share of world exports by one per cent the resulting gains in income could lift 128 million people out of poverty. ... If the nations of the WTO were to adopt one and only one human welfare measure, elimination of [subsidies in trade barriers] should be the measure.[33]

---

[28] Joseph Stiglitz, *Making Globalization Work* (2006), p. 68.   [29] Ibid., p. 77.
[30] Ibid.   [31] Ibid., pp. 80–1.
[32] Ibid., pp. 85–6; *see also* Kenneth A. Bamberger and Andrew Guzman, "Keeping Imports Safe: A Proposal for Discriminatory Regulation of International Trade," *Cal. L. Rev.*, (2008), p. 1445 (arguing that encouraging competition among United States and foreign companies, while simultaneously enforcing safety regulations, would significantly benefit U.S. consumers).
[33] Eleanor M. Fox, "Globalization and Human Rights: Looking Out for the Welfare of the Worst Off," *N.Y.U. J. Int'l L. & Pol.*, 35 (2002), p. 211. But

Indeed, "[r]ich countries have cost poor countries three times more in trade restrictions than they give in total development aid."[34]

Five years after the WTO's Uruguay Round, protesters disrupted the next round scheduled to begin Seattle in 1999. Following the debacle of the "Battle in Seattle," the WTO convened in a more remote location – Doha, Qatar – to avoid large protests.[35] Although the Doha Round was touted as a "development round," again, there were few real concessions to the developing states.[36] Even before the Great Recession, legal scholars such as Andrew Guzman[37] and Chantal Thomas[38] questioned how effectively the WTO could support the developing states and their people, even if that were its objective.

see Department of Economic and Social Affairs, "The Millennium Development Goals Report 2007," (2007), p. 28 (noting that the elimination of trade barriers benefits some developing states at the expense of others).

[34] Stiglitz, *Making Globalization Work* , p. 78.

[35] See "The Battle in Seattle," *Economist*, November 27, 1999, p. 21; Paul Reynolds, "Eyewitness: The Battle of Seattle," BBC News, December 2, 1999, http://news.bbc.co.uk/2/hi/amercias/547581.stm. Several scholars have analyzed the "Battle of Seattle" in the larger context of global governance. See for example Richard B. Bilder and Richard Falk, "Recent Books on International Law," *Am. J. Int'l L.*, 96 (2002), pp. 264 and 267 (reviewing Susan Marks, *The Riddle of All Constitutions: International Law, Democracy, and the Critique of Ideology* (2000) and Gregory H. Fox and Brad R. Roth, *Democratic Governance and International Law* (2000)).

[36] Some argued that the collapse of the Doha Round of WTO talks precluded agreement on effective measures to "lift millions out of poverty, curb rich countries' ruinous farm support and open markets for countless goods and services." "The Future of Globalisation," *Economist*, July 29, 2006, p. 11.

[37] See for example Andrew Guzman, "Trade, Labor, Legitimacy," *Cal. L. Rev.*, 91 (2003), pp. 885–9 (discussing the dilemmas posed by the integration of the ILO Core Rights Labor Standards into the WTO).

[38] Chantal Thomas, "Should the World Trade Organization Incorporate Labor and Environmental Standards?," *Wash. & Lee L. Rev.*, 61 (2004), pp. 347, 379–86, 401–3 (explaining some of the difficulties in negotiating common agreements); Elissa Alben, Note, "GATT and the Fair Wage: A Historical Perspective on the Labor-Trade Link," *Colum. L. Rev.*, 101 (2001), pp. 1411–20 (putting the relationship between labor and trade in historical perspective).

As Olivier De Schutter, the UN Special Rapporteur on the Right to Food, noted in 2011, "[T]he WTO continues to pursue the outdated goal of increasing trade for its own sake rather than encouraging more trade only insofar as it increases human wellbeing. It therefore treats food security policies as an unwelcome deviation from this path."[39] By 2011, the financial crisis in the United States had become a food crisis in much of the world. De Schutter addressed the WTO a month before a key summit:

> Trade did not feed the hungry when food was cheap and abundant, and is even less able to do so now that prices are sky-high. Global food imports shall be worth 1.3 trillion USD in 2011, and the food import bills of the least developed countries have soared by over a third over the last year. The G20 has acknowledged that excessive reliance on food imports has left people in developing countries increasingly vulnerable to price shocks and food shortages. The WTO must now do the same.[40]

He was ignored.

II WOMEN IN DEVELOPING STATES

A The Impact of the Great Recession

The Harvard study which first documented the shrinking women drew on surveys from 1994 through 2008. Researchers analyzed data on 365,000 adult women in 54 low and middle-income countries, noting changes in birth cohorts starting with those born in 1945, and ending with those born in 1983.[41] The women measured ranged in age from 25 to 49, to exclude those who were still growing or beginning to shrink with age. Height, according to the researchers, is a "reliable indicator of childhood nutrition, disease and poverty."[42]

---

[39] "Food security hostage to trade in WTO negotiations," available at www.srfood.org/index.php/en/component/content/article/1774
[40] Ibid.   [41] Subramanian et al., "Height of Nations," p. 1.
[42] Ibid. But see Gardiner Harris, "Malnutrition in Well-Fed Children is Linked to Poor Sanitation," *New York Times*, July 15, 2014, p. A1 (describing

The richest 20 percent of women in these countries grew. Women's heights declined in the poorest 40 percent in 14 African countries and stayed the same in 21 states in Africa and Latin America. This indicates inadequate food and healthcare, and probably inadequate housing and education. As explained below, this is a clear violation of well-established human rights. But the surveys began well before the Great Recession and ended just when it began. There is no more information on this *particular* group of women.

There are other studies, but evidence of the Great Recession's impact on women in developing states is necessarily impressionistic and anecdotal. First, as the Bank noted in 2012, "Lags in data availability mean that 2008 is the most recent year we can make a reliable global estimate."[43] Second, as the contributors to *The World's Women, 2010*[44] recognize, there is little agreement regarding measurement standards or methods. As the authors of *The First CEDAW Impact Study* explain:

> We have used stories, research, statistics, reports, local, regional and world conferences, and a myriad of indicators to assist in this critical task. A multidimensional, multifaceted approach is needed – as diverse as the lives and experiences of women.[45]

Both *The World's Women* and *The First CEDAW Impact Study* reports, along with other recent studies, show real progress in some areas, such as declining gender disparities in youth literacy rates,[46] a decline

---

scientific studies linking stunting from malnutrition to poor sanitation rather than lack of food).

[43] Shaohua Chen and Martin Ravallion, "An Update to the World Bank's estimates of consumption poverty," March 1, 2012, http://econ.worldbank .org.povcalnet.

[44] UN Dep't Econ. & Soc. Aff., "The World's Women 2010: Trends and Statistics," at xii, UN Doc. ST/ESA/STAT/SER.K/19, UN Sales No. E.10. XVII,11 (2010).

[45] Andrew Byrnes and Jane Connors, "Introduction," in Marilou McPhedran et al., *The First CEDAW Impact Study* (Final Report) 11 (2001). [Hereinafter *First CEDAW Impact Study*].

[46] Ibid., p. viii.

in maternal mortality rates,[47] and the decline of female genital sur-
geries ("FGS").[48]

But women in developing states continue to lag. Women comprise
roughly 60–80 percent of the export manufacturing workforce in the
developing world, a sector hard hit during the economic crisis.[49] In
Arab states, fewer than one third of women are in the labor force.[50] In
sub-Saharan Africa and South Asia, 80 percent of women workers are
in "vulnerable employment"; that is, low-income jobs with few rights.[51]

Even if data were available, moreover, it rarely reflects *intra*-house-
hold distribution, which overwhelmingly favors males.[52] Women bear
the brunt of poverty in poor households.[53] In Pakistan and Yemen,
for example, girls in the poorest quintile are far more likely to leave
primary school than boys.[54] Where households lack access to clean
water and energy, similarly, women do most of the additional work
and suffer most of the harmful health effects.[55] Women and girls often
eat last, and if there is not enough, they do not eat at all.

B The Empty Promise of Human Rights

Several legally binding international treaties, including the Economic
Covenant,[56] the Convention on the Rights of the Child, and the
Convention Against All Forms of Discrimination Against Women
("CEDAW" or the "Women's Convention"),[57] expressly require

---

[47] Denise Grady, "Maternal Deaths in Sharp Decline Across the Globe," *New
York Times*, April 14, 2010, p. A1 (citing study in the *Lancet* showing a
"significant drop worldwide in the number of women dying each year from
pregnancy and childbirth, to about 342,900 in 2008 from 526,300 in 1980").
[48] Ibid., p. x.
[49] UNIFEM, "Facts and Figures on Women, Poverty and Economics,"
www.unifem.org/gender_issues/women_poverty_economics/facts_figures
.php.
[50] Ibid.   [51] Ibid.   [52] See for example "The World's Women 2010".
[53] "The World's Women 2010," p. 168.   [54] Ibid.   [55] Ibid.
[56] International Covenant on Economic, Social and Cultural Rights, adopted
December 16, 1966, 993 U.N.T.S. 3 (entered into force January 3, 1976).
[57] G.A. res.34/180, 34 GAOR Supp. (No. 46) at 193, UN Doc. A/34/46, entered
into force September 3, 1981.

states to assure their people adequate food, shelter, and healthcare. Article 11 of the Economic Covenant, for example, requires states to assure an "adequate standard of living" and Article 12 requires states to provide healthcare. These obligations have been set out in detail in voluminous white papers. But the same lack of infrastructure and accountability, along with pervasive corruption, that undermine effective environmental and labor standards in developing states – and that make these states so appealing to foreign investors – make these assurances of basic human rights empty rhetoric there.

1 The International Bill of Rights

The International Bill of Rights consists of the Universal Declaration of Human Rights,[58] the Economic Covenant,[59] and the Civil and Political Covenant.[60] The Universal Declaration assures the civil and political rights familiar to Americans from our own Constitution, as well as less familiar economic, social and cultural rights, such as the right to health and the right to work. The holistic conception of rights set out in the Universal Declaration was rejected during the Cold War. Despite rhetoric about the interdependence of civil/political rights and economic, social and cultural rights, two 'separate but equal' covenants were drafted and entered into force in the 1970s.

a Civil and Political Rights

Since the end of the Cold War and the collapse of the Soviet Union in the early 1990s, economic rights have been have been marginalized. Social safety nets have been slashed and the rhetoric of 'freedom' – especially free markets – dominates. As Upendra Baxi explains:

> [T]he paradigm of the Universal Declaration of Human Rights is being steadily supplanted by a trade-related, market-friendly,

---

[58] Universal Declaration of Human Rights, G.A. Res. 217 (III) A, UN Doc. A/RES/217(III) (December 10, 1948).

[59] International Covenant on Economic, Social and Cultural Rights, adopted December 16, 1966, 993 U.N.T.S. 3 (entered into force January 3, 1997).

[60] International Covenant on Civil and Political Rights, adopted December 19, 1966, 999 U.N.T.S. 171 (entered into force January 3, 1976).

human rights paradigm ... [This] insists ... upon the promotion
and protection of the collective rights of global capital in ways that
"justify" corporate well-being and dignity over that of human
persons.[61]

The Washington Consensus promised that free markets and free
trade would bring wealth and prosperity. And they have – but mostly
for investment banks and hedge funds. Goldman Sachs, for example,
recently reported that its profits – $1.93 billion – doubled in the
second quarter of 2013.[62] For those at the bottom, including women
in the lowest quintiles in developing states, life is harder than it was
for their grandmothers.

Now, in an era of unprecedented global inequality, "rights" are
generally understood as "civil and political rights." In theory, civil and
political rights should enable vulnerable groups to claim a fair share of
the pie, especially if an entitlement is already set out in existing law.
But women's civil and political rights cannot be realized in developing
states in the same ways that they may be realized in better-off countries. Developing states lack the requisite infrastructure – the courts,
lawyers, and critical mass of rights-literate women for whom civil and
political rights are a priority – that make these rights useful in
developed states. Indeed, many women in developing states remain
unaware of their human rights.[63] This may be attributable, in part, to
women's disproportionate illiteracy.[64] Despite the proliferation of

[61] Upendra Baxi, "Voices of Suffering and the Future of Human Rights,"
   Transnat'l L. & Contemp. Probs., 8 (1998), p. 125.
[62] Susanne Craig, "Goldman, Its Profit Doubling, Sees Hope for U.S. Recovery
   but Doubts for Global Growth," *New York Times*, July 17, 2013, p. B3.
[63] Barbara Stark, "Women's Rights," in David Forsythe (ed.), *Oxford
   Encyclopedia of Human Rights*, 5 (2009), p. 341. See also *First CEDAW Impact
   Statement*, p. 18 (noting that, "awareness of [CEDAW's] potency as an
   instrument to amend domestic legislation is often limited."); Martha
   C. Nussbaum, *Women and Human Development: The Capabilities Approach*,
   pp. 113-14 (describing the impact of a government-sponsored consciousness-
   raising program in India).
[64] "The World's Women 2010," p. viii (noting that, "women account for two
   thirds of the world's 774 million adult illiterates – a proportion that is
   unchanged over the past two decades").

laws addressing women's human rights, and fora in which such claims may be brought, few women in developing states have actual access to either.

b Economic Rights

Most developed states, with the conspicuous exception of the United States, have long recognized basic economic and social rights. Before the Great Recession, these states also had the resources to assure these rights. Women's rights to healthcare, including prenatal and maternity care, and an adequate standard of living, were the norm. This was reflected in the long lifespans and low maternal mortality rates taken for granted in most of the OECD states.[65] But even in Europe, where basic economic rights were part of the culture and incorporated in domestic law, they have been cut.

The European Commission, the European Central Bank, and the IMF have insisted on austerity in response to the Great Recession. This is generally attributed to Germany's bitter experience of inflation and the determination of its prime minister, Angela Merkel, to avoid it at all costs. These costs include women's health, which has already declined.[66]

Women in developing states, in contrast, have had negligible experience with economic rights. If the state provided any assistance, it has usually gone to the male head of the family, although, as the Bank notes, giving it to women is more effective: "A host of studies suggests that putting earnings in women's hands is the intelligent thing to do to speed up development and the process of overcoming poverty. Women usually reinvest a much higher portion in their families and communities than men, spreading wealth beyond themselves."[67]

---

[65] "The World's Women 2010," pp. vii-viii.

[66] David Stuckler and Sanjay Basu, "How Austerity Kills," *New York Times*, May 13, 2013, p. A21.

[67] World Bank, *The World Bank and Gender Equality: At a Glance* (Hereinafter World Bank, *Gender Equality*) http://web.worldbank.org (noting further that, "This could be one reason why countries with greater gender equality tend to have lower poverty rates.") at www.unifem.org/gender_issues/ women_poverty_economics/facts_figures.php. See also, "Study Finds Educating Women Saves Children," *New York Times*, September 17, 2010,

The real problem with economic rights is that they can only be claimed against the *state*; there is no larger pool, no "common heritage,"[68] from which women may draw, benefiting their states as well as themselves. Because of this, women in developing states can only get more if *others* in developing states get less. Women in developing states rarely have the political clout to claim their economic rights.

2 *Women's Rights*

'Human' rights, of course, include the rights of women as well as the rights of men. Nondiscrimination has been a cornerstone of international human rights since 1948. Women, like men, are entitled to all of the protections and assurances set out in the Universal Declaration, the Civil Covenant and the Economic Covenant. Women are even singled out for special treatment in Article 10 of the Economic Covenant, which assures mothers special protections while pregnant and after giving birth.

But feminists have long noted that existing human rights were not enough.[69] First, as a practical matter, women in fact remain second-class citizens, subordinated throughout the world, despite their equal treatment in these foundational human rights instruments. Second,

---

p. A7 (citing study published in the *Lancet* stating that "giving young women an education resulted in saving the lives of more than four million children worldwide in 2009").

[68] In 1967, Arvid Pardo of Malta suggested in the General Assembly that the deep seabed should be considered the "common heritage of mankind." Lori F. Damrosch et al., *International Law* 1446 (5th ed. 2009). *See also* UN Declaration on the Establishment of a New International Economic Order (NIEO), G. A. Res. 3201 (S-VI), UN Doc. A/9556 (May 1, 1974).

[69] Important early examples of the burgeoning scholarship on women's human rights include: Natalie Hevener, *International Law and the Status of Women* (1982); Rebecca Cook, (ed.), *Human Rights of Women* (1994); Kelly Askin and Dorean Koenig (eds.), *Women's Human Rights*; Dorinda Dallmeyer (ed.), *Reconceiving Reality* (1993); Julie Peters and Andrea Wolper (eds.) *Women's Rights, Human Rights* (1995); Arvonne Fraser, "Becoming Human: The Origins and Development of Women's Human Rights," *Hum. Rts. Q.*, 21 (1999), p. 853.

from a more theoretical perspective, feminists exposed the gendered assumptions of human rights discourse itself. Human rights law incorporates a male perspective, they explained; it focuses on issues that affect men more than women, or that affect men differently than they affect women. Rights, historically, are claims of the citizen against the state. But citizens, historically, were male and their claims reflected the interests, concerns, and social reality of men. In Aristotle's *polis*, men alone were citizens, and therefore rightholders.[70] Civil rights, such as the right to freedom of expression, assume a capacity for participation in public life, for moving about freely in the world. Historically, and in much of the contemporary world,[71] this does not reflect women's experience.

Women's human rights did not become a focus of international law until the 1990s.[72] Faced with the dearth of law addressing women's experience, women's advocates sought empirical data to substantiate that experience.[73] They also demanded the disaggregation of existing

---

[70] D. Brendan Nagle, *The Household as the foundation of Aristotle's Polis* (2006).

[71] See for example Caryle Murphy, "Saudi Women Demand Driving Rights," *Galloway Family Foundation*, June 15, 2011, www.gallowayfoundation.com/ europe/2011/20110615-saudi_arabia.html (observing that the driving ban is increasingly upsetting Saudi women, who now make up more than half of the country's university students. Graduating in record numbers, they are looking for jobs and they want to drive themselves to work, to the shopping mall, to the grocery store and to their children's schools). See also "The Plight of the Afghan Woman," *Afghanistan Online*, www.afghan-web.com/woman/ (noting the remnants of the Taliban rule under which women were forbidden to work or leave the house without a male escort).

[72] Henry J. Steiner and Philip Alston, *International Human Rights in Context* (2nd ed. 2000), pp. 158–9 (noting that, "of the several blind spots in the early development of the human rights movement, none is as striking as that movement's failure to give violations of women's (human) rights the attention . . . that they require"). This is not to suggest that they were ignored. For an account of the long years of hard work by the Commission on the Status of Women (CSW), created in 1946, see Stark, "Women's Rights," pp. 344–9.

[73] See for example Marilyn Waring, *If Women Counted* (1988), pp. 74–91 (noting that women's work is economically invisible; it does not appear in national statistics).

data on the basis of sex. They pressed for new laws on multiple fronts, including human rights and humanitarian law, expanded interpretations of existing law, and developed new fora in which to present these new claims.

In addition to the prohibitions on discrimination cited above, several human rights instruments explicitly focus on women. The most important, the legally binding CEDAW, was adopted by the General Assembly in 1979[74] and came into force in 1981.[75]

CEDAW addresses women's actual subordination as well as the gendered assumptions of human rights law. First, CEDAW requires states to address discrimination in fact as well as in law, including discriminatory "social and cultural patterns of conduct." Second, CEDAW, authorizes "temporary special measures aimed at accelerating *de facto* equality"; that is, the state may take temporary affirmative measures to level the playing field to compensate for historical discrimination. Third, CEDAW explicitly addresses reproduction and reproductive work, requiring state support for both and further requiring states to educate men regarding their responsibility for reproductive work.

Women's advocates have also expanded the available fora in which claims arising under these new laws may be brought. In addition to international tribunals, such as the ICC and the ad hoc criminal tribunals, these include regional courts, such as the European Court

---

[74] See Marsha A. Freeman, "Convention on the Elimination Against Women," in *Human Rights Encyclopedia*, p. 331 (noting that the adoption was "in time for a signing ceremony at the opening of the Second World Conference on Women held in Copenhagen, Denmark, in 1980").

[75] In addition to CEDAW, instruments focusing on women include: the Optional Protocol to the Convention on the Elimination of All forms of Discrimination Against Women, G.A. Res. 54/4, annex, UN GAOR, 54th Sess., Supp. No. 49 (Vol. I), UN Doc. A/RES/54/4 (October 15, 1999) the Convention on Consent to Marriage, Minimum Age for Marriage and Registration of Marriages, adopted November 7, 1962, 521 U.N.T.S. 231 (entered into force December 9, 1964), Convention on the Nationality of Married Women, 193 U.N.T.S. 135, entered into force July 7, 1954, Convention on the Nationality of Married Women, G.A. Res. 1040 (XI), (August 11, 1958).

of Human Rights and the Inter-American Court of Human Rights, the sessions of the human rights treaty committees, and national courts.[76] In addition, women are the subjects of innumerable soft law initiatives, including the Millennium Development Goals ("MDGs").[77]

Although women's human rights remain a distinct regime, the *principle* of gender equality has been "mainstreamed,"[78] that is, widely incorporated in international instruments and policies across the board. The Bank, for example, has a policy, procedure, strategy, and action plan on gender.[79] While well-intentioned, as Hilary Charlesworth explains, "[mainstreaming] has allowed the reduction of resources for specialized women's units within UN agencies."[80]

Most developing states have ratified most of the major human rights treaties.[81] As Oona Hathaway notes, however, monitoring

[76] See for example Rachel A. Cichowski, "Women's Rights, the European Court, and Supranational Constitutionalism," *L. & Soc'y Rev.*, 38 (2004), p. 489 (focusing on the role of the European Court of Justice in the creation of women's rights), See also *A, B and C* v. *Ireland*, 25579/05 [2010] ECHR 2032 (December 16 2010) (holding that Ireland had failed to implement the constitutional right to a legal abortion in violation of Article 8's guarantee of the right to respect for private and family life).

[77] United Nations, *Millennium Development Goals Report 2011*, UNSales No. E.11.I.1, available at www.unhcr.org/refworld/docid/4e4211%208b2.html (the promotion of gender equality and empowerment of women is the third Millennium Development Goal).

[78] Nicholas Pialek, "Is This Really the End of the Road for Gender Mainstreaming? Getting to Grips with Gender and Institutional Change," in Antony J. Bebbington et al. (eds.), *Can NGOs Make a Difference? The Challenge of Development Alternatives* (2007), p. 281 (noting that the "transition from gender-rich policy to gender-poor practice is frequently cited as an example of policy evaporation"). Hilary Charlesworth, "Not Waving but Drowning: Gender Mainstreaming and Human Rights in the United Nations," *Harv. Hum. Rts J.*, 18 (2005), pp. 1, 13.

[79] The International Criminal Court (ICC), as well as the ad hoc criminal tribunals, similarly, all address women's rights.

[80] Charlesworth, "Not Waving but Drowning," p. 13.

[81] See United Nations Treaty Collection, United Nations, available at http://treaties.un.org/Pages/UNTSOnline.aspx?id=1 with list of Least Developed Countries (LDCs), "Least Developed Countries: About Least Developed

and enforcement are minimal.[82] It is left to non-governmental organizations (NGOs), already spread thin,[83] to pressure states in which human rights are often perceived as a low priority, lacking the political urgency of assuring security (or "public order") and addressing never-ending disasters. As Paul Collier points out, moreover, few NGOs head to the developing states where the "bottom billion" subsists, where the risks are high, and the likelihood of a good outcome are low.[84]

Women's human rights are incorporated in a greater range of international regimes than most norms, and more fora are available in which to vindicate these rights. But all of these new laws, fora, and policy initiatives have failed to significantly improve the well-being of the poorest women in developing states, or even to allow them to maintain the level of well-being enjoyed by previous generations.

III POSSIBILITIES

Part I has shown how the multiple regimes that comprise globalization have effectively overcome the obstacles posed by the fragmentation of international law. Globalization works quite well – moving capital freely around the world, generating massive profits, at least for some. But globalization makes many lives worse. Because developing states do not want to be at the mercy of the IMF when the next crisis hits, they hold massive reserves, which they could otherwise invest in schools, roads, clinics, and emergency food relief. Those who win

---

Countries," UN-OHRLLS, http://222.un.org/special-rep/ohrlls/ohrlls/
UNOHRLLS/new/en/ldc/related/58/index.html.

[82] Oona Hathaway, "Do Human Rights Treaties Make a Difference?" *Yale L. J.*, 111 (2002), p. 1935.

[83] Ibid., p. 2008 ("As a consequence, the failure of a country to comply with its treaty obligations is, in most cases, unlikely to be revealed and examined except by already overtaxed NGOs").

[84] Paul Collier, *The Bottom Billion: Why the Poorest Countries Are Failing And What Can Be Done About It* (2007), p. 4("The World Bank has large offices in every major middle-income country but not a single person residing in the Central African Republic").

"the race to the bottom" work long hours, in often unsafe conditions, for whatever Walmart or Fung & Li, the massive global contractor for the garment industry, decides to pay.

Part II has shown how the regime of women's human rights, in contrast, has been effectively gutted by the fragmentation of international law, at least for the bottom quintiles of women in low- and middle-income states. Those whose lives have been made worse by globalization, along with those for whom it is a mixed blessing, cannot rely on "women's human rights" to protect them from violence and exploitation, or to feed and educate their children. The regime of international law intended to protect the most vulnerable remains words on a page – or a screen they can't afford and couldn't power – which many cannot even read.

This part considers some options. Would more fragmentation provide greater security for women in developing states? Would less fragmentation (or greater coordination) be more constructive? Less fragmentation regarding some regimes does not, of course, preclude *more* fragmentation of others, or even greater coordination among increasingly fragmented regimes. What lines can be crossed, and by whom? This section focuses on a few major developments, and explains why some are more promising than others.[85]

A More Fragmentation

Some seek complete fragmentation – the separation of the West from the rest, the end of globalization. For them, the threat posed by the West is not so much destabilized currencies, as immorality, apostasy, the endless corruptions of a godless consumer culture. Some link this to the wars in Iraq and Afghanistan and call it a "war against Islam," justifying violence. The United States calls them "terrorists," and treats them as enemies or criminals. As Dianne Otto explains, "terrorist" has become a convenient catch-all category for some governments, who use it to scapegoat gays, lesbians, and transgendered people, among others.

---

[85] See Chapter 3: Dianne Otto, "Decoding Crisis in International Law."

Some still argue that developing states should reject "development." They should sever ties with international investment firms
that have been all too willing to gamble with their national currencies,
and international organizations like the IMF that have prescribed
"austerity" for developing states while commending stimulus in the
United States.

That ship has probably sailed, at least for large swathes of the
developing world. China is already heavily invested in Africa and
Latin America. As Saskia Sassen notes, some developing states have
already committed their land to biofuels, trading away food security.
Even those she calls "the expelled," subsisting on garbage dumps in
the outer rings of the new global cities, want refrigeration, electricity, and cellphones.[86] This part explains how non-state actors, as
well as states, are creating alternatives to international regimes,
some of which explicitly focus on women in developing states. Many
depend on the transnational movement of goods or services,
whether coordination with IOs is sought or not. Even those focusing
on national policy, like Jamaica, affect international trade regimes.
In different ways, most contribute to the ongoing fragmentation of
international law.

1 Non-state Actors and Privatized Foreign Aid

There is growing support for fragmented, small-scale aid, as opposed
to the massive failed development projects of an earlier era. Nicholas
Kristof, for example, touts "privatized foreign aid."[87] In a special

[86] Saskia Sassen, Lecture, Law & Society Annual Meeting, Boston, June 2013.
[87] Nicholas Kristof, "The D.I.Y. Foreign Aid Revolution," *New York Times
Magazine*, October 24, 2010. There are, of course, scores of well-intentioned
and effective efforts to promote well-being throughout the LDCs that benefit
women, even if they do not focus on them. Nor are these efforts necessarily
grounded in "rights" claims. See for example Michael Kimmelman, "Rescued
by Design," *New York Times*, October 23, 2011, p. 1 Arts (reviewing show in
the UN visitors' lobby showcasing projects, from a community cooker fueled
by refuse in Kibera, Kenya to floating community lifeboats that serve as
schools, libraries, and health clinics in Bangladesh); *Small Fixes*, Special Issue
of *New York Times Science Times*, September 27, 2011, p. D1 (describing "low-
cost innovations that are making a big difference" from biodegradable toilet

Women's Empowerment Issue of the *New York Times Magazine*,[88] he describes a school in Nepal,[89] a factory in Rwanda,[90] and an international organization, *Run for Congo Women*.[91] He concedes that:

> It's fair to object that activists like Doyne are accomplishing results that, however noble, are minuscule. Something like 101 million children aren't attending primary school around the world, so 220 kids in Doyne's school constitute the teensiest drop in the bucket ... All that is true – but it's equally true if you happen to be that drop in the bucket, Doyne is transforming your life.[92]

Kristof argues that free markets promote women's human rights. Tina Rosenberg, similarly, claims that "[e]very week someone comes up with an ingenious product for the world's poor: a new water filter, vitamin packet, solar lamp."[93] This is a familiar premise: markets spur technology and innovation, and thus benefit those at the bottom as well as those at the top. Rosenberg is especially enthusiastic about a new business model called Living Goods, which combines microfinance with a familiar franchise, the Avon Lady. Living Goods, by selling health products door to door, provides a delivery system.[94] The strength and appeal of these claims reflect the strength and appeal of market rhetoric.

But many are skeptical. Peter Buffet, whose father, Warren Buffet, gave him a charitable foundation to manage, describes his dilemma:

> Inside any important philanthropy meeting, you witness heads of state meeting with investment managers and corporate leaders. All are searching for answers with their right hand to problems that others in the room have created with their left. There are

bags to drinking straws that filter out pathogens). See also Scott L. Cummings, book review, reviewing Lucie E. White and Jeremy Perelman (eds.) *Stones of Hope: How African Activists Reclaim Human Rights to Challenge Global Poverty* (2012), *J.Legal Educ.*, 61 (2012), p. 711 (inspiring accounts of self-help activity by Africans).
[88] *Women's Empowerment Issue*, New York Times Magazine, October 24, 2010.
[89] Ibid., p. 49.
[90] Ibid., p. 50.   [91] Ibid., p. 51.   [92] Ibid.
[93] Tina Rosenberg, "The 'Avon Ladies' of Africa," *New York Times*, October 14, 2012, p. 9.
[94] Ibid.

plenty of statistics that tell us that inequality is continually rising.
At the same time ... the non-profit sector has been steadily
growing ... It's a massive business, with approximately $316
billion given away in 2012 in the United States alone and more
than 9.4 million employed.[95]

Others point out that a significant portion of aid dollars never leaves
the developed states.[96] Instead, it pays the salaries of consultants,
bureaucrats and technical advisors in Washington and Geneva.[97]

As Stiglitz, Collier, and others have shown, moreover, markets do
far more for the financiers and investment banks which control them,
and the states that support them, than for women in developing
states.[98] Even in India, a major success story, there is little mobility
for women at the bottom. A survey completed in 2011 of Dalit
women entrepreneurs in Delhi and Hyderabad found that most made
less than $100 a month from their business. As researcher Annie
Namala characterizes such businesses: "These are basically survival
enterprises."[99]

2 Sovereign States

Some progressive scholars, having spent much of their careers challenging state sovereignty, find themselves looking to the state as a
refuge from neoliberal hegemony. Brad Roth and Sharon Lean look
to the state to protect its people from the vicissitudes of global

---

[95] Peter Buffett, Op. Ed "The Charitable-Industrial Complex," *New York Times*,
July 26, 2013.

[96] See for example Oxfam Am., *Smart Development: Why U.S. Foreign Aid
Demands Major Reform* (2008), pp. 22–4.

[97] See Ibid., pp. 19, 22, 24 (pointing out that the United States frequently
includes clawback provisions in aid packages); see also *The World Bank,
Implementing the Bank's Gender Mainstreaming Strategy: FY08 Annual
Monitoring Report 11* (June 2009)(Hereinafter *Gender Mainstreaming*) (noting
that "Competition for Gender Action Plan (GAP) funding rarely elicits 'new'
work on gender. In the first call for proposals, 66 percent of proposals
submitted were from Bank staff who already worked on gender issues").

[98] See Part III, Section B.

[99] Lydia Polgreen, "Scaling Caste Walls With Capitalism's Ladders," *New York
Times*, December 21, 2011, pp. A1, A12.

markets.[100] While poor women in developing states have many reasons to distrust their states, state measures, such as national capital controls, may be all the protection they can hope for from the next global tsunami, whether food riots, "hot money," or another round of IMF "austerity."

Some states have taken steps to protect their people from the ongoing crises of global capitalism.[101] Jamaica, for example, initiated a "food security" program ten years ago to reduce the country's dependence on foreign imports.[102] National farmers had scaled back in the 1990s and 2000s, unable to compete with global agribusiness. The food shortages of 2008, when foreign producers kept their food for their own people, were a harsh reminder that the island was still vulnerable. Jamaica and other states in the Caribbean re-committed to domestic agriculture with a renewed sense of urgency. Antigua and Barbuda expect to grow half their own food in 2013.[103] Haiti, where food riots erupted in 2008, is constructing silos for "strategic food reserves."[104] By reducing their dependence on foreign producers, these states hope to insulate themselves from volatile global markets.

States also seek to counter Western influence or domination by forging alliances with similarly situated states. The BRICS (Brazil, Russia, India, China, and South Africa) for example, recently met to form the New Development Bank as an alternative to the World Bank.[105] They are also considering pooling their foreign reserves as a bulwark against future currency crises.[106] At the same time, however, other alliances seem to be fraying. As the governor of Nigeria's central bank recently wrote: "China is no longer a fellow underdeveloped economy – it is the world's second biggest, capable of the same

[100] *See* Chapter 7: Brad Roth and Sharon F. Lean, "A Bolivarian Alternative? The New Latin American Populism Confronts the Global Order."
[101] See, Damien Cave, "As Cost of Importing Food Soars, Jamaica Turns to the Earth," *New York Times*, August 4, 2013, p. A6.
[102] Ibid.   [103] Ibid.   [104] Ibid.
[105] Simon Romero, "Emerging Nations Bloc to Open Development Bank," *New York Times*, July 16, 2014, p. A9; Lydia Polgreen, "Group of Emerging Nations Plans to Form Development Bank," *New York Times*, March 27, 2013, p. A4.
[106] Ibid.

forms of exploitation as the West. It is a significant contributor to Africa's deindustrialization and underdevelopment."[107]

B Less Fragmentation

In response to the ongoing fragmentation of international law, some scholars urge greater integration of regimes and suggest mechanisms for reconciling them. This may well be necessary, at least to safeguard some interests. As noted above, however, efforts to "mainstream" women's human rights seem to have backfired, diffusing already-scarce resources.[108] At the same time, as set out in Part II, existing regimes for promoting women's rights, and existing mechanisms for vindicating them, offer little for poor women in developing states.

Financial institutions that rely on globalization, on the other hand, are thriving. The six largest investment banks enjoyed an estimated average increase of 20 percent in earnings during the second quarter of 2013.[109] Public pressure seems to be easing. At the World Economic Forum at Davos this year, "there appear[ed] to be a growing sentiment that the banks have taken enough abuse."[110] In 2013, the twenty-five highest earning hedge fund managers in the United States earned $21.15 billion.[111]

It is clear, however, that the underlying problems that led to the crises remain unresolved. Rather, "the banks that created risky amalgams of mortgages and loans during the boom – the kind that went so wrong during the bust – are busily reviving the same types of investments that many thought were gone for good."[112] Indeed, as of November 2013, the Justice Department along with other authorities in Britain, the EU, Switzerland, and Hong Kong were investigating

---

[107] Ibid.   [108] See notes 78–80.

[109] Greta Morganstern, "Bankers Are Balking At Tighter Suspenders," *New York Times*, July 4, 2013, p. B1.

[110] Jack Ewing, "In Davos, Atmosphere For Bankers Improves," *New York Times*, January 21, 2013, p. B1.

[111] Alexandra Stevenson, "Hedge fund Moguls' Pay Has the 1% Looking Up," *New York Times*, May 6, 2014, p. B1.

[112] Nathaniel Popper, "Wall St. Redux: Arcane Names Hiding Big Risk," *New York Times*, April 19, 2013, p. A1.

"the world's biggest banks for rigging the world's biggest market," that is, the $5.3 trillion a day foreign currency exchange market.[113] This requires less fragmentation and greater harmonization, if not integration, of international regimes.

1 International Regulation

In 2009, the UN Commission of Experts on Reforms of the International Monetary and Financial System, chaired by Stiglitz, called for "global economic governance."[114] The President of the General Assembly, Miguel d'Escoto, demanded "new global institutions, authorities and advisory boards."[115] They made a compelling fairness argument: the "Group of 192" – all the member states of the United Nations – should participate in setting the rules for the global economy. These rules should not be left to the G8, or even the G20. Absent international regulation, countries with lax regulation "compete[ed] to attract financial services" in a desperate "race to the bottom."[116] The Experts Report, and d'Escoto's demand, were ignored by the G9.[117]

a Banks

During the Great Recession, hundreds of billions of dollars were spent bailing out banks in the United States, the United Kingdom, and Germany, among other states. The fear was that national

---

[113] "Editorial, Another Banking Scandal," *New York Times,* November 22, 2013, p. A28.

[114] *Report of the Commission of Experts of the President of the UN General Assembly, Reforms of the International Monetary and Financial System,* September 21, 2009.

[115] Neil MacFarquhar, "At U.N., A Sandinista's Plan for Recovery," *New York Times,* May 25, 2009 (noting that d'Escoto's initiative breached UN etiquette: "[T]raditionally, before any conference, the General Assembly president appoints a couple of ambassadors as 'facilitators' who consult widely and then propose a working document").

[116] Joseph E. Stiglitz, "A Real Cure for the Global Economic Crackup," in *The Nation,* July 13, 2009, p. 11.

[117] MacFarquhar, "At U.N., A Sandinista's Plan for Recovery."

financial systems would collapse if they were allowed to fail. The banks were "too big to fail, to manage, to regulate, and to prosecute."[118] If the banks are to remain intact, as the Dodd-Frank reform law assumes, the rules governing them must be scaled accordingly. The rules on derivatives to be applied under Dodd-Frank, for example, would have to apply to foreign branches and affiliates of American banks, as well as to hedge funds that operate here but are incorporated elsewhere.[119] Oversight of the $700 trillion derivatives markets is fiercely resisted, however, by Wall Street as well as by top finance ministers in Britain, Russia, Japan, and Germany.[120]

In a separate but related development, the Federal Reserve proposed rules requiring American subsidiaries of foreign banks to maintain capital and liquidity in the United States.[121] Michel Barnier, the European commissioner in charge of internal markets, rejected the proposal and warned that if the Fed did not back down the new rules "could spark a protectionist reaction" from other countries and bring on "a fragmentation of global banking markets and regulatory frameworks."[122]

The Fed also proposed that the biggest banks be required to hold extra capital.[123] Banks could avoid this requirement by becoming smaller, so that their failure would not pose the same threat to the economy.[124] A bipartisan bill was recently introduced in the Senate which would require banks with over $500 billion to hold capital worth 15 percent of their assets.[125] This leverage ratio would be fixed. Unlike the international banking regulations set out in Basel III, there would be no adjustment for "perceived risk" by the

---

[118] "Editorial, After the 'London Whale'," *New York Times*, March 22, 2013, p. A28.

[119] Ibid.

[120] Eric Lipton, "Banks Resist Strict Control of Foreign Bets," *New York Times*, May 1, 2013, p. A1.

[121] Floyd Norris, "From Federal Reserve, A New Chill to Banks From Abroad," *New York Times*, April 26, 2013, p. B1.

[122] Ibid.

[123] Peter Eavis, "A New Fed Thought for 'Too Big to Fail' Banks: Shrink Them," *New York Times*, May 4, 2013, p. B5.

[124] Ibid.   [125] Ibid.

banks themselves.[126] Another bipartisan bill would resurrect Glass--Steagall, forcing banks to shed their trading operations.[127]

The European Parliament, similarly, has completed a plan to reform its troubled banking system. The new plan establishes a common rule book for managing failing banks and guarantees on deposits, among measures intended to contain risk.[128] Whether risk can be managed as well – as it can be exploited remains an open question in a global system that still allows huge profits to be made by gambling with other peoples' money.

b Tax Havens

Tax havens like the Cayman Islands provide safe havens for wealthy Americans and Europeans, as well as dictators in developing states. Because such havens are unregulated, state tax authorities are unable to track assets hidden there.[129] In addition, as Krugman notes, tax havens "distort the flow of capital, helping to feed even-bigger financial crises."[130]

In 2009, the G20 asked the OECD to list states according to their commitment to international transparency. Only four countries were put on a blacklist (not including the Caymans) and all were upgraded to a gray list within a week.[131] Fragmentation may be more productive than this kind of tepid regulation. Bilateral arrangements, like the recent agreement between Switzerland and the United States,[132] may

---

[126] Ibid.

[127] Peter Eavis, "Senators Introduce Bill to Separate Trading Activities From Big Banks," *New York Times*, July 12, 2013, p. B3.

[128] James Kanter, "European Parliament Approves Laws to Overhaul Troubled Banking System," *New York Times*, April 16, 2014.

[129] Joseph Stiglitz, *Freefall*, pp. 217–18.

[130] Paul Krugman, "Treasure Island Trauma," *New York Times*, March 22, 2013, p. A29. See generally Nicholas Shaxson, *Treasure Islands* (2011).

[131] Joseph Stiglitz, *Freefall*, p. 346 n. 14.

[132] See Agreement Between U.S. and Switzerland for Cooperation to Facilitate the Implementation of FATCA, February 13, 2013. But see Stephen J. Dunn, "Beware of Swiss Banks Urging Offshore Voluntary Disclosure to IRS," *Forbes*, June 8, 2014, www.forbes.com (noting risks to bank customers).

well be more effective in the short run. But in the long run, the G20's rhetorical support for new standardized tax treaties may matter more simply because anything short of international regulation invites capital flight to wherever banks remain unbound.

2 Crossing Lines

As noted in the ILC Report, specialists within the proliferating networks that comprise international law speak their own esoteric languages. Globalization itself has shown that some networks can be linked, especially when teams of savvy lawyers are paid top dollar to do so. In general, however, these networks are not porous; line crossing is difficult. Those who are fluent in financial and economic jargons, moreover, are often more interested in increasing profits than distributive justice.

But growing numbers of sophisticated international legal scholars, such as Dan Danielsen,[133] along with economists like Krugman and Stiglitz, continue to expose the deliberately complex machinations of the global financial networks. They track who benefits, and who pays. Their work shows that crossing lines is possible, and why it is necessary.

IV CONCLUSION

As Krugman and other economists have explained, before the deregulation of financial markets the waves of financial crises that have overtaken states since the early 1980s were virtually unknown.[134] Since then, however, the crises have been unrelenting: "Mexico, Brazil, Argentina and Chile in 1982. Sweden and Finland in 1991. Mexico again in 1995. Thailand, Malaysia, Indonesia and Korea in 1998. Argentina again in 2002. And, of course, the more recent run of disasters: Iceland, Greece, Portugal, Spain, Italy, Cyprus."[135]

---

[133] Dan Danielsen, "Economic Approaches to Global Regulation: Expanding the International Law and Economics Paradigm," *J. Int'l Bus. & L.*, 10 (2011), p. 23.

[134] Paul Krugman, "Hot Money Blues," *New York Times*, March 25, 2013, p. A23.

[135] Ibid.

The future of the shrinking women cannot be assured by existing women's rights regimes. But *other* international law regimes still have the capacity, if not the political will, to rein in risktakers on Wall Street, in London and in Shanghai. The hedge fund managers and investment bankers at ICBC (Industrial and Commercial Bank of China), JP Morgan Chase, HSBC and Bank of America are a resilient group.[136] A few have been chided, and even fewer jailed, but many are eager to replace them and create new, even more exotic financial instruments; to take brave, wild risks with other peoples' money. The future of the shrinking women, some of whom live in states unlikely to weather yet another global crisis, may well depend on international law regimes which they cannot imagine, and which are oblivious to them.

---

[136] See for example Peter Eavis, "The Wall St. Recovery," *New York Times*, July 4, 2014 (noting that most of the $3 trillion gained in the 12 months through have gone to "wealthier households").

PART III   Sovereign States

5 CORPORATE POWER AND INSTRUMENTAL STATES: TOWARD A CRITICAL REASSESSMENT OF THE ROLE OF FIRMS, STATES, AND REGULATION IN GLOBAL GOVERNANCE

Dan Danielsen

I FIRMS, STATES, AND MODERN POLITICAL ECONOMY: IDEOLOGICAL STRUGGLE FROM WITHIN A COMMON CONCEPTION

Since the global financial crisis began in 2008, a commonly proffered view among political progressives and conservatives alike is that the central issue for achieving economic stability and growth in the global economy is finding the appropriate level of public oversight of the economy. Progressives suggest that the level of regulatory oversight is too little and too deferential to the influence of "the regulated," while conservatives assert that, on balance, there is too much regulatory interference with markets, distorting the efficiency of private transactions and disrupting the tendency of markets to self-correct through private reallocation of resources when imbalances occur. While these two perspectives might seem oppositional or contradictory, a shared conception in both accounts is that the nation-state is the primary institutional mechanism for setting the background conditions for the smooth operation of the economy. From this perspective, whether the global economy functions well or badly depends on whether the nation-state, and by extension the global regulatory institutions by and large created by nation-states, create an appropriate legal architecture to facilitate private economic transactions while maintaining an appropriate level of regulatory oversight to reduce the likelihood of either regulatory capture by firms or regulatory over-reach by states. The ideological struggle, to the extent there is one on this score, turns on what is "appropriate" both with respect to the content of the background rules that structure markets and the scope and implementation of the regulatory oversight functions.

Juxtaposed to this vision of the proper role for the "public" regulator is a conception of the "private" economic actor and its proper role in the system. While private economic actors are expected to abide by the rules of the game set by the public regulatory system, they are also expected, if not encouraged like Adam Smith's self-interested individuals, to follow their (natural?) proclivity to seek their own advantage. Doing so is expected to be accomplished in large part through risk-taking, including regulatory risk-taking that might challenge regulatory limits. If the "rules of the game" are too constraining on private choice, then some transactions that by definition would be welfare-enhancing for the parties to them (because, the story goes, they would otherwise not enter into them) will be discouraged or precluded by the over-zealous rules. Moreover, by reducing the welfare-gains the parties would otherwise have generated had they been permitted to transact, total output is also reduced, thereby reducing total social welfare. If, on the other hand, the rules are too loose, private transactional gains might come at the expense of general welfare by creating adverse effects (or externalities) on third parties that exceed the welfare gains of the parties by transacting.

In a sense, this conception of the global public "regulator" evokes something akin to a mechanical system (not so much in terms of actual function as aspiration) – a largely public regulatory system that if properly calibrated could ensure the smooth operation of a largely private market system. From this perspective, it follows that private economic actors are and should remain "self-interested," leaving public regulators to provide for the general welfare by endeavoring to achieve the proper regulatory balance for structuring markets – allowing the productive dynamism of private economic autonomy to flourish while ameliorating externalities and spillover affects to the extent they reduce aggregate welfare and providing "public goods" where private actors are insufficiently incentivized to do so. Thus, from this vantage point, maintaining the private, "self-interested" orientation of economic actors is important both for inducing welfare-increasing private transactions and for signaling when the public regulatory system might be misaligned with the enhancement of general welfare.

Despite the air of natural inevitability that seems to pervade this familiar description of (prescription for?) the global political and economic order, the system, even by its own account, seems quite fragile. The proper calibration of the regulatory state and by extension, the global public regulatory order, seems more wish than reality – rarely if ever achieved or achievable. This seems particularly true at the global level where national interests and global welfare may often conflict and the challenges to and costs of productive coordination (as well as competition) among states and other public regulatory institutions can be quite high. Of course, despite the apparent fragility of the system on the one hand, and the difficulty of achieving the appropriate regulatory balance on the other, proponents of this view of political economy treat the consequences of "state" or "regulatory failure" as significant – when the regulatory system comes too misaligned, regulating too much or too little – one foreseeable result is crisis (economic, political, or both).

Moreover, since in this conception, the public *acts* and the private *reacts*, it is perhaps better, on balance, if the public acts less in the global arena. For conservatives, this means shifting the balance of global regulatory governance in the direction of facilitating and supporting private ordering mechanisms and self-regulatory systems. For political liberals and progressives, this means focusing regulatory attention on correcting "market failures." Some types of "market failures" treated as justifying regulatory oversight include situations where economic activity produces more adverse effects on third parties than benefits to the parties engaged in the activity; or where asymmetric access to market information may lead some parties to gain advantage over or others or to enter into welfare-reducing transactions; or where collective action problems or other conditions producing high transaction costs may discourage welfare-enhancing transactions; or where private incentives are insufficient to lead to an adequate supply of "public goods," such as education or transport or public safety or market information. In any case, whether viewed from the conservative or the liberal perspective, economic crises seem an inevitable, if regrettable, part of the operation of this system even if better calibration of the regulatory system and levels of public oversight were able to reduce the frequency and severity of the crises.

The view of the global economic and regulatory order I've described could be seen as a mélange of contemporary ideological positions loosely reflective of the struggle between Washington Consensus neo-liberals on the one hand, and post-Washington consensus (political) liberals on the other.[1] Yet the genealogy of these general (if sometimes contradictory) notions of a proper relation between state and economy – a limited public regulatory state whose primary function is the creation and preservation of a private economic order – has a history that extends well beyond contemporary debates over the merits of neo-liberal political and economic reforms of the past 30 years. It is perhaps because these conceptions of "state," "economy," and their proper relations are so deeply embedded in the development of modern political economy since the Enlightenment that they continue to exert so much influence on contemporary understandings of the functioning, problems, possibilities, and limits of the global economic and regulatory order across the political spectrum.[2]

---

[1] For a short introduction to these debates, see Joseph E. Stiglitz, "Is there a Post-Washington Consensus Consensus," in Narcis Serra and Joseph E. Stiglitz (eds.) *The Washington Consensus Reconsidered: Towards a New Global Governance* (2008), pp. 41–60, 46–7 (associating Washington Consensus neo-liberals with "market fundamentalism" and Post-Washington Consensus liberals with "a balanced role for markets and government").

[2] See, for example John Locke, *The Second Treatise on Government* (Thomas P. Peardon (ed.), The Bobs–Merrill Company, 1952; 1690), pp.70–3 (asserting that the justification for and appropriate limits of government is the protection of individual liberty and property for the public good); John Stuart Mill, *Principles of Political Economy* (Sir William Ashley (ed.), Augustus M. Kelley Publishers, 1987; 1848), pp. 881–8 (treating all government action as interference, the basis for governmental action as the protection of person and property and the legitimacy of government action as a function of the economic effects of carrying it out); Karl Marx, "On the Jewish Question," in *Karl Marx Early Writings* (Rodney Livingstone and Gregor Benton (trans.), Penguin Classics, 1992; 1843), pp. 229–30 (arguing that the purpose of the state after the political emancipation of the French and American Revolutions was

II AN ALTERNATIVE VISION: WHY IT IS NEEDED AND WHAT IT MIGHT LOOK LIKE

Despite its historical provenance and contemporary pervasiveness, the conception of a (mostly public) regulatory system charged with and responsible for securing the (mostly smooth) functioning of a global economy driven by (mostly private) self-interested economic actors, is neither helpful as a means of describing the actual operation of the global economic and regulatory order as it currently exists, nor useful in explaining why a public global order intended to promote general welfare is leading to increasing asymmetries in power and resources both among states and within states. Moreover, framing the central issue of political economy to be the creation/preservation of a proper (natural?) relation between public state and private economy, regulator and regulated, general welfare and individual gain through the careful avoidance of the Scylla of regulatory capture of public authorities by private firms on the one hand and the Charybdis of over- or under-regulation by states that may reduce public welfare and precipitate crises on the other, makes it more difficult to recognize or address significant aspects of and issues with the global order.

In particular, two problems with this pervasive conception stand out. First, the conception is premised on a sharp divide between "public" and "private" that makes it difficult to engage the diverse, complex, highly entangled, and interdependent relations among states, regulatory institutions and firms we see all around us or to explain the impact of those relations on the structure, content, and operation of the

protecting the "Rights of Man" which he defines as "liberty," "property," "equality," and "security" about which he states: "[N]ot one of the so-called rights of man goes beyond egoistic man ... The only bond which holds [individuals] together is natural necessity, need and private interest, the conservation of property and their egoistic persons."); Michel Foucault, *The Birth of Biopolitics, Lectures at the Collège de France* 1978–1979 *(Graham Burchell (trans.), Michel Senellart (ed.), Picadore, 2008; 1979), pp. 3–25 (arguing that in the middle of the eighteenth century the main conception of government shifted from* raison d'État *constrained only by external limits imposed by divine and natural law to the notion of the self-limiting state governed and constrained by the rationality of political economy).*

governance system and the economy locally and globally. Second, the notion that each nation-state bears the sovereign responsibility for balancing the gains and excesses of self-interested private economic actors within its jurisdiction obscures the radical asymmetries in power, capacity, and resources among states, regulatory institutions and firms that are significant to regulatory and distributional outcomes both in individual states and across the global system as a whole.

We need only look out at the world to recognize that there are significant asymmetries in the bargaining power, resources, and capacities of states and of firms that affect their relative abilities to advance or protect their interests in the global economy. When we bring together the complex, multiple, and inter-penetrated relations between "public" and "private" entities as traditionally conceived with the pervasive inequalities and power asymmetries among and between states and firms, it becomes quite difficult if not impossible to generalize about either the ability of firms to capture public regulatory power and advantage or the ability of states (or other public regulatory institutions) to secure the success or control the excesses of self-interested firms either at home or globally. A conception of global governance able to incorporate these two ubiquitous aspects of the contemporary global order would seem to require much more nuanced, particularized, and messy accounts of the structure and operation of the global economic and regulatory system, including accounts of the legal, institutional, and other mechanisms that shape the current and future distribution of power and resources in the system.

We might begin by theorizing the global economic and regulatory order we see in operation rather than one premised on counterfactual notions of a "public" regulatory order and a "private" economy. Such an order would reflect a dynamic, continuous, and cumulative co-production of states and firms with different baseline allocations of power, resources and capacities, bargaining over, making, adapting, and resisting the rules of the game on the one hand and anticipating, making and reacting to each other's assertions of power on the other.[3]

---

[3] For an alternative account of state sovereignty and corporate power as mutually constitutive, see Joshua Barkan, *Corporate Sovereignty: Law and Government under Capitalism* (2013), pp. 1–9.

Such a conception of continuous bargaining, assertion, and adaptation to constantly changing legal, economic, cultural, and political conditions is not consistent with the hypothetical steady state equilibrium premised by mainstream economics or a single optimally efficient allocation of power or resources as is often suggested in the law and economics literature on bargaining. Such a conception would nevertheless be useful in helping to explain the production of relatively stable configurations of power and advantage that could reinforce inequalities and shape future bargaining among players in the system.[4]

Michel Foucault captures the flavor of the dynamic processes I have in mind, albeit describing a somewhat different context. He states:

> Inasmuch as the government of men is a practice which is not
> imposed by those who govern on those who are governed, but a
> practice that fixes the definition and respective positions of the
> governed and the governors facing each other in relation to each
> other, "internal regulation" means that limitation is not exactly
> imposed by one side or the other, or at any rate not globally,
> definitely and totally, but by, I would say, transaction, in the very
> broad sense of the word, that is to say, "action between," that is to
> say, by a series of conflicts, agreements, discussions, and
> reciprocal concessions: all episodes whose effect is finally to
> establish de facto, general, rational division between what is to be
> done and what is not to be done in the practice of governing.[5]

Seeing the global order as a dynamic system emerging from the actual practice of states and firms and perpetually defining and redefining the boundaries among public and private, governors and governed, and legitimate and illegitimate assertions of authority, invites us to rethink the central questions that have dominated the study of political economy since the Enlightenment. More specifically, it invites us

---

[4] For a fascinating discussion of the ways in which asymmetries in resource
  endowments can lead through processes of cumulative causation to vicious
  cycles of increasing inequality, see Gunnar Myrdal, *Economic Theory and Under-
  Developed Regions* (Harper Torchbooks, 1971; 1957), pp. 11–38.
[5] Michel Foucault, *The Birth of Biopolitics* , p.12.

to shift the focus of study from how to produce and maintain an appropriate (if not always optimal) balance between "public" order and "private" initiative to consider the practical meaning and implications of regulation, intervention, public welfare, and crisis in circumstances where state and firm, rule and transaction, public and private, governor and governed blur and blend in ways that challenge simple conceptions of agency, control, and domination.

Perhaps more importantly, moving from a conception of the global order premised on the authority and efficacy of public regulatory power to limit the excesses of private economic activity without diminishing its tremendous productive capacity to a conception of global economic governance as a complex co-production of states and firms invites us to consider the "firm" as more than a convenient institutional form for carrying out private initiative. It becomes among the most significant institutions in modern life. From this new vantage point, exploring the significance of the "firm" requires looking beyond the processes by which corporate power shapes state power, to consider much more broadly the social, psychological, political, and economic significance of the firm as an allocator of resources, a form of group life, an aggregator of resources, a coordinator of collective projects, a creator of social relations, and a significant influence on the structure of work, family, community, and identity.[6]

Foucault once again captures something of what I'm suggesting, though in talking about the state. As you read the following quotation, imagine substituting "the firm" for "the state." Foucault says:

> The state[/firm] is not a cold monster: it is the correlative of a particular way of governing. The problem is how this way of governing develops, what its history is, how it expands, how it

---

[6] For some diverse examples of work exploring the social and cultural implications of "the firm" as well as its economic and political ones, see Thorstein Veblen, *The Theory of Business Enterprise* (1904); Paul A. Baran and Paul M. Sweezy, *Monopoly Capital: An Essay on the American Economic and Social Order* (1966); Herbert Marcuse, *One-Dimensional Man* (1964); William M. Dugger, *Corporate Hegemony* (1989); John L. Comaroff and Jean Comaroff, *Ethnicity, Inc.* (2009); and Joshua Barkan, *Corporate Sovereignty*.

contacts, how it is extended to a particular domain, and how it invents, forms and develops practices.[7]

In short, I'm suggesting that we need to investigate the firm with every bit as much ingenuity, rigor, and tenacity as lawyers, social scientists, philosophers and humanists have applied to the study of the state. While undertaking such an investigation of "the firm" is beyond the scope of this essay, it is to the firm and its complex role in the global order that we now turn.

A Firms "Govern" but Do They "Rule"?

While the pervasiveness and significance of the firm in the structure and operation of the global regulatory and economic order might be subject to debate, that firms are not only subject to public regulation but also produce it at both the national and the transnational levels seems an indisputable fact of modern life.[8] I have argued elsewhere that firms "govern" in a variety of ways including through their interpretations, reactions and challenges to extant legal rules, through their business practices and structures, through direct political or economic pressure on regulators from lobbying to bribes, through supplying de facto rules where none exist, through evading rules by doing business elsewhere or threatening to do so, through industry organizations and coordinated standard setting, through public relations and marketing campaigns, sponsored research studies and other forms of public knowledge production, through playing regulatory institutions against each other, through arbitrage of conflicts and ambiguities in often complex, overlapping and sometimes contradictory regulatory regimes to which they may be subject locally, nationally and/or globally.[9] Through these diverse mechanisms, and many others, firms contribute to the global regulatory and economic order, shaping both its substantive content and its distributional effects.

---

[7] Michel Foucault, *The Birth of Biopolitics* , p. 6.

[8] See for example Joshua Barkan, *Corporate Sovereignty*, pp. 1–4.

[9] See Dan Danielsen, "How Corporations Govern: Taking Corporate Power Seriously in Transnational Regulation and Governance," *Harv. Intl L. Rev.*, 46 (2005), p. 412.

In their book *Empire* Hardt and Negri describe the impact of the transnational firm on global governance as follows:

> The huge transnational corporations construct the fundamental connective fabric of the biopolitical world in certain important respects. Capital has indeed always been organized with a view toward the entire global sphere, but only in the second half of the twentieth century did multinational and transnational industrial and financial corporations really begin to structure global territories biopolitically. Some claim that these corporations have merely come to occupy the place that was held by the various national colonialist and imperialist systems in earlier phases of capitalist development, from nineteenth-century European imperialism to the Fordist phase of development of the twentieth century. This is in part true, but that place itself has been substantially transformed by the new reality of capitalism. The activities of corporations are no longer defined by the imposition of abstract command and the organization of simple theft and unequal exchange. Rather, they directly structure and articulate territories and populations. They tend to make the nation-states merely instruments to record the flows of the commodities, monies and populations that they set in motion.[10]

From this perspective, one might conclude that the state is a mere instrumentality of corporate power, and as such, has been transcended as the main institutional form for global governance. To a certain extent, one might see this passage as an extreme version of the conception of political economy with which I began this essay – the struggle to retain public control over the private economy lost, perhaps entirely, to corporate capture. Yet, to recognize that corporate actors shape, participate in and sometimes engage directly in making the global order does not necessarily lead to the conclusion that they control it, at least not in any coordinated, hegemonic sense.

Like governments and quasi-governmental institutions, corporate actors are diverse – in terms of size, power, interests, business needs and regulatory goals. They can be large or small. They can be local, regional or global in terms of production systems or markets. They can be highly mobile or geographically bound. They can be narrow in

[10] Michael Hardt and Antonio Negri, *Empire* (2000), p. 31.

business focus or quite diversified in their business activities. They can be monopolists, oligarchs, or major or minor players in highly competitive industries or markets. They can be vertically integrated or highly disaggregated in complex supply chains. They may focus on short-term gain or long-term profit. They may rely on constant technological innovation and intellectual property investment or efficient exploitation of well-established technologies through sophisticated global strategies of sourcing and production cost management. Even from this brief and incomplete catalog of diversity among firms as to business type, strategy and perspective, it would be difficult to credibly suggest that a single or overarching business interest could be articulated or advanced that could direct the activities of regulators to the benefit of business generally without adversely affecting the interests of at least some powerful business and social actors elsewhere in the system. The "logic of capitalism" is not sufficiently determinate to overcome the fact that regulation rarely creates only winners.

For example, consider a domestic environmental regulation designed to promote cleaner energy through the reduction of greenhouse emissions from power producers. Such a regulation may benefit solar, wind, hydroelectric, and nuclear power producers; engineers, designers, and manufacturers of equipment used by those producers locally and globally; workers in those industries; areas and regions where such power production is most feasible; areas, regions, or nations where the technological capacity to develop and/or produce the equipment and knowhow necessary for this form of power production is most advanced and perhaps that portion of the public that values better air quality or worries about the consequences of global warming or that supports environmental regulation even if it increases energy prices in the short term or imposes economic hardship on some groups. At the same time, such a regulation may harm traditional power producers based on fossil fuels, extractors, and refiners of coal and oil locally and globally; engineers, designers, and manufacturers of equipment and technology used in these industries locally and globally, workers in all these industries, areas, or regions where alternatives to fossil fuel energy production are less feasible; areas, regions, or nations where the technological capacity to develop and/or produce the equipment and knowhow necessary to produce alternative

energy is less advanced or nonexistent, as well as that portion of the
public that due to economic hardship or otherwise would trade
cleaner air for cheaper energy or that believes concerns about global
warming to be overblown or that opposes environmental regulation
that may lead to an increase in energy prices in the short term or that
imposes economic hardship on some groups.

Generalizing from this example, we can see that a regulatory
change in one jurisdiction that may lead to an economic advantage
for a particular firm or group of firms may not similarly advantage, or
may actually disadvantage, competitor firms in that jurisdiction. We
can also see that a regulatory change may not affect only competitors –
it might produce spillover effects that advantage or disadvantage other
firms locally or globally, as well as diverse nonfirm constituencies. To
the extent that regulatory changes such as the hypothetical environmental rule described result from influence or capture by a firm or
group of firms, one would expect that firms would most often pursue
regulatory advantage when it conferred just that – a disproportionate
gain for them relative to their competitors nationally or globally,
regardless of its impact on third-party firms and other constituencies.
In other words, the struggle among firms or industry groups for
advantage *over other firms* even within the same jurisdiction or industry may work at cross-purposes with or undermine efforts to coordinate activities among firms for shared advantage vis-à-vis public
regulators both locally and globally.

Moreover, even if one or more firms were able to capture some
states or regulators for some purposes, we could not easily conclude
that business advantage achieved in one regulatory context would
translate into consistent business advantage across the global economy as a whole. As a consequence, one might reasonably expect that
many firms would need to employ different regulatory and business
strategies in different jurisdictions if the goal were securing economic
advantage in global operations. But deploying different business or
regulatory strategies would likely lead to new complexities even if it
also produced the potential for new sources of economic gain. For
example, such different strategies might produce different effects on
competitors and different spillover effects on third party firms and
other constituencies both within and outside each jurisdiction,

resulting in different configurations of bargaining, influence, resistance, and counter-strategy among both firms and regulators locally and globally.

For all these reasons, it seems likely that efforts by firms or industry groups to capture some relevant segment of regulatory authority, whether within or among nation-states, would be but one among many available strategies for seeking advantage in the complex global economic order. And, it would not be easy with so many rival firms and groups seeking regulatory control for their own purposes. Moreover, even if firms exert significant influence and occasionally even capture public regulatory institutions to promote their advantage, and even if some firms predictably win more regulatory advantages and a larger share of the global economic surplus than others, this does not mean that there is a generalizable "firm" or common business perspective on global regulatory authority. To put this point differently, without imagining some shared and consistent business interest that could both trump the drive for particular firm advantage and steer corporate power toward particular forms of public institutions and regulatory structures, asserting that "firms rule" would seem to tell us little more about the particularities or distributional consequences of the current global order than asserting, as has historically been the case, that "states rule."

While all "states" may be formally equal in some international law definition kind of way, different states with different interests, structures, resources, and goals rule differently, with different effects, to the benefit of different constituencies. We might expect the same of firms, and looking at the behavior of firms, we can see a great diversity of business strategies, goals, and governance practices. More fruitful inquiries might explore questions such as which states? Which firms? How rule? For whose benefit? With what constraints? Through what concrete practices? My point here is that shifting our focus from a theory *public rule* to *corporate rule* seems only to shift our gaze from one illusory conception of political economy to another. If we remain focused on the behaviors of states and firms we see manifesting all around us, it becomes harder to conclude that firms "rule" – in the sense of consistently control or dominate nation-states or the global regulatory order – except perhaps in ad hoc, disaggregated, incoherent, and incomplete ways similar to those frequently attributed to states by many scholars and policymakers narrating the decline of national sovereign power.[11]

B. States "Govern" but Do They "Rule"?

Turning now to the "public" side of the story, one reason it seems unconvincing to treat "the firm" as the "new global sovereign" is in part because of the undeniable fact that regulation promulgated by nation-states both at the domestic level, and at the global level through bi-lateral or multi-lateral institutions comprised of nation-states, undeniably has a significant impact on the behavior firms both domestically and globally. Yet, to suggest that public regulation

---

[11] Narratives of the decline of state sovereignty and claims of the emergence of a new world order of limited state power and policy autonomy abound in public international law discourse. Seefor example Louis Henkin, *International Law Politics and Values* (1995), p. 10 ("For legal purposes at least, we might do well to relegate the term sovereignty to the shelf of history as a relic from an earlier era."); Boutros Bourtros-Ghali, *Empowering the United Nations* (1992), pp. 71, 89, 98–9 ("While respect for the fundamental sovereignty and integrity of the state remains crucial, it is undeniable that the centuries-old doctrine of absolute and exclusive sovereignty no longer stands ... Related to this is the widening recognition that states and their governments cannot face or solve today's problems on their alone."); Secretary-General Kofi Annan, *Annual Speech to the General Assembly*, UN Doc SG/SM/7136, GA/9596 (September 20, 1999) ("State sovereignty, in its most basic sense, is being redefined by the forces of globalization and international cooperation ... In short, it is not the deficiencies in the [UN] Charter which have brought us to this juncture, but our difficulties in applying its principles to a new era: an era when strictly traditional notions of sovereignty can no longer do justice to the aspirations of peoples everywhere to attain their fundamental freedoms."); John H. Jackson et al., *Legal Problems in Economic Relations: Cases, Materials and Text* (5th ed., 2008), p. 1. ("Despite all the talk about sovereignty and independence, these concepts can mislead when applied in today's world economy. How 'sovereign' is a country with an economy so dependent on trade that its government cannot readily affect the real domestic interest rate, implement its preferred tax policy, or establish an effective program of incentives for business or talented individuals? Many governments face such constraints today including, increasingly and inevitably, the United States.")

affects firm behavior is not necessarily to suggest that states control or manage firms or the economy effectively, coherently or in the service of a "public interest" that reflects an aggregation of the collective interests of their constituents. This may in part be a function of the fact that, as public choice theorists so frequently remind us, states are themselves made up of diverse interests, institutions and constituencies engaged in struggle over the present and future distribution of power, prestige, votes and/or resources in their own regulatory jurisdictions and institutions.[12] Moreover, sometimes portions of the regulatory apparatus get captured for particular purposes by well-organized interests (including, as we've already seen, firms or groups of firms) as well as by political or institutional constituents within the governance institutions themselves. Such capture may lead states or institutions to take or refrain from taking action that benefits some powerful interests or players at the expense of others or that results in a reduction of aggregate general welfare.

Multiply the diverse interests and divisions within each nation-state and each transnational regulatory institution comprised of states by the number of countries and transnational regulatory institutions that make up the "public" global regulatory order and add to that the diverse interests trying to capture institutional power and special advantage from these states and institutions and it becomes quite

---

[12] For a general overview of public choice theory, see Gordon Tullock, "Public Choice," in Steven N. Durlauf and Lawrence E. Blume (eds.), *The New Palgrave Dictionary of Economics* (2nd ed., 2008), available at www. dictionaryofeconomics.com/articleid=pde2008_P000240doi:10.1057/ 9780230226203.1361. For some classics examples of public choice analysis, see Duncan Black, "The Unity of Political and Economic Science," *The Econ. J.*, 60 (1950), p. 506; Anthony Downs, *An Economic Theory of Democracy* (1957); Anne O. Krueger, "The Political Economy of the Rent Seeking Society," *Am. Econ. Rev.*, 64 (1974), p. 291; William C. Mitchell and Michael C. Munger, "Economic Models of Interest Groups: An Introductory Survey," *Am. J. Pol. Sci.*, 35 (1991), p. 512. For representative examples of public choice analysis in international law and regulation, see Paul B. Stephan, "Barbarians Inside the Gate: Public Choice Theory and International Economic Law," *Am. U. J. Int'l L. & Pol'y*, 10 (1995), p. 745; Paul B. Stephan, "Accountability and International Lawmaking: Rules, Rents, and Legitimacy," *Nw. J. Int'l L. & Bus.*, 17(1996–7), p. 470.

difficult to have any confidence that the regulatory activity of states or international institutions reflects an effective aggregation of the collective interests of their respective constituencies or an increase in aggregate global welfare.[13] Without some reasonable assurance that the global "public" regulatory system deploys its regulatory power to manage the economy in a way that leads to increased global welfare most of the time? usually? not infrequently?, it would be difficult to justify continued fealty to a conception of global governance that relies on a "public" regulatory regime to manage the "private" economy in the public interest on the hope that it can overcome interest-group capture and achieve something like a proper balance between laissez-faire and regulatory oversight of economic activity.

At the same time, it is becoming increasingly difficult under current global conditions for states to secure domestic or global economic advantage through assertions of sovereign regulatory power. Looking first to powerful states, while it would be hard to deny that the domestic legal rules of jurisdictions like China or the United States produce local and global effects, the effects may not be the ones intended, and they may not result from conscious assertions of sovereign will over the global economy. For example, China's domestic wage regulations shape wage rates around the globe putting

---

[13] See for example Eric A. Posner, *The Perils of Global Legalism* (2009), pp. 94–9 (arguing that the proliferation of international legal norms reflects efforts by the most powerful states to maintain power in the face of increasing fragmentation of the sovereign order); Anthony Anghie, *Imperialism, Sovereignty and the Making of International Law* (2004) (arguing that since its inception international law has consistently reflected the imperial power and ambitions of colonizer [later the developed world] by the colonized [later the developing world]); Ha-Joon Chang, *Bad Samaritans: The Myth of Free Trade and the Secret History of Capitalism* (2008), p. 19–39 (arguing that the developed world uses trade agreements and international institutional arrangements to extract higher levels of growth and prosperity at the expense of the developing world); but see Joel Trachtman, *The Economic Structure of International Law* (2008), pp. 9, 10, and 37 (asserting that "[t]he state acts as agent of its citizens[,]" public welfare maximization reflects the maximization of the regulatory concerns of states, and that "for analytical purposes, [he] assume[s] national laws to be perfect expressions of constituent preferences").

pressure on higher wage jurisdictions to lower domestic wages while simultaneously calling into being lower wage strategies in other jurisdictions that undercut China's economic advantage. Or consider the fact that while U.S. mortgage rules and home ownership promotion policies during the 2000s produced an economic boom for a time at home they also brought down the global financial system when the real estate bubble burst, resulting in sustained hardship both at home and abroad.

Adding to these complex challenges is that fact that sometimes the rules of relatively weak jurisdictions, at least in terms of political power or economic clout, can affect the economic sovereignty of even the most powerful states. For example, Delaware corporate law shapes business practice globally, though not by institutional design or sovereign hegemony, but through the decisions and ordinary business practices of Delaware-incorporated firms which make up a significant percentage of the world's largest firms. Similarly, the bank secrecy laws of countries like the Bahamas, Guernsey, Luxembourg, Lichtenstein all challenge the fiscal sovereignty of the world's most economically powerful states – again not by assertions of sovereign power or even global economic clout outside their territories but by the magnetic force their domestic rules enact on global capital flows.

Domestic rules such as the ones just described seem important to understand precisely because their economic effects do not result from extraterritorial sovereign application. Rather, the effects of these rules are transnationalized through often ordinary economic activity of firms sometimes undertaken in reaction or in relation to the rules.[14] Moreover, the magnitude of the transnational economic effects of these rules often do not easily correlate with traditional sources of international sovereign authority such as political or military power or market size. Some of the sovereign rulemakers in the examples just described are, by international economic and political standards, weak players in the global system. Nevertheless, in some circumstances, their rule-making produces significant economic effects that

---

[14] For a discussion of the transnationalization of domestic rules through private economic activity, see Dan Danielsen, "Local Rules and a Global Economy: An Economic Policy Perspective," *Transnat'l Legal Theory*, 1 (2010), pp. 52–7.

even the world's most powerful states have difficulty combating or
containing. Finally, from a political perspective, these rules evidence
a disjuncture between the political constituencies responsible for
the adoption or implementation of the rules and the economic constituencies affected by them. This disjuncture between economic
effects and the political and institutional mechanisms for addressing
them poses complex challenges for the legitimacy and functioning of
the global order that cannot easily be addressed through traditional
conceptions of territorial sovereignty or consensual sovereign deference to international norms or institutions.[15] This disjuncture seems
particularly important in circumstances where the economic benefits
of the global order are so inequitably distributed and when the presumption of formal sovereign equality is belied by significant differences in the abilities of states to shape their economic destinies
through regulation.

In such circumstances it is perhaps not surprising to look to the
nation-state and to sovereign consent-based efforts by nation-states
working through international institutions to manage the "private"
economy for the "public" good. Yet, even if we set aside the concern
about interest group or firm capture and assume states effectively
aggregate the interests of their constituents, there seems to be no
reason to conclude that the promotion by grossly unequal individual
states of their respective national interests in the global order is likely
to lead to an increase aggregate global welfare rather than further
increasing the power and resources of the most powerful states.
Moreover, if national rules domestically applied can lead through
the pursuit of ordinary business activity to widespread and diverse
global consequences even in the absence of sovereign intent, it seems
unlikely that even powerful states could exercise effective regulatory
control over economic welfare within their geographic territories,

---

[15] For a concise and interesting perspective on this problem, see Dani Rodrick,
One Economics, Many Recipes: Globalization, Institutions, and Economic Growth
(2007), pp. 195–6 (arguing that economic globalization and its benefits come
at the cost of undermining the strength and effectiveness of nation-state
institutions, perhaps leading, in the long run, to a global politics to match a
global economy).

let alone effectively shape the behavior of economic actors in the global economy in their national interest.

It could be that imperialist dreams of economic domination by sovereigns lives on and continues to shape the behavior of states, perhaps as a kind of institutional or cultural path dependence harkening back to the days when empire meant economic power secured through the assertions of sovereign authority, military power and economic clout, yet in the current global order the ability of even the most powerful states to secure consistent economic advantage abroad while securing welfare gains for citizens at home seems to be significantly diminished, even if some states frequently capture disproportionate economic spoils while others seem to lose almost systematically. Thus, while states can affect economic behavior locally and globally, some states more effectively or more consistently than others, to suggest that states "rule" in the sense of control or dominate private economic activity would seem to overstate both their role and their capacity in the contemporary global order.

III IF NOT STATES OR FIRMS, BUT STATES AND FIRMS, THEN WHAT?

V.I. Lenin argued in 1916 that world capitalism would mature into regimes of monopolist firms and great power states dividing and dominating the world for economic exploitation.[16] Perhaps, this is where we have come to. Or perhaps, as Hardt and Negri suggest in the passage quoted earlier, the proliferation of business power and what Thorstein Veblen calls pecuniary "business principles"[17] into every state, legal order, and culture across the globe suggests that business has already triumphed – the age of imperialism of states has

---

[16] V.I. Lenin, *Imperialism The Highest Stage of Capitalism A Popular Outline* (Martino Publishing, 2011; English trans. 1939), pp. 88–89

[17] For a discussion of the evolution of pecuniary norms into the governing principles of business enterprise, see Thorstein Veblen, *The Theory of Business Enterprise* , pp. 66–91. See also Thorstein Veblen, *The Theory of the Leisure Class* (1899).

been or is in the process of being replaced by an age of imperialism by firms.[18] While each has some appeal, neither seems to capture adequately the complexity or diversity of the regulatory and business practices we regularly see in the contemporary global economy or the roles and relations among states and firms in the construction or operation of that order.

In seeking a more compelling, realistic, and nuanced account of states, firms and the construction and functioning of the global order, I would like to return us to Foucault. More particularly, I would like to return to Foucault's notion of governance as the playing out of processes of "conflicts, agreements, discussions, and reciprocal concessions" in the ordinary practices of states and firms in pursuing their interests through which "a de facto, general, rational division of what is to be done and what is not to be done in the practice of governing" is dynamically produced.[19] As we have seen, while regulatory power is not evenly distributed and the ability of states to shape economic activity either outside or inside their jurisdictions is limited, regulation still matters – can shift power relations, produce distributional effects. Similarly, while the power of firms is not evenly distributed or consistently effective at obtaining either individual or collective advantage and conflicting interests both within and among firms challenge the articulation or the implementation of a coherent global governance policy agenda, corporate power still matters. There are predictable winners and losers, but there are also surprises. The system does not seem random in its distribution of power and resources globally even if it also does not seem governable in any systemic or hegemonic sense by either what has traditionally been conceived as "public" or "private" power.

In such circumstances, the challenge will be finding new institutional and political mechanisms for contesting the pervasive inequities in power, resources and well-being across the globe. Doing so will require us to look beyond the dream of autonomous and effective public regulatory oversight as the solution and periodic capture by firms of regulatory institutions as the problem to be solved. More

---

[18] See Michael Hardt and Antonio Negri, *Empire* , pp. 31–4, 304–9.

[19] Michel Foucault, *The Birth of Biopolitics* , p.13.

particularly, we will need to reconsider what we mean by and what we can expect from "the firm," "the state," "regulation," and "markets" when we loosen our attachment to a stable distinction between "public" and "private" ordering or the "legal rules" and the "transactions" that result from, for lack of a better term, "bargaining" between and among states and firms over the content of rules and the allocation of resources in the global order.

A related challenge will be discovering the potentialities as well as the limits of influence and intervention in what may appear to be a chaotic and ungovernable system of governance. If neither the state nor the firm can control the system, to what institutional forms or mechanisms might we look? If states and firms co-produce both the regulatory order and the economy then they will also both be implicated in the production as well of the possible amelioration of systemic risk and crisis. Perhaps more significantly, if neither state nor firm is wholly regulator or regulated, public or private, hegemonic or helpless, we will need to develop a much better understanding of the variety and diversity of the complex and dynamic processes – both and neither public nor private –through which we are governed globally, including the ways in which our shifting conceptions of "state" and "firm," "public" and "private," "appropriate regulation" and "legitimate self-interest," "intervention" and "laissez-faire" themselves emerge through these processes of bargaining, conflict and compromise rather than simply existing as the "natural" background preconditions from which the global order develops or upon which it depends.

Doing so will require the development of both concepts and analytic methods than enable us to trace dynamic processes of cumulative causation and patterns of interdependence, shifting advantage, adaptation and crisis across a broad range and diversity of local and global actors and in a variety of cultural and institutional contexts. We might begin by producing numerous, detailed, particular, and necessarily partial studies of some of the diverse and multiple processes of bargaining, assertion, resistance, cooperation and adaptation among states, firms and other institutional players in relation to particular changes in global economic conditions or in pursuit of particular regulatory changes in the global system. In the development of such studies we should include an investigation of whether and if so how these processes are affected by the relative distribution of power, resources, capacities and other endowments of the players and the relative impact of these processes on the players themselves and the broader global system. Such new, if partial, accounts should help to illuminate particular inflection points of mutual advantage, interdependence, vulnerability and resilience among the players studied as well as whether particular institutional configurations seem more likely to create or exacerbate advantages among some players or more equitable distributions of power and well-being. This information might lend support to state-focused regulatory strategies or mechanisms for ordering led by firms or may suggest previously unexamined sites or modes of intervention based on new institutional formations to bring about more equitable distributions of power, resources, and advantage both in present conditions and in future economic and governance relations. Of course, there is no way of knowing what the ramifications or potential of this more dynamic institutional approach to political economy and global governance might be until we give it a try.

At least one thing seems certain. What I'm proposing will take us a long way from the conception political economy comprised of public states, private firms and the creation of appropriately limited public regulatory structures that has dominated political and economic philosophy and theory for some three hundred years. There is comfort in familiar concepts and institutional expectations even when they seem to take us quite far from the world we see around us. But, as we have seen, these familiar and comfortable conceptions of global political economy neither reflect the hybridity, multiplicity and complexity of contemporary relations between states and firms they purport to describe nor help to explain why a system premised on public oversight of private power in the interest of general welfare persists in producing ever-increasing asymmetries in power and resources both between states and between firms and states.

There are good reasons to suspect that an alternative conception of global political economy that better reflects the complex, dynamic and inter-connected activities of states and firms we observe as they pursue their interests locally and globally should also better enable us to imagine the institutional mechanisms necessary to bring about the more equitable order we hope to create. Moreover, we are no means alone in traveling this complex institutionalist path. Excellent examples of some of the analytic strengths and policy insights that can be derived from dynamic institutional analyses of economic and social phenomena can be found in the work of more historic forebears such as Thorstein Veblen and Gunnar Myrdal or more contemporary scholars such as Joshua Barken and Neil Fligstein.[20]

Doubtless as we endeavor to capture more complexity, variety, and particularity in our accounts of the diverse arrangements of power, institutions and resources that comprise the contemporary global order, we will find ourselves in a messier, more uncertain and less coherent world than the one premised on public order and private initiative with which I began this essay. Perhaps critics will claim, as they often have with institutionalists past, that complexity and particularity are inconsistent with generalizable theory and that simplifying models are better able to guide us in what to do. Of course, the value of theoretical insights based on simplifying models can only be measured against the relative merits of alternative accounts in capturing the phenomena they seek to understand or explain and policy prescriptions based on models that, by virtue of their underlying assumptions, bear little resemblance to the concrete practice of social actors may do more harm than good. What seems undeniable is that the dominant conceptions of the political economy of the global order do not reflect the observable phenomena either at the level of description or prescription. We can and must do better. In the spirit of Foucault and the very best of our institutionalist forebears, my hope is that by beginning to explore the concrete practices of the governance regime we observe all around us, in the gaps and conflicts in the logics of the regime's self-articulation, we will invent new ways of seeing, modes of understanding, strategies of resistance and mechanisms for progressive transformation.

---

[20] See Thorstein Veblen, *The Theory of Business Enterprise*; Gunnar Myrdal, *Economic Theory and Under-Developed Regions*; Joshua Barkan, *Corporate Sovereignty: Law and Government under Capitalism*; Neil Fligstein, *The Architecture of Markets: An Economic Sociology of Twenty-First-Century Capitalist Societies* (2001).

6 GLOBAL ECONOMIC INEQUALITY AND THE POTENTIAL FOR GLOBAL DEMOCRACY: A FUNCTIONALIST ANALYSIS

Andrew Strauss

INTRODUCTION: EINSTEIN AND FREUD

Sigmund Freud, from whose book *Civilization and its Discontents*[1] this volume takes its inspiration, engaged in an exchange of letters with Albert Einstein in the early 1930s.[2] Einstein, concerned that technological advances meant that war might destroy humanity, attempted to engage Freud in a dialogue and in the forming of an organization of moral and intellectual elites to promote his cause of world government. Freud answered Einstein's call for thoughtful correspondence, but was not optimistic about a program for world government. After all, as he had argued in *Discontents*, humans had aggressive instincts and impulses that were at odds with global harmony, and Freud was doubtful, given the then state of cultural evolution, that these could be contemporaneously overcome in the furtherance of an effective world authority.

Helping shape the distinctive perspectives of Einstein and Freud are contrasting methodological assumptions, each of which has in various guises been reflected in the Western philosophical tradition

I would like to thank Barbara Eckman for her very helpful research assistance with this chapter.

[1] Sigmund Freud, *Civilization and its Discontents*, in James Strachey (trans.), *Standard Edition of the Complete Psychological Works of Sigmund Freud*, vol. XXI (1961).

[2] *See Why War? A Correspondence Between Albert Einstein and Sigmund Freud* (1991 edition).

since the time of the Greeks. Einstein, the rationalist, presupposed with Kant and many others the possibility that human behavior and society in general could be molded to the dictates of human reason.[3] Freud, an heir to the psychological turn in our understanding of ourselves that began decidedly with Hume, and was most powerfully advanced by Nietzsche, saw our passions and other hidden forces from within our psyches as the central drivers of our social institutions.

Today most students of global institutions implicitly reject the assumptions of both Einstein and Freud. The World Federalists, who have long followed a political strategy derived from their Kantian belief that a rational response to the human condition should lead nations to suspend their rivalries and create a world federal state, are distinctly out of step.[4] Likewise, most professional observers of global institutions (behavioral economists aside) eschew a Freudian understanding of such institutions as an amalgam of the complex psychology that make up individuals.

Rather, what is implicit in the approach of most observers today is a third method that might be thought of as that of the political scientist. This method, which can be traced back most definitively to Machiavelli, assumes that social institutions are the sum total of an underlying social dynamic resulting from a kind of reductionist notion of collective and individual self-interests often associated with Hobbes.

Functionalism, as originally conceptualized by David Mitrany in the 1930s, is informed by such an understanding.[5] For Mitrany and his later adherents, international organizations emerge as a result of the needs of global actors to tackle specific problems that cannot be

---

[3] Part of Einstein's purpose, however, in attempting to enlist Freud comes out of a recognition of the importance of the psychological dimension to the change he was promoting. See *See Why War?*, p. 2 ("The ill success, despite their obvious sincerity, of all the efforts made during the last decade to reach this goal [of a supranational organization] leaves us no room to doubt that strong psychological factors are at work which paralyze these efforts").

[4] For a comprehensive history of the world federalism movement, including the development and evolution of the ideology of world federalism, see Joseph Preston Baratta, *The Politics of World Federation: From World Federalism to Global Governance* (2004).

[5] See generally David Mitrany, *The Progress of International Government* (1933).

solved in the absence of international cooperation. Unlike most world federalists or other rational idealists, they do not assume the workability of grand schemes for global governance, but rather, for them, global change comes about as a result of people individually and collectively pursuing concrete self-interested objectives. Thus, to take one example, for functionalists, the International Civil Aviation Organization was created by states in 1944 because they could not independently secure the safety of their newly airbound citizens over the global commons.[6] Contemporary regime theorists such as Robert Keohane and Joseph Nye have further developed and refined the idea that states create international regimes in self-interested response to collective action problems.[7]

The thesis that I wish to develop in this chapter is that a functionalist view of the development of global institutions suggests that the structural inequalities in global income that were a primary cause of the global economic crisis of 2008, and that continue to endanger the world economy, have the potential to provide the political preconditions for a global regime that can help redress those inequalities. To do so, however, such a regime must empower the less economically well off through representation, and the regime itself must have the practical ability to influence global economic policy. Such a regime, I will argue, must be fundamentally democratic in its character. If it were to be brought into existence, a democratic regime, representative of the global public, would likely weigh in on many issues beyond income inequality. Environmental concerns, including climate change, human rights, and international conflict resolution are only a few of the areas where a parliament might be argued to have salutary value. A focus on economic inequality as a matter of great saliency today, however, presents a useful case study for both the political viability and utility of such an institution.

---

[6] David Mackenzie, *ICAO: A History of the International Civil Aviation Organization* (2010).

[7] See for example Robert Keohane and Joseph Nye, "Between Centralization and Fragmentation: The Club Model of Multilateral Cooperation and Problems of Democratic Legitimacy," available at http://papers.ssrn.com/sol3/papers.cfmabstract_id=262175.

I THE MACROECONOMIC PROBLEM OF GLOBAL INCOME INEQUALITY AND THE GREAT RECESSION

A strong – even compelling – case can be made that income inequality worldwide was a primary cause of the 2008 economic crisis and that it continues to endanger the global economy. The thesis that income inequality poses a danger to economic health lays claim to a distinguished pedigree. To name two of the inequality thesis's most notable twentieth-century adherents, Marriner Eccles, a Federal Reserve Chairman during the Roosevelt administration, and the famed economist John Kenneth Galbraith, both saw the rise in inequality in the 1920s as a major cause of the Great Depression.[8] Among the many contemporary observers supporting the view that income inequality was among the primary causes of the Great Recession, former IMF Chief Economist Raghuram Rajan makes the argument forcefully in his 2010 book *Faultlines*[9] as does former Labor Secretary Robert Reich in his 2011 book *Aftershock, the Next Economy and America's Future*.[10]

While the varied proponents of the inequality thesis have different emphasis and perspectives, they all share a common grounding in John Maynard Keynes's depression-era upending of classical

---

[8] For Eccles's views, see Marriner Eccles, *Beckoning Frontiers* (1951); for Galbraith's views, see John Kenneth Galbraith, *The Great Crash, 1929* (1954).

[9] Raghuram G. Rajan, *Fault Lines: How Hidden Fractures Still Threaten the World Economy* (2010).

[10] Robert B. Reich, *Aftershock: The Next Economy & America's Future* (2011). See also Gustav Horn et. al., "From the Financial Crisis to the World Economic Crisis: The Role of Inequality," IMK Policy Brief, Institut für Makroökonomie und Konjukturforschung (2009), p. 10. Other economic observers sounded the alarm before 2007. See Thomas I. Palley, "Economic Contradictions Coming Home to Roost? Does the U.S. Economy Face a Long-Term Aggregate Demand Generation Problem?," *J. Post Keynesian Econ.*, 25 (2002), p. 9; Heather Boushey and Christian E. Weller, "Inequality and Household Economic Hardship in the United States of America, Working Papers," United Nations, Department of Economic and Social Affairs (2006); Robert H. Franck, *Falling Behind: How Rising Inequality Harms the Middle Class* (2007); Robert Pollin, "The Growth of U.S. Household Debt: Demand-side Influences," *J. Macroeconomics*, 10 (1988), p. 231.

economic theory.[11] At the root of the Keynesian understanding is the notion that for an economy to function at full capacity, sufficient aggregate demand for goods and services must exist to absorb that capacity.[12] If for some reason, such demand ceases to exist, producers will respond by lowering production, and cancelling or putting on hold plans to invest in expansion.[13] Lower production and less investment means the elimination of workers who can no longer be productively utilized.[14] In what becomes a vicious cycle, the newly jobless workers are forced to cut back on their own consumption, further reducing demand and causing further economic contraction.[15]

The reason that high levels of income inequality affect aggregate demand and begin this unfortunate cycle is that the wealthier people become, the lower their marginal propensity to consume. Every additional dollar obtained by someone who is living at the subsistence level will tend to be spent on basic necessities, such as feeding the family or paying the rent, while an additional dollar garnered by someone of wealth, whose consumer needs are likely to already be mostly satiated, is more likely to be saved.[16] Thus, as income becomes highly concentrated, wealth is transferred from the less well off, who will consume, to those better off, who will save, and when this happens, sustaining the Keynesian demand that drives the economy becomes problematic.[17]

---

[11] See generally John Maynard Keynes, *The General Theory of Employment Interest and Money* (1936).

[12] Ibid.   [13] Ibid.   [14] Ibid.   [15] Ibid.

[16] Ibid., p. 97. There is a good deal of empirical support for this rather self-evident proposition that with increasing wealth there is a diminishing marginal propensity to consume. See for example Ulrike Stein, "Zur Entwicklung der Sqarquoten der privaten Haushalte-ein Auswertung von Haushaltsdaten des SOEP," IMK Working Paper 10 – 2009 (2009) (finding that in 2007 the top income quartile of Germans had an average saving rate of 15.8 percent, the second quartile of 9 percent, the third of 8 percent and the bottom of 4.1 percent).

[17] As Keynes put it: "up to the point where full employment prevails, the growth of capital depends not at all on a low propensity to consume but is, on the contrary, held back by it; and only in conditions of full employment is a low propensity to consume conducive to the growth of capital. Moreover, experience suggests that in existing conditions savings by institutions and

The period of globalization leading up to the 2008 financial crisis corresponded to a period of income inequality within countries and thus very likely established the preconditions for the deficiency in aggregate global demand I have described. The most common way economists measure income inequality is with an equation that they call the Gini Coefficient. Named after Corrado Gini, the Italian sociologist who worked out its formulation, the Gini coefficient is used to measure inequality in a frequency distribution.[18] Thus, when applied to income distribution, a Gini coefficient of zero indicates perfect equality (everyone has the same income), and a Gini coefficient of one indicates maximum inequality (only one person has all the income).[19]

Given the premium that communist ideology put on economic equality, it is not surprising that countries transitioning away from planned economies saw their Gini coefficients rise significantly.[20] When China, for example, abandoned its "iron rice bowl policy" following the reforms of Deng Xiaoping in the 1980's, income inequality exploded.[21] This inequality has become even more pronounced in the last decade leading China to have a Gini coefficient higher than the United States.[22] This rise in inequality has not been

through sinking funds is more than adequate, and that measures for the redistribution of incomes in a way likely to raise the prosperity to consume may prove positively favourable to the growth of capital." John Maynard Keynes, *The General Theory of Employment Interest and Money* , pp. 373–4.

[18] Corrado Gini, *Variabilità e Mutabilità* (1912).

[19] Corrado Gini, *On the Measure of Concentration with Special Reference to Income and Statistics* (1936).

[20] See Branco Milanovic and Lire Ersado, "Reform and Inequality During the Transition: An Analysis Using Panel Household Survey Data, 1990–2005," Policy Research Working Paper 4780, The World Bank Development Research Group Poverty Team (2008) (examining the rise of income inequality in 26 post-communist countries during the period from 1990–2005 and concluding that its scale was unprecedented).

[21] OECD, *Economic Surveys of China* (2010), p. 147.

[22] Int'l Labour Org. [ILO], "Income Inequality as a Cause of the Great Recession? A Survey of Current Debates," Conditions of Work and Employment Series No. 39 (prepared by Till van Treeck and Simon Sturn), p. 27. One reason for China's high Gini coefficient is the very well-known gap

limited to transitional economies. Developing countries generally have tended to experience a significant rise in inequality during the period of neoliberal globalization which began in 1989.[23]

The trend was similar in the developed world. In 2007 the American economy, for example, was roughly 60 percent larger than it was in the 1970s. Yet, the inflation adjusted income of the median male worker actually decreased over the period.[24] The missing gains almost all found their way to those at the upper end of the income stratum. The wealthiest 10 percent of Americans went from appropriating around 35 percent of national income in the 1970s to a full 50 percent in 2007.[25] Even more dramatically, during this period, the now infamous upper 1 percent expanded their take of national income from under 10 percent in the 1970s to 23 percent in 2007.[26]

Most other advanced industrial countries followed this same trajectory toward inequality. According to the OECD, its member states

between relatively high urban and relatively low rural incomes, however, urban inequality in itself has increased to the point where it is almost as large as the Gini coefficient for total household incomes in the United States. See also Edward Wong, "Survey in China Shows a Wide Gap in Income," *New York Times*, July 19, 2013, p. A9 (reporting on a Peking University survey finding that in 2012 households in the top 5 percent income bracket accounted for 23 percent of China's total household income while those in the bottom 5 percent accounted for only 0.1 percent and estimating China's Gini coefficient to be 0.49).

[23] See Branko Milanovic, "Can We Discern the Effect of Globalization on Income Distribution? Evidence from Household Surveys?" *World Bank Econ. Rev.*, 19 (2005), p. 21 (describing the increased inequality in developing countries and suggesting causal factors related to economic openness). But see, Leonardo Gasparini, Guillermo Cruces and Leopoldo Tornarolli, "Recent Trends in Income Inequality in Latin America," in Branko Milanovic (ed.) *Globalization and Inequality* (2012), p. 172 (arguing that inequality has been decreasing in Latin America over the last five to ten years although it continues to be among the most unequal regions in the world).

[24] See Robert B. Reich, *Aftershock* , p. 19 (extrapolating earnings figures from Bureau of Economic Analysis and U.S. Census Bureau figures).

[25] See Emmanuel Saez, "Striking it Richer, The Evolution of Top Incomes in the United States (Updated with 2011 estimates)" (2013), available at http://emlab.berkeley.edu/~saez/saez-UStopincomes-2011.pdf).

[26] Ibid.

had an average Gini coefficient of 0.29 in the mid-1980s.[27] By the late 2000s, however, this average had increased by almost 10 percent to 0.316, having risen in seventeen of the twenty-two OECD countries for which sufficient data is available.[28] It grew by more than 4 percent in Finland, Germany, Israel, Luxemberg, New Zealand, Sweden, and the United States.[29] The only exceptions were Turkey, Greece, France, Hungary, and Belgium which registered either no increase or small declines in their Gini coefficients.[30]

Certain high Gini coefficient countries, most notably Germany, Japan, and especially China, lacking sufficient internal Keynesian demand to absorb their excess production, attempted to compensate through exports.[31]

The United States in particular was a net absorber of global surplus production. Given its own increasingly unequal distribution of income, and the corresponding financial constraint on those middle and poorer Americans, with the highest marginal propensity to consume, such consumption had to be financed. As is now well known, such financing to a great extent took the form of easy access to consumer credit, most characterized by home mortgage loans.[32]

In the expansion of consumer credit, the United States was again not alone. In the years leading up to the Great Recession, consumer debt soared throughout the industrialized world. According to the International Monetary Fund, between 2002 and 2007, the ratio of household debt to income went up by an average of 39 percent until peaking at 138 percent.[33] In Denmark, Iceland, Ireland, the Netherlands, and Norway, debt rose to more than 200 percent of household income.[34]

---

[27] OECD, *Divided We Stand: Why Inequality Keeps Rising* (2011), p. 22.
[28] Ibid.   [29] Ibid.   [30] Ibid.
[31] See Michael Pettis, *The Great Rebalancing: Trade, Conflict, and the Perilous Road Ahead for the World Economy* (2013), pp. 1–26.
[32] Raghuram G. Rajan, *Fault Lines* , pp. 21–45. A significant part of global surplus production was (and continues to be) absorbed by the U.S. government financed by large federal deficits.
[33] "World Economic Outlook: Growth Resuming, Dangers Remain," International Monetary Fund 89 (2012), available at www.imf.org/external/pubs/ft/weo/2012/01/pdf/text.pdf).
[34] Ibid.

Of course, global aggregate demand could not be maintained indefinitely by consumers taking on higher and higher levels of debt, and when the inevitable happened, and consumers began to default (triggered by the subprime home mortgage collapse in the United States), the demand necessary to fuel the economy could no longer be sustained. The most enduring economic contraction since the Great Depression was upon us. Some governments stepped in to create demand with old fashioned Keynesian fiscal (government spending) and monetary policy (central bank lowering of interest rates to encourage consumption and investment), but maintaining the political will for those policies has been an uphill battle. Now, in this period of economic difficulty, both those who have been disadvantaged by the increasingly unequal distribution of income, as well as those who have been advantaged, have a joint interest in reviving the global economy. It is to understanding the practical case for global democracy as an impetus to sustaining such a revival that I will now turn.

II GLOBALIZATION AND THE PROBLEM OF UNEQUAL DISTRIBUTION OF INCOME

The increasing inequality of income around the world that we have just chronicled poses significant questions of distributive justice. One does not have to go so far as John Rawls – whose famous difference principle holds that income disparities are only justifiable to the extent they improve the lot of the least well off – to recognize the ethical challenge posed by such large-scale inequality.[35] The argument that I wish to make in this chapter is not, however, fundamentally normative in character. Rather, with reference to functionalist analysis, I intend to demonstrate that such income inequality provides an economically instrumental rationale for global democracy.

Significantly contributing to the income inequality phenomenon is the globalization system that allows industrial enterprises to raise funds on global exchanges and sell their products to global markets

---

[35] See generally John Rawls, *A Theory of Justice* (rev. ed. 1999), p. 266.

regardless of where they set up shop. The result is a mismatch between the realm of the nation-state, whose confines limit the mobility of most workers, and the transnational realm of footloose commerce. While workers with specialized skills in global demand can command generous salaries, less skilled workers, the supply of which is in global surplus, have lost negotiating leverage. The advantage goes to firms that can keep their compensation in check by transferring production offshore, or by buying from global suppliers, who themselves must keep compensation low to match foreign competitors.[36]

Is there a way around globalization's tendency toward exacerbating income inequality? The model of industrial relations that became most accepted in the twentieth century would answer that question by looking to governments to establish worker protection laws establishing minimum wages, making termination of employment and plant closings difficult, and securing collective bargaining rights.[37] The ability of governments, however, to maintain pro-worker industrial policies of this kind has itself come under assault by the same competitive dynamics of globalization that pits workers against workers around the globe. Countries must compete for investment capital, and countries with more stringent worker protections find themselves at a competitive disadvantage.[38] The example of worker protective sclerotic France is often held out as one to be avoided if governments want to attract the international capital that allows their economies to flourish.[39]

---

[36] See for example Joseph E. Stiglitz, *The Price of Inequality: How Today's Divided Society Endangers our Future* (2012), p. 60 (maintaining that, "[t]he threat of capital outflow, should workers get too demanding about rights and wages, keeps workers' wages low").

[37] See generally Bruce E. Kaufmann, *The Global Evolution of Industrial Relations: Events, Ideas and the IIRA* (2005).

[38] See for example Joseph E. Stiglitz, *The Price of Inequality*, p. 60. ("Competition across countries for investment takes on many forms – not just lowering wages and weakening worker protections. There is a broader 'race to the bottom,' trying to ensure that business regulations are weak and taxes are low.")

[39] See for example Steven Erlanger, "Memo From France: A Proud Nation Halts Its Slow Decline," *New York Times*, August 25, 2013, p. 6.

Alternatively, countries could compensate those who have wound up on the wrong side of the global income divide by resorting to redistributionist social welfare programs that were also held out as a model in the twentieth century.[40] Unfortunately, however, governments are similarly hampered in their capacity to tax global enterprises to fund such programs by the ease with which they can relocate to more tax friendly jurisdictions that globalization makes possible.[41]

These kinds of constraints on the abilities of individual governments to act alone means that the most promising strategy to counter increasing inequality in the age of globalization are ones that globally harmonize worker protections and other social welfare policies. But putting such policies in place has been elusive. Despite efforts in the International Labour Organization, the World Trade Organization and even the G20, at the end of the day, the political will has not been sufficient to create strong global social welfare standards. On its face, this is paradoxical. If those lacking in economic privilege had the political clout to secure the implementation of strong worker protection and redistributionist policies in many countries during the twentieth century, then why couldn't they aggregate their clout to convince governments collectively to harmonize such policies?

While the answer is not simple, the unique dynamics of the interstate politics that defines the international system is of primary importance. Before the onslaught of globalization, the battle for worker protections and redistributionist policies were fought separately in each state. If the forces opposing such policies were successful in one country, it had little impact on the ability of other countries to pursue such policies. Now, because the competitive dynamics of globalization described above mean that any harmonization initiative must secure the participation of all states (or at least all of the states with any significant productive potential) the forces opposing such

---

[40] See for example Harold L. Wilensky, *Rich Democracies: Political Economy, Public Policy and Performance* (2002), pp. 211–16.

[41] See generally Joseph E. Stiglitz, *The Price of Inequality* , p. 278. ("Our system of global competition encourages firms to locate on the basis not of global efficiency but of tax competition ... [i]t distorts the global economy and undermines the ability to impose fair taxation on capital.")

initiatives have gained a significant advantage. If they can capture policy in just a few, or even one of the states that are necessary for a harmonization agreement, they can effectively veto the ability of the rest of the world to maintain such policies.

To make matters even harder for the forces of worker protections and equitable redistribution, the architecture of the global system is not congenial to the ability of citizens to coalesce transnationally. Within national parliamentary systems, those citizens in the middle and lower income stratums constitute a large percentage of the electorate, generally allowing them to wield considerable power at the ballot box. What is more, through the pluralist democratic structures that are adjunct to parliamentary process,[42] such citizens can overcome geography as well as their many other ethnic, religious and ideological cleavages to join forces on behalf of their common economic interest.[43]

The role of citizens in the international system is quite different. Because international law is created by states, rather than through parliamentary voting by citizen elected representatives, the interstate system does not facilitate opportunities for citizens to formally participate in the law making process.[44] Without any institutional structure for bringing disparate communities together, language, ethnicity, religion, culture, nationalist ideology, and distance all conspire to make a collective response on behalf of common economic interests extremely difficult. For the most part, this means that the voices of those in the middle and lower income stratums are subsumed by those of their governments, regardless of whether such governments are captured by the interests of the wealthy or compromised in their ability to respond to inequality by the dynamics of globalization.

---

[42] For example, political parties and interest groups that lobby legislative bodies.

[43] See generally David Held, *Models of Democracy* (2006), pp. 160–4.

[44] For one of the classic works discussing the limits of citizen politics in the international system, see Margaret E. Keck and Kathryn Sikkink, *Activist Beyond Borders* (1998). Other scholars have focused on participation by civil society organizations and epistemic networks in the international system. For some of the more influential works on participation by civil society organizations see Jessica T. Mathews, "Powershift," *Foreign Aff.*, Jan./ Feb. 1997, p. 50; Jackie Smith, *Social Movements for Global Democracy* (2008).

III FUNCTIONALISM

Pioneered by David Mitrany, whose writings spanned the period from the 1930s to the 1970s, functionalism was an attempt to find an intermediate position in international relations theory between what it regarded as the utopian legacy of Woodrow Wilson's belief in legally engineered grand transformations of the global institutional order and a bleak realist understanding that saw states as immutably locked in a Hobbesian competition that tended toward war.[45] Functionalism held that international organizations could gradually play an ever greater role in human affairs as both governments and sub-state actors came to realize that regulatory matters requiring transnational cooperation could best be addressed at the transnational level through international organizations.[46]

A defining characteristic of functionalism is the nature of these organizations. They are to be designed to address the discreet problems that arise in defined areas of governance. By way of examples, Mitrany pointed to the need globally to coordinate intercontinental shipping, aviation and broadcasting.[47] Thus, Mitrany's vision was of a myriad of distinct international organizations all functioning independently in their own realms. As these organizations took on increasing importance, functionalists believed that this would create a *spillover* effect. Political actors would gradually come to shift their political loyalties and activities to the international realm.[48]

The primary implements of functionalist analysis were taken up in the 1950s by Ernst Haas and others to both explain and predict the transfer of rule-making authority from national governments to the

---

[45] See generally David Mitrany, *The Progress of International Government*.
[46] See David Mitrany, *A Working Peace System* (1966), pp. 93–7.
[47] Ben Rosamond, *Theories of European Integration* (2000).
[48] See Leon Lindberg, *The Political Dynamics of European Economic Integration* (1963), p. 5 (explaining from the functionalist perspective, "[p]olitical integration is the process whereby political actors in several distinct national settings are persuaded to shift their loyalties, expectations and political activities toward a new centre, whose institutions possess or demand jurisdiction over the pre-existing national states").

European Union in what came to be called neofunctionalism.[49] Neo-functionalism has in many ways defined the European integrationist project. Whether in neofunctionalism's prescription for step-by-step incrementalism that has become the European project's hallmark, or the early strategic primacy given to the technical governance of economic arrangements, the neo-functionalist canons read like manuals to the construction of what today has become the European Union.[50]

Knocked around by the inevitable vicissitudes of a bold movement toward continental integration, neofunctionalism eventually fell out of favor. The most defining moment came in the 1970s when Haas, himself, declared that the theory was obsolete.[51] After the so-called "empty chair crisis," precipitated by French President Charles de Gaulle having put the brakes on the pace of integration in the mid

---

[49] For Haas's classic book inaugurating neofunctionalism, see Ernst Haas, *The Uniting of Europe* (1958). For other influential works, see Leon Lindberg, *The Political Dynamics of European Economic Integration* and Philippe Schmitter, *Neo-Neo-functionalism* (2004).

[50] For example the French Schuman Declaration of May 9, 1950 (proposing the nascent institution that would one day become the European Union) embodies the neofunctionalist notion that narrowly tailored technical institutions of an economic nature could evolve far beyond their humble beginnings:
"Europe will not be made all at once, or according to a single plan. It will be built through concrete achievements which first create a defacto solidarity. The coming together of the nations of Europe requires the elimination of the age-old opposition of France and Germany. Any action taken must in the first place concern these two countries. With this aim in view, the French Government proposes that action be taken immediately on one limited but decisive point. It proposes that Franco-German production of coal and steel as a whole be placed under a common High Authority, within the framework of an organization open to the participation of the other countries of Europe. The pooling of coal and steel production should immediately provide for the setting up of common foundations for economic development as a first step in the federation of Europe, and will change the destinies of those regions which have long been devoted to the manufacture of munitions of war, of which they have been the most constant victims."
See Press Conference, Robert Schuman, French Foreign Minister (May 9, 1950), transcript available at www.robert-schuman.org/robert-schuman/declaration2.htm.

[51] See Ernst Haas, *The Obsolescence of Regional Integration Theory* (1975).

1960s, Haas became disillusioned that the predicted transfer of loyalties had not materialized in his expected timeframe.[52] Regardless of the vagaries of their fashionability, most of the insights from functionalism and neofunctionalism are more or less taken for granted today among the architects of Europe's future and are now subsumed into what has become regime theory and constructivism.[53]

In fact, looking back almost a century since functionalism's founding, the theory's early adherents seem almost prescient in their presaging of the development of the international system generally over the course of the twentieth century. The organizations that had universal pretentions such as the League of Nations and the United Nations have generally not lived up to their founder's aspirations, and grand schemes for world government, fashionable in the periods following both world wars, never came close to getting off the ground. What has been successful have been functionally focused international organizations such as the World Trade Organization, the Bretton Woods organizations, the World Health Organization, the International Labour Organization and the like. While the United Nations lays claim to many as nominally part of the "UN family," in reality most important international organizations are created by independent treaties and function independently of the United Nations in all important matters. As functionalism predicted, these organizations were established because of a perceived need to address concrete problems of a transnational nature and have tended to accrue greater powers incrementally over time. They have also had important spill-over effects on the global system as a whole. As the current saliency of the discussion over fragmentation demonstrates, these organizations have developed a complex ecology that has evolved into an institutional order commonly thought of as our system of global governance.

---

[52] See James Caporaso and John Keeler, *The European Union and Regional Integration Theory, in The State of the European Union* (1995) (chronicling of the rise and fall of neo-functionalist theory).

[53] For an argument that neofunctionalism accurately predicted how European *legal* as opposed to *political* integration would proceed, see Anne-Marie Burley [Slaughter] and Walter Mattli, "Europe before the Court," *Int'l Org.*, 41, (1993), p.47.

For our purposes, what can be most productively distilled from functionalism and neofunctionalism are the insights that the greatest political impetus for the establishment of a new international organization are concrete problems that can be most effectively addressed internationally, that single regimes are more likely to be politically viable than overarching constitutional schemes, and that over time such organizations are likely to grow in influence as they gain the loyalties of their constituents. As I will now discuss, these insights from functionalism can help us understand why the creation of a Global Parliamentary Assembly (GPA) is now a viable political project.

IV FUNCTIONALISM, INEQUALITY, AND THE VIABILITY OF A GLOBAL PARLIAMENTARY ASSEMBLY

Critics claim that a GPA is a utopian project that cannot be realized.[54] In making this assertion they conflate the introduction of an independent functionalist representative institution of limited powers with grand legalist schemes for comprehensive world government. They confuse the step-by-step organic vision of global institutional development that the functionalists saw as the practical way forward with the revolutionary one that they considered unworkable. Certainly, a parliament of a plenary nature is a unique kind of functional institution, different from more narrowly-focused organizations designed to address discreet areas of governance. Nevertheless, it meets the

---

[54] See for example Paul Kennedy, *The Parliament of Man, The Past, Present and Future of the United Nations* (2006), p. 214 ("The practical and political problems with this sort of utopian thought are numerous."); Kenneth Anderson, "Accountability as 'Legitimacy': Global Governance, Global Civil Society and the United Nations," *Brooklyn J. Int'l L.*, 36 (2011), p. 871 ("Some dreamers dreamed – and still do – of a planetary parliament directly elected by populations around the world. Most others – even many who are otherwise deeply committed to the political ideals of global governance in a globally federal system – accept that planetary democracy in that sense is meaningless and unachievable.") (footnote omitted).

functionalist test of being a self-contained entity with its own specific mission, and after over half a century of proliferating functional organizations, global system coherence can be most effectively achieved by an institution whose function is to link these organizations. Mitrany, himself, anticipated the potential need for such an institution[55] and prescribed that it be conceived with reference to the same functionalist principles as apply to the initiation of other international organizations:

> As the whole sense of this particular method is to let activities be organized as the need for joint action arises and is accepted, it would be out of place to lay down in advance some formal plan for the coordination of various functions. Coordination too, would in that sense have to come about functionally.[56]

In this period of authoritarian resurgence, if the international system is to meaningfully further democracy by example (rather than mere rhetoric), it is appropriate that a representative parliament would play this coordination role. Because it is well established in the popular imagination that parliaments promulgate laws and oversee agencies of government, a GPA, once realized, would be poised to evolve over time into playing a central role in the international system as the vertical link to the citizenry and the horizontal link between the various international organizations.

True, however, to the functionalist understanding of how the international system develops incrementally, the GPA should not initially be given formal powers of law-making and oversight. At this point in history such a bold grant of authority would almost certainly be rejected by governments jealous of their own prerogatives. In accepting such a concession to reality, the question then becomes

---

[55] "The question will be asked . . . in what manner and to what degree the various functional agencies that may thus grow up would have to be linked to each other and articulated as parts of a more comprehensive organization. It should be clear that each agency could work by itself, but that does not exclude the possibility of some of them or all being bound in some way together, if it should be found needful or useful to do so." David Mitrany, *A Working Peace System*, p. 107. That indeed is the test.

[56] Ibid.

whether a GPA lacking in formal powers could actually have an impact on income distribution and by extension the global economy.

I have rehearsed arguments above that globalization has exacerbated the problem of economic inequality, that the resulting lack of aggregate demand threatens the health of the global economy, and that the domestic realm is limited in its ability to redress the problem. A GPA could provide the political underpinnings for such redress. Unlike the current configuration of power, a GPA would facilitate citizens' ability to organize transnationally, and it would overcome the capacity of those who wish to maintain the economic status quo to block equality initiatives by winning the day in single jurisdictions. Able to coalesce in the parliament's democratic space, supporters of greater economic equality could petition the organization to endorse their programs. Despite the GPA's lack of formal powers, as the world's only body with a direct claim to represent the global citizenry as a whole, its decisions would likely be very influential and serve as reference points for discussion and debate.

As the planet's organized citizenry began to reconfigure itself beyond the limitations of separate and discreet orbits around national parliaments into a new common orbit around a GPA, over time the parliament's formal powers might well come to reflect this new political reality. Not only would the organized citizenry be inclined toward supporting the legal force of legislative results that were fashioned in response to their input, but an existing GPA could powerfully lobby governments on behalf of expanding its own powers. In a world where democratic elections have become the litmus test for legitimate governance at the local, provincial and national levels, GPA's claim to exercise increasing authority in the name of the global citizenry would be hard to resist.

If a parliament would give an effective global voice to those representing the less economically well off, then wouldn't those powerful elements of the economic elite whose wage costs and tax burdens have been kept low by the current global configuration of power resist the GPA based upon their perception of self-interest? No doubt many would. As I have discussed, however, everyone has a shared interest in a global economy that can function at as close to full capacity as possible. It is said in the United States that President Franklin

Roosevelt "saved capitalism" by using Keynesian tools to create a social safety net and stimulate demand in response to the Great Depression.[57] Many in the moneyed class opposed Roosevelt, but with his core of support among the working class, enough believed it to be either ethical or in their own enlightened self-interest to support him, for his plans to be implemented. As this discussion of economic inequality reveals, a GPA is at least in part about establishing a global political structure that could support a social safety net, and the same dynamic could at some point potentially play out in its creation.

It is one thing, of course, for a functional argument to be useful and viable as a practical political project and quite another to actually get the institution off the ground. The potential organizational catalyst for such a parliament has been building primarily around the German based, Campaign for a United Nations Parliamentary Assembly.[58] The organization holds conferences, issues papers, and builds political support for an international parliament. To date, over 1,000 past and present national parliamentarians and other moral authority figures have endorsed the Campaign's call for a parliament associated with the United Nations.[59]

Mirroring these organizational developments has been a growing academic discourse. In addition to the work that Richard Falk and I have done proposing a GPA, leading scholars of cosmopolitan democracy such as Daniele Archibugi and David Held are widely cited,[60] and many others have contributed to the broader discussion of global democracy.[61]

---

[57] See Arthur M. Schlesinger, Jr., *The Age of Roosevelt: The Crisis of the Old Order; The Coming of the New Deal; and The Politics of Upheaval* (1959) (arguing famously that Roosevelt saved capitalism from self-destruction and preserved democracy from authoritarianism of both the left and right).

[58] See the Campaign's website at www.unpacampaign.org/

[59] http://en.unpacampaign.org/support/index.php.

[60] For representative works, see Daniele Archibugi and David Held (eds.) *Cosmopolitan Democracy: An Agenda for a New World Order* (1995); Daniele Archibugi, *The Global Commonwealth of Citizens: Toward Cosmopolitan Democracy* (2008).

[61] The literature in the field has grown large. For a representative sampling of works by those both supporting a parliamentary approach and those opposing

Finally, and most importantly, the project for the first time has found its way onto the United Nations agenda. Both the United Nations Human Rights Council and the General Assembly have begun considering the matter. In October of 2011 the Human Rights Council adopted Resolution 18/6 calling for "the promotion of a democratic and just international order,"[62] and in December of 2012, the General Assembly adopted Resolution A/Res/67/175 on "the promotion of a democratic and equitable international order."[63] In their respective resolutions, each of the bodies in very general language affirms that a democratic and equitable international order requires "the promotion and consolidation of transparent, democratic, just and accountable international institutions in all areas of cooperation, in particular through the implementation of the principle of full and equal participation in their respective decision-making mechanisms."[64] The latest General Assembly resolution A/Res/68/175 passed in December 2013 goes further, and in more specific language declares that everyone is "entitled to a democratic and equitable international order,"[65] and that among the requirements of such an order is "the

one, see Raffaele Marchetti, *Global Democracy: For and Against: Ethical Theory, Institutional Design and Social Struggle* (2008); Tony McGrew, *Transnational Democracy: Theories and Prospects* (Institute for History, International and Social Studies, 2004); Philip Pettit, "Democracy National and International," *The Monist*, 89 (2006), p. 301; Andrew Moravcsik, "Is there a Democratic Deficit in World Politics? A Framework for Analysis," *Gov't & Opposition*, 30 (2004), p. 336; Robert E. Goodin, "Global Democracy: in the Beginning," *Int'l Theory*, 2 (2010), p. 175; Daniel Bray, "Pragmatic Cosmopolitanism: A Deweyian Approach to Democracy Beyond the Nation-State," *Millennium J. Int'l Studies*, 37 (2009), p. 683; Pila-Noora Kauppi, Jo Leinen, Graham Watson, Gérard Onesta, *The Case for Global Democracy: Advocating a United Nations Parliamentary Assembly* (2007); Pascal Lamy, *Toward World Democracy* (2005); Mattias Koenig-Archibugi, "Is Global Democracy Possible," *Eur. J. Int'l Rel.*, 17 (2011), p. 519.

[62] H.R.C. Res 18/6, UN Doc. A/HRC/RES18/6 (October 13, 2011).

[63] G.A. Res. 67/175, UN Doc. A RES/67/175 (December 20, 2012).

[64] H.R.C. Res 18/6, ¶ 6(g), UN Doc. A/HRC/RES18/6 (October 13, 2011); H.R.C. Res 18/6, UN Doc. A/HRC/RES18/6 (October 13, 2011). G.A. Res. 67/175, ¶ 4(g), UN Doc. A RES/67/175 (December 20 2012).

[65] G.A. Res. 68/175, ¶ 5, UN Doc. A RES/68/175 (December 20, 2013).

right to equitable participation of all, without any discrimination, in domestic and global decision-making."[66] This places within the realm of international discussion how all seven billion citizens on the planet can equitably participate in global decision-making without discrimination outside of some sort of parliamentary structure.

The Human Rights Council in its resolution 18/6, decided to establish a mandate for an independent expert on the promotion of a democratic and equitable international order in part to, "identify best practices in the promotion and protection of a democratic international order at the local, national, regional and international levels,"[67] and the General Assembly in its resolution calls for cooperation with the independent expert.[68]

The independent expert, Alfred de Zayas, in his subsequent reports to both the Human Rights Council[69] and the General Assembly has called for consideration of a parliament.[70] He wrote, for example, in his report to the General Assembly:

> Among other civil society initiatives, the launching of a World Parliamentary Assembly or United Nations Parliamentary Assembly is worth exploring. As former Secretary-General Boutros Boutros-Ghali stated: "A United Nations Parliamentary Assembly – a global body of elected representatives –could invigorate our institutions of global governance with unprecedented democratic legitimacy, transparency and accountability." The idea is to remedy democracy deficits by giving voice to global public opinion, including citizens in global decision-making through elected officials. Such an Assembly could be set up by a vote of the General Assembly under

---

[66] G.A. Res. 68/175, ¶ 5 (h), UN Doc. A RES/68/175 (December 20, 2013).

[67] H.R.C. Res 18/6, ¶ 14 (b), UN Doc. A/HRC/RES18/6 (October 13, 2011).

[68] G.A. Res. 67/175, ¶ 13 & 14, UN Doc. A RES/67/175 (December 20, 2012).

[69] Independent Expert on the Promotion of a Democratic and Equitable International Order, *Report of the Independent Expert on the Promotion of a Democratic and Equitable International Order, Alfred-Maurice de Zayas, delivered to the Human Rights Council*, UN Doc. A/HRC/24/38 (July 1, 2013).

[70] Independent Expert on the Promotion of a Democratic and Equitable International Order, *Report of the Independent Expert on the Promotion of a Democratic and Equitable International Order, Alfred-Maurice de Zayas, delivered to the General Assembly*, UN Doc. A/68/284 (August,7, 2013).

Article 22 of the Charter or it could be created on the basis of a new international treaty between governments, followed by an agreement linking it to the United Nations. Neither mechanism requires Charter amendment or reform. Global decisions would gain greater legitimacy through citizen input and involvement in an independent World Assembly with consultative functions, or in a United Nations Parliamentary Assembly representing people as well as states.[71]

De Zayas recommends Article 22 of the Charter and an independent treaty as the two most viable vehicles for creating the GPA. I agree.[72] The Charter under Article 22 provides that "the General Assembly may establish such subsidiary organs as it deems necessary for the performance of its functions."[73] Article 22 has the advantage that, unlike the treaty process, a General Assembly resolution could bring the GPA into being without the cumbersome requirement of state ratification.[74]

Resorting to Article 22, however, is not without its own drawbacks. Perhaps most significant, garnering the requisite support for the approval of the GPA within the General Assembly is likely to require problematic political concessions. A lowest common denominator parliament, for example, might allow for authoritarian regimes to appoint members to the GPA, or even worse, orchestrate elections that would produce sham results. This would undermine the legitimacy of the organization and compromise its ability to act as a counterweight to authoritarianism.[75]

This is why Richard Falk and I have favored the GPA being initiated as an independent treaty body[76] adopted by whichever

---

[71] *Id* ¶ 23 and 24.

[72] See Andrew Strauss, "On the First Branch of Global Governance," *Widener L. Rev.*, 13 (2007), p. 347 (describing four potential ways of creating a global parliament and concluding that the treaty approach is the most practicable).

[73] UN Charter, art. 22.

[74] For further discussion, see Andrew Strauss, "On the First Branch of Global Governance," pp. 352–4.

[75] Ibid.

[76] Professor Falk and I have made the case for a treaty-based approach in several publications, including *Foreign Affairs* and *The Nation*. See Richard Falk and Andrew Strauss, "Toward Global Parliament," *Foreign Aff.*, 80 (2001), p. 212;

internationally progressive countries were willing to be pioneers.[77] Countries that are truly supportive of the GPA's democratic mission are likely to create the best, most democratic organization. Even twenty to thirty such countries (as long as they are economically and geographically diverse) would be enough to found the GPA, and opposing countries in the General Assembly could not stand in their way. Once the parliamentary initiative gained momentum, their less enthusiastic peers in the United Nations would have an incentive to take part rather than be sidelined, and there might even come a time when it would be politically untenable for authoritarian governments to deny their people the right to vote in the only globally elected body.

The treaty agreed to by the founders would establish the legal structure for elections to be held within their national territories including a voting system and electoral districts. In addition, an operational framework for the GPA, including its mandate and limitations on its powers would be included in the treaty as would a provision for future accession by other countries. Any country could later join the GPA so long as it was willing to meet its obligations under the treaty, the most important of which would be to allow its citizens to vote representatives to the GPA in free and fair elections.

The treaty could include provisions defining the GPA's initial role vis-à-vis the United Nations, and once established the parliament

Richard Falk and Andrew Strauss, "Toward a Global Parliament," *The Nation*, September 22, 2003, p. 28.

[77] A standalone treaty organization whose membership may not be the same as the United Nations is not a novel concept. Most major international bodies such as the Bretton Woods organizations, the World Trade Organization and the World Health Organization, to name but a few, have been created in this way. Most significant, this approach was used to establish the International Criminal Court, whose membership famously does not include the United States, nor for that matter Russia or China (though Russia is a signatory). In the case of the International Criminal Court, specific treaty provisions align that organization's processes with those of the United Nations. Most significant are terms providing for the Security Council to refer criminal cases to the Court.

could enter into a relationship agreement with that body.[78] Though begun independent of the United Nations, the GPA would be meant to strengthen it. Part of the GPA's treaty-based responsibilities, for example, could be to weigh in with its own vote on issues such as global income inequality. General Assembly resolutions are themselves largely recommendatory, and by insinuating a democratic voice into the process, the resolutions that passed both bodies would be more noticed and deemed more legitimate. Backed by the weight of popular authority over time, perhaps the General Assembly and the GPA could evolve together into a truly bicameral legislative system capable of producing binding legislation.

V CONCLUSION: RETURNING TO EINSTEIN AND FREUD

While Freud did not accept the presumed supposition that a compelling case for a world authority to avoid war could in itself be the impetus for such an authority, he did maintain a dynamic view of history. Influenced profoundly by German Romanticism, he believed that human civilization evolves as the individual psyche evolves, in the eternal struggle between the instincts of love (Eros, sexuality, that which unites) and death (aggressiveness and destruction).[79] In this sense Freud and Einstein, together with the politically scientific functionalists, all share a common perspective that embraces the reality of historical change. And, by almost any measure, we are living in a time of tremendous historical dynamism.

Viewed from the vantage point of the individual human psyche, today more of us on the planet than ever before have access to the

---

[78] The UN Charter provides that: "The Economic and Social Council may enter into agreements with any" agency "established by intergovernmental agreement and having wide international responsibilities." UN Charter art. 63, para. 1; ibid. at art. 57, para. 1. These agreements "defin[e] the terms on which the agency concerned shall be brought into relationship with the United Nations[,]" and "shall be subject to approval by the General Assembly." UN Charter art. 63, para. 1.

[79] See Sigmund Freud, *Civilization and its Discontents*.

education that allows us, in Freud's terms, to be "strengthening the intellect" so as to "master our instinctive lives."[80] Seen alternatively from Einstein's rationalist orientation, the increasingly rapid globalization of the planetary social order that technology has wrought has intensified the reflective case that we create a viable international system. Similarly, as I have argued in this chapter, in this globalized world, the dynamics of the functionalist variant of the political scientific tradition leads self-interested actors in the direction of collective action.

The extent to which the dynamism of the system will translate into any particular global institutional innovation is unknown. If planetary civilization, however, is to continue the long-term trend toward parliamentary democracy and toward greater planetary social integration, then presumably these two trend lines will at some point converge in the establishment of a globally democratic institution. That day may not be as far off as some people might imagine. For decades now the international community has been experimenting successfully with transnational parliamentary institutions, the most well-known of which is the citizen elected European Parliament.[81] Our functionalist study of the role that income inequality could play in the establishment of a GPA provides a framework for understanding the social mechanisms animating such an institutional development and presages the role that such an institution could play.

---

[80] Ibid., pp. 11–12. For example, according to the World Bank, in just the short period between 2004 and 2012, the worldwide percentage of children enrolled in secondary school increased from 63 percent to 73 percent. See The World Bank, Working for a World Free of Poverty, School Enrollment, Secondary, available at http://data.worldbank.org/indicator/SE.SEC.ENRR/countries/1W?display=graph.

[81] That democratic body has come to have significant powers as one of the three law-making institutions of the European Union. Among the more well-known of the other institutions are: the citizen-elected Central American Parliament, in operation since 1991; the ten-year-old Pan-African Parliament, composed of members elected by African national parliaments; the Council of Europe's parliamentary assembly composed of members of national parliaments; and the Organization for Security and Cooperation in Europe, the North American Treaty Organization and Mercosur parliaments also composed of national parliamentarians.

PART IV   International Political Crisis

7 A BOLIVARIAN ALTERNATIVE?

The New Latin American Populism Confronts the Global Order
Brad R. Roth and Sharon F. Lean

INTRODUCTION

"Chávez vive, la lucha sigue" is a ubiquitous slogan in Venezuela and the aligned countries of the Bolivarian Alliance for the Peoples of Our America (ALBA).[1] The slogan might be recast as a question. Over the course of his fourteen-year tenure (notoriously interrupted for two tumultuous days in April 2002), Venezuelan President Hugo Chávez Frías not only initiated extraordinary institutional and social transformations in his own country, but launched or instigated a series of challenges to the global economic, political, and legal orders – challenges reminiscent of an earlier generation of efforts to revise the terms of international order in favor of the global South.[2] These

---

[1] Translated as "Chávez lives, the struggle continues!" this is a rallying cry of *chavistas,* supporters of the late Venezuelan President Hugo Chávez and his "Bolivarian" revolution.

[2] Hugo Chávez was first elected president in 1998. In 1999, he called three elections: to convene a constitutional assembly, to elect representatives to the constituent assembly and to approve a new constitution. José E. Molina and Carmen Pérez B., "Radical Change at the Ballot Box: Causes and Consequences of Electoral Behavior in Venezuela's 2000 Elections," *Latin Amer. Politics & Soc.,* 46:1 (2004), p. 103. The 1999 constitution set the terms for the "Bolivarian revolution," which promised participatory democracy, economic and political sovereignty, and a redistribution of Venezuela's oil wealth to benefit the poor. The nation changed its name from "Republic of Venezuela" to "Bolivarian Republic of Venezuela," invoking independence

developments have represented a resurgence, albeit in modified form, of the state socialism and Bandung nationalism[3] that once countervailed (both institutionally and ideologically) the global system's dominant forces. The Alliance has established mechanisms to orchestrate substantial flows of international trade and development assistance both among and beyond its member states, flows that have effectively (and not coincidentally) underwritten local political movements that articulate a common set of social values. But with Chávez's death in March 2013, coinciding with a sharpening of Venezuela's political divisions and a deepening of its economic slide, it has become unclear to what extent the ALBA challenge will outlive its progenitor.

The polarized internal and intergovernmental responses to the policies of Chávez and his fellow leaders of the Bolivarian Alliance – most centrally, Bolivia's Evo Morales, Ecuador's Rafael Correa, and Nicaragua's Daniel Ortega, along with Cuba's redoubtable Fidel and Raul Castro – have found expression in the sharply contradictory assessments

hero Simón Bolívar and his vision of a united South America. But not all sectors of Venezuelan society supported these changes: on April 11, 2002, in the wake of a massive opposition rally beset by deadly clashes of still-controverted origin, the Venezuelan military removed Chávez from office in what has become known as a "civil society coup." Omar Encarnación, "Venezuela's Civil Society Coup," *World Policy J.*, 19:2 (2000), p. 38. The following day, a junta led by Chamber of Commerce president Pedro Carmona announced the abrogation of the Constitution, the dissolution of the National Assembly, and the dismissal of the sitting justices of the Supreme Court. But on April 13, another massive demonstration – this one by Chávez supporters – prompted a counter-coup that restored the constitutional order. See Gregory Wilpert, "The 47-Hour Coup That Changed Everything," VenezuelaAnalysis.com (April 13, 2007), http://venezuelanalysis.com/analysis/2336. These events were famously captured in the documentary, "The Revolution Will Not Be Televised" (Power Pictures, 2003).

[3] After the Bandung (Indonesia) Conference founding the Non-Aligned Movement in 1955, "'Bandung' soon came to resonate nostalgically [as] the collective, symbolic moment of decolonization when charismatic revolutionary leaders like Sukarno, Nasser, Nehru, and Zhou Enlai dominated world headlines ... Bandung ... came to acquire a multitude of emotive meanings for generations of oppressed peoples." Naoko Shimazu, "Guest Editorial: Places in Diplomacy," *Political Geography*, 31:6 (2012), p. 336.

of academic commentators. Indeed, the scholarly accounts of developments on the ground are so thoroughly incommensurable – focusing on such different aspects of local realities and measuring success or failure by such divergent criteria – that it is almost impossible to arrive at a balanced description (let alone evaluation) of the project's impact.[4]

From one perspective, the Bolivarian Alternative represents the emergence of a viable long-term model for implementing social justice, solidarity among peoples, and resistance to First-World domination. For Mohsen al Attar and Rosalie Miller, writing in the tradition of Third World Approaches to International Law (TWAIL), the ALBA is the long-awaited vehicle for an egalitarian international project that redresses the disparities and predations within and among societies:

> Now that a strong united bloc has formed to reverse the staggering inequalities permeating contemporary global society, there is an opportunity to construct an international legal regime that more accurately reflects the histories, cultures and voices of more than a privileged few. In short, the Bolivarian Revolution provides the structural (state) and popular (people) support needed to shift discussion away from the dominant Eurocentric international legal regime towards a dynamic pluralist alternative.[5]

The material effects are manifest in countries experiencing a large net inflow of ALBA resources. In Nicaragua, for example, "development cooperation has effected the reinstitution of free health care and basic education as human rights, and subsidised cooking-gas supply and school meal schemes."[6]

According to supporters, the results are not merely beneficent, but fundamentally democratic, in transnational and participatory ways

---

[4] For a discussion of the difficulties in assessing the competing empirical claims, see Christopher David Absell, "The ALBA-TCP: Looking with Keen Eyes," *Revista Problemas Del Desarrollo*, 169:43 (2012), p. 73 (English version available at www.probdes.iiec.unam.mx/en/revistas/v43n169/body/v43n169a4_1.php).

[5] Mohsen Al Attar and Rosalie Miller, "Towards an Emancipatory International Law: The Bolivarian Reconstruction," *Third World Q.*, 31:3 (2010), p. 352.

[6] Thomas Muhr, "(Re)constructing Popular Power in Our America: Venezuela and the Regionalisation of 'Revolutionary Democracy' in the ALBA–TCP Space," *Third World Q.*, 33:2 (2012), p. 236.

that conventional calls for "democratization" systematically neglect.[7] ALBA sponsors structures for popular input into the implementation of regionally coordinated development programs.[8] In the words of Thomas Muhr:

> the regionalisation of revolutionary democracy implies the (re) construction of popular power in three complementary ways. First, the Council of Social Movements provides the structure for the exercise of direct democracy through a pluri-scalar governance regime, through which a transnational organised society is constructed. Second, the democratisation of the organisation of production with socialist orientation (social, state and private ownership) is promoted through regional production and trade chains through which the power of global capital is challenged. Third, participatory democracy promotion means the reduction of inequality in human development and protagonism.[9]

From a different perspective, however, ALBA development projects are little more than payoffs by (principally) Venezuela to political allies. Beyond its public enterprises' substantial portfolio of politically-targeted foreign direct investments and loans, Venezuela has emerged as an outsized provider of South–South aid, committing an estimated $17 billion to transnational "social investment" projects between

---

[7] For a critique of the emerging international "right to democracy" as neglecting both active mass participation and accountability of transnational decision-making processes, see Susan Marks, *The Riddle Of All Constitutions: International Law, Democracy, and the Critique Of Ideology* (2000), pp. 50–100. For a range of views about the democratic entitlement, see Gregory H. Fox and Brad R. Roth (eds.), *Democratic Governance And International Law* (2000).

[8] This sponsorship itself has implications for the quality of democratic participation. According to David Smilde, "when Venezuela's Bolivarian government speaks of participatory democracy, it starts from a neomarxist view that sees civic autonomy as a fiction that favors the hegemony of dominant interest groups at the same time that it leaves the majority passive. In this perspective it is the government itself that needs to organize, facilitate and even fund such popular mobilization in order to democratize society." David Smilde, "Seeing and Not Seeing Venezuela's Bolivarian Democracy," unpublished paper, n.d., p. 11, http://svs.osu.edu/documents/ DavidSmilde_SEEINGANDNOTSEEING.pdf.

[9] Muhr, "(Re)constructing Popular Power in Our America," p. 237.

1999 and 2007.[10] According to Javier Corrales and Michael Penfold, this assistance is far from pure humanitarianism: "Billed as investment in social services, it in fact consisted largely of unaccountable financing for political campaigns, unelected social movements, business deals, and political patronage by state officials."[11]

Whatever their virtues or vices, such payouts lack any clearly sustainable economic or political logic. The Chávez government reportedly diverted substantial oil revenues from the investments needed to maintain productive capacity, auguring a potential breakdown of the engine that drives most of the Alliance's projects.[12] Venezuela's generosity cannot, in any event, be expected to withstand a change of government. Such a change – or alternatively, a paralyzing social confrontation in the wake of an unsettled electoral outcome – is a real possibility in the near term, given the narrow (1.5 percent) and controverted margin of victory for Chávez's successor, Nicolás Maduro, in the April 2013 Presidential election; a constitutional provision invites a recall effort after three years.[13]

---

[10] Javier Corrales and Michael Penfold, *Dragon in the Tropics: Hugo Chávez and the Political Economy of Revolution in Venezuela* (2011), p. 106. Only China and Saudi Arabia rival Venezuela in South–South aid, and only the latter rivals Venezuela in aid as a percentage of Gross National Income. Ibid., p. 105.

[11] Javier Corrales and Michael Penfold, *Dragon in the Tropics* , p. 109.

[12] Javier Corrales and Michael Penfold, *Dragon in the Tropics* , pp. 85–90. On the other hand, widely proclaimed past predictions of Venezuela's impending economic demise have proved unfounded (or at least premature). See Mark Weisbrot, "Disinformation Still Clouds the U.S. Debate on Chávez's Legacy in Venezuela," *The Guardian* (January 9, 2013), available at www.theguardian .com/commentisfree/2013/jan/09/us-debate-chavez-venezuela-legacy.

[13] The Maduro Administration received a boost from the December 2013 nationwide municipal elections, which yielded a 6.5 percent plurality for the pro-government parties (49.24 percent to 42.72 percent). The *chavistas* retained the mayoralties of a large majority of municipalities. Ewan Robertson, "Results of Venezuelan Municipal Elections Announced (Updated)," VenezuelaAnalysis.com (December 8, 2013), http://venezuelanalysis.com/ news/10227. Nonetheless, for several months in early 2014, a sense of crisis prevailed, as opposition demonstrators demanding the President's resignation clashed violently with security forces and pro-Government vigilantes. Although the confrontations do not appear to have led to a broadening of the

Moreover, however much popular participation may have been incorporated into the setting of local priorities for resources allocated to social projects,[14] critics allege that the Alliance's leading political movements have systematically undermined political pluralism and dismantled mechanisms of horizontal accountability in their respective countries. A persistent charge is a sharp diminution of the transparency of governmental operations – above all, as to state finances. For its adversaries, *chavismo* represents a mobilization, not of the less well-off in general, but of a select combination of underprivileged and privileged client constituencies – including wealthy contractors and military elites[15] – bound together by favoritism in the allocation of state resources and in the application of law.[16] Whatever their egalitarian pretensions, argue Corrales and Penfold, the left-wing populists of

opposition's base, the seemingly perpetual economic and political crises have further eroded popular confidence in Maduro's leadership. For an analysis of the political implications of the clashes, see Alejandro Velasco, "Venezuela's Polarizations and Maduro's Next Steps," NACLA (March 11, 2014), available at http://nacla.org/news/2014/3/11/venezuelas-polarizations-and -maduro%E2%80%99s-next-steps.

[14] See Luis Vicente León and David Smilde, "Participatory Democracy in Venezuela?, in Understanding Populism and Political Participation: The Case of Venezuela," in Adam T. Stubits (ed.), *Woodrow Wilson Center Update on the Americas, No. 3* (April 2009), p. 9: "Under the Chávez administration, the most readily recognizable forms of participation are 1) the government's attention to people's demands, 2) passive participation in state subsidies, also known as missions, and 3) the creation of the communal councils, although these lack a chain connecting them with the central government. Under this structure, where the potential for *caudillismo* is great and the potential for institutional democracy is low, community participation in self-government can be high when the issues are strictly local and routine, but in matters that reach beyond – to the city, state, or nation – participation is low."

[15] Javier Corrales and Michael Penfold, *Dragon in the Tropics* , pp. 144–9.

[16] For Corrales and Penfold, such unprincipled favoritism as an intended consequence of de-institutionalization is the quintessence of "populist" politics. For a non-pejorative application of the "populist" label to *chavismo*, see Kirk Hawkins, *Venezuela's Chavismo And Populism In Comparative Perspective* (2010), p. 247 ("a discourse or worldview that celebrates the people's will and its unmediated expression as the ultimate repository of goodness").

the *chavista* brand are more akin to right-wing populists than to left-wing democrats; the bottom line is the concentration of power in the hands of an unaccountable leadership, no longer bridled by previously existing institutional safeguards against arbitrariness and corruption.[17]

It is against this backdrop of divergent accounts that one must begin to make sense of the Bolivarian challenge to the normative order. This chapter will describe in brief the ALBA system and its trade and aid flows, and will go on to assess the Alliance's prospects as a source of resistance to the global trade and investment order. The chapter will further address the challenges that the ideology and practice of leading Alliance members pose to the international legal order's dominant understandings of human rights, democracy, and state sovereignty.

I A BRIEF HISTORY OF ALBA

The *Alianza Bolivariana para los Pueblos de Nuestra América* (ALBA) arose in the context of the backlash against neoliberal globalization that began in the 1990s, in large part as a response to the U.S.-backed proposal to create a Free Trade Area of the Americas (FTAA). Official negotiations towards an FTAA, first discussed at the 1998 Summit of the Americas meeting in Santiago, Chile, began in earnest at the 2001 Americas Summit in Quebec, Montreal. At the Quebec summit, Hugo Chávez took to the podium to pronounce his opposition to any regional trade agreement led by the United States and built on the principles promoted by the International Monetary Fund and World Bank.[18] Later in 2001, at a summit of the Association of Caribbean States, Chávez went further, proposing the idea of an alternative regional integration project.[19]

---

[17] Javier Corrales and Michael Penfold, *Dragon in the Tropics*, p. 149.
[18] For a succinct discussion of the FTAA debate in the Summits, see Alfredo Toro, "El Alba Como Instrumento De 'Soft Balancing'," *Pensamiento Propio*, 16:33 (January–June 2011), pp. 162–4.
[19] See ALBA-TCP, "History of Alba-Tcp," n.d., www.alba-tcp.org/en/contenido/history-alba-tcp.

Three years later, ALBA came into being through an agreement between Venezuela and Cuba, signed by Presidents Hugo Chávez and Fidel Castro on December 14, 2004. The preamble to this agreement describes the effort as a critical response to the proposal to create the FTAA and to perceived U.S. imperialism in the hemisphere: "the Free Trade Area for the Americas (FTAA) is the most accomplished expression of the appetites of domination over the region ... it would constitute a deepening of neo-liberalism and create levels of dependence and subordination without precedent in case it enters into force."[20]

The initial ALBA agreement outlined twelve basic principles, which continue in place as of 2013. They include the principle that trade and investment among countries should be instruments not only for growth, but also for "just and sustainable development." Countries should receive differential treatment on the basis of their level of development, and integration should be built on economic cooperation rather than competition, to promote "a productive, efficient and competitive specialization ... [and] balanced economic development in every country." Fighting poverty is a stated principle, along with state-provided health care and literacy programs. The preservation of the cultural identity of the peoples and care for the environment are also integral goals, along with integration of energy, communications and transportation sectors. Finally, the principles propose the creation of alternative financial institutions and a social emergency fund to reduce the dependence of member states on neoliberal international financial institutions and private lenders.[21]

The debut of the initial two-state alliance at the end of 2004 coincided with a cycle of national elections that marked a pronounced shift to the Left in regional politics. During the wave of transitions to democracy that swept Latin America in the 1980s, citizens elected leaders from parties of the Right and Center-Right, who largely

[20] See ALBA-TCP, "Alba-Tcp Building an Interpolar World: 2004–2010 Summits," (Caracas, Venezuela: Executive Secretariat ALBA-TCP, 2011), www.alba-tcp.org/public/documents/pdf/Ingles/BuildinganInterPolarWorld .pdf, p. 6.

[21] For a complete, translated text of the twelve basic principles, see Ibid., pp. 7–8.

embraced neoliberal economic policies. As time went on these policies, and the limited top-down form of "polyarchy" that characterized the Latin American regimes, failed to satisfy voters.[22] As the region shifted Left between 2004 and 2006, ALBA grew. After the 2005 election of Evo Morales, Bolivia became the third state to join ALBA. With the accession of Bolivia on April 26, 2006, the alliance became officially known as ALBA-TCP (Alianza Bolivariana para los Pueblos de Nuestra América-Tratado de Comercio de los Pueblos, or People's Trade Agreement).

In 2007, the same day that Daniel Ortega of the Sandinista Front (FSLN) was sworn in as president of Nicaragua, that country signed on. Ecuador, similarly, ratified the agreement in June 2009, shortly after Rafael Correa was elected to a second term in office under a new (2008) constitution. By 2013, ALBA counted nine member states: Venezuela, Cuba, Bolivia, Nicaragua, Ecuador, Dominica, Antigua and Barbuda, St. Vincent-Grenadines and Santa Lucia. Suriname began the process of accession in early 2012, and at the same time Haiti affirmed its status as a "permanent guest member."[23] Honduras, which had joined in 2008, withdrew in the aftermath of the 2009 coup against Manuel Zelaya that returned the Right to power in that country (The Honduran National Congress ratified its departure from ALBA on January 12, 2010). The nine ALBA states, together, account for 12.6 percent of the population of the region, and 10 percent of the region's GDP.[24]

---

[22] On the left turn in Latin American politics, see Matthew R. Cleary, "Explaining the Left's Resurgence," *Journal of Democracy*, 17:4 (2006), p. 35; Raúl L. Madrid, "The Origins of the Two Lefts in Latin America," *Pol. Sci. Q.*, 125:4 (2010), p. 587. On the idea of polyarchy as low-intensity democracy, see William I. Robinson, *Promoting Polyarchy: Globalization, U.S. Intervention And Hegemony* (1996), pp. 49–52.

[23] See ALBA-TCP, "Resolution of Member Countries of the ALBA on the Entry of Haiti, Santa Lucia y Surinam [sic] as Special Guest Members," (XI Cumbre, Caracas, Venezuela, 5 February 2012), www.alba-tcp.org/en/ contenido/resolution-member-countries-alba-entry-hait%C3%ADsanta -lucia-y-suriname-special-guest-members, p. 1.

[24] Author's calculations based on 2012 data from the World Bank. Data are available online at http://data.worldbank.org/.

Given the ALBA's ideological orientation, it is notable that other states where the Left holds power have opted not to join. Uruguay, where Tabaré Vázquez of the *Frente Amplio* won the presidency in 2004, provides a first example. Although Vázquez restored Uruguay's relations with Cuba and generally employed an anti-neoliberal discourse during his presidency (2004 to 2009), he also "negotiated an investment-protection agreement with the United States, sent his finance minister to Washington to explore the possibility of forging a free-trade agreement, and... refused to attend Morales' inauguration as president of Bolivia."[25] Uruguay further consolidated its leftward orientation in 2009 with the election of Jose Mujica, an ex-Tupamaro also from the *Frente Amplio*, but the Uruguayan government has maintained its orthodox economic orientation, and has not chosen to enter ALBA.[26]

El Salvador, where the candidate of the revolutionary Left party, the FMLN, won the presidency in 2009, is another example. President Mauricio Funes explained that El Salvador would refrain from joining ALBA *because* of the Alliance's ideological component. The Funes government sought instead to develop a foreign policy that would transcend the idea of ideological friends and enemies.[27] The contrast with Nicaragua is especially vivid. Peru, where Ollanta Humala took office in 2011, is another notable non-participant in ALBA-TCP. Humala, who had a warm relationship with Hugo

---

[25] See Jorge G. Castañeda, "Latin America's Left Turn," *For. Aff.*, 85:3 (2006), p. 36.

[26] Uruguay has, however, joined two of ALBA's initatives: Telesur and the Sucre.

[27] See Josette Altmann Borbón, "Alba: From Integration Alternative to Political and Ideological Alliance," in *Latin American Multilateralism: New Directions* (September 2010), pp. 27, 30, available at www.iadb.org/intal/intalcdi/PE/2010/06396.pdf (published as Josette Altmann Borbón, "El Alba: Entre Propuesta De Integracion Y Mecanismo De Cooperacion," *Pensamiento Propio*, 16:33 (2011), p. 185). Funes's ostensibly more radical successor, one-time FMLN guerrilla commander Salvador Sanchez Ceren, is unlikely to change course substantially, especially given the extreme narrowness of his 2014 Presidential election run-off victory.

Chávez, and who spoke favorably of ALBA during his first (unsuccessful) bid for the presidency in 2006, chose not to join the Bolivarian alliance once in office, stating a preference to reinforce Peru's regional ties through other multilateral mechanisms, including UNASUR and the Andean Community.[28]

Since its beginning in 2004, ALBA has undertaken numerous initiatives designed to advance the Alliance's declared principles. ALBA's first initiative brought Cuban medical personnel to staff clinics in poor neighborhoods in Venezuela, a program called "Barrio Adentro." Cuba provided this human capital in exchange for subsidized Venezuelan oil for Cuba. Other initiatives include Petrocaribe, an alliance in which Venezuela provides oil to its neighbors in the Caribbean Basin at favorable rates; Telesur, an alternative television network which began full-time broadcasts in 2005; the ALBA Bank, started in 2008 and its electronic currency the Sucre, launched in 2010; and the *grannacionales*, supranational enterprises for the production of food and medicine.

However, as is the norm for multilateral institutions in Latin America, ALBA is a presidentialist institution with a comparatively low degree of institutionalization, with most of its activities planned at periodic summit meetings. This structure has contributed to a situation in which the actions of ALBA do not match its aspirations. As Altmann Borbón has put it, ALBA has produced "a glut of signed agreements from presidential summits, and it is impossible to fulfill all of them[;]... in the end much remains [limited to] the political discourse."[29] In 2009, the Alliance created a Permanent Council and appointed a Secretary General, in an effort to provide better follow-through and implementation for decisions made in summit meetings.

[28] On Humala's expressed admiration for Chávez, see Jorge G. Castañeda, "Latin America's Left Turn," p. 41; on his pragmatic behavior once in office, see "Humala Afirma Que Perú No Se Alineará a La Alba De Chávez Y Castro," *El Comercio* (June 22, 2013).

[29] Josette Altmann Borbón, "Alba: From Integration Alternative to Political and Ideological Alliance," p. 29.

II ALBA AS AN ALTERNATIVE TO THE GLOBAL ECONOMIC ORDER

For all of its significance as a source of assistance to developing economies within and beyond its membership, ALBA lacks the economic diversity to present its own member states with a comprehensive alternative to global markets and First-World sources of investment capital, and its dependency on Venezuelan oil wealth and political motivation impairs its utility as a model susceptible of emulation elsewhere. It is best understood as a mechanism for the promotion of particular political interests, arising as part of a broader trend of Latin American experimentation with new forms of intergovernmental economic and political coordination.

The regionalist impulse in Latin America is at an historic high, encompassing summitry, regional and sub-regional economic integration mechanisms, the creation of new regional institutions, and continued activities of longstanding institutions such as the OAS.[30] New regional groupings in this logic include, in addition to ALBA, UNASUR (Union of South American Nations, created in 2008 on a Brazilian initiative to reinvigorate the South American Community of Nations); and CELAC (the Community of Latin American and Caribbean States, created in 2010 at a meeting in Cancun, Mexico). All three are multifunctional institutions, and all exclude the United States and Canada. They represent overlapping yet distinct attempts to balance U.S. power in the region. They also balance power among the more powerful Latin American states in the region: UNASUR is a Brazilian-led initiative; CELAC affords Mexico a larger role, and ALBA positions Venezuela at the helm. Thus, ALBA is just one among a menu of options for heads of state seeking venues for multilateral cooperation in multiple arenas without the United States as the principal partner. The existence of these options helps to explain the absence of some presumably ideologically compatible states in ALBA.

---

[30] Legler and Burns describe this as "dynamic multilateralism," in Thomas Legler and Lesley Martina Burns (eds.), *Latin American Multilateralism: New Directions* (2010), p. 6.

However, whereas many of Latin America's multilateral institutions arguably play a part in spreading the dominant capitalist model by institutionalizing global structures of political and economic domination, ALBA, in contrast, is openly opposed to global and regional capitalism. It advocates a different form of Latin American multilateralism and seeks to redefine regional integration – political, social and economic – within a project of "twenty-first century socialism."

Petrocaribe, an initiative designed to foster energy independence and social investment, facilitates Venezuelan crude oil exports to seventeen states that have joined the Petrocaribe alliance, not all ALBA members.[31] Countries that are part of Petrocaribe have ninety days to pay 40 percent of the value of oil they import and pay off their remaining bill on credit extended over a twenty-five-year period at very low interest rates (between 1 and 2 percent).[32] Under the terms of the agreement, recipient states are encouraged to redirect monies saved towards social programs, and a portion of payments on the balance go into an ALBA fund for social and infrastructure development in the importing country. By all accounts, Petrocaribe has provided a significant source of revenue for Caribbean Basin countries – dwarfing, for example, U.S. assistance and Inter-American Development Bank lending. It has also allowed Venezuela to penetrate oil markets previously dominated by other oil producers (although it is an open question whether this will be a profitable strategy for Venezuela). *Latin American Monitor*, a publication of Business Monitor International, reported in 2008 that "the PetroCaribe deal has become the largest single source of concessional finance to the Caribbean, and that Venezuela has surpassed Mexico as Central America's dominant oil supplier."[33] Furthermore, Petrocaribe

---

[31] The eighteen Petrocaribe members include ALBA members Venezuela, Cuba, Nicaragua, Antigua and Barbuda, Dominica, St Vincent, and the Grenadines and St Lucia, plus Bahamas, Belize, Dominican Republic, Grenada, Guatemala, Guyana, Haiti, Honduras, Jamaica, St Kitts and Nevis, and Suriname.

[32] See Petrocaribe, *Acerca de Petrocaribe* (2009).

[33] "Petrocaribe: Crude Appeal Strains U.S. Ties," *Latin America Monitor*, 25:9 (2008), p. 2.

has improved both energy security and infrastructure development for refining, storing and distributing gas and oil for Caribbean states that previously had very little capacity in these areas.[34] However, these gains rely on a non-renewable energy source that fluctuates in price on the global market and depends fundamentally on the generosity of Venezuela government and the fortunes of the state-run oil company, PDVSA – aspects that render the program's sustainability uncertain.

The ALBA Bank, an initiative launched at the Sixth ALBA Summit in 2008, is currently functioning. Through this mechanism, the organization created a shared unit of account in 2010. Although modeled on the Euro, the Sucre (Unified System for Regional Compensation), is not to date used as circulated currency. Rather, it is a virtual currency used for international payments related to trade among adherent countries, which include Venezuela, Bolivia, Cuba, Ecuador, and as of 2013, Nicaragua, and Uruguay. The Sucre seeks to protect the monetary sovereignty of constituent states by reducing their dependency on the U.S. dollar and to further regional economic integration by facilitating intraregional trade in goods other than petroleum. It had demonstrated some modest potential to advance these goals by the close of its second year of operation.[35]

Notwithstanding ALBA's significant contributions as an alternative to the global economic order,[36] it is important to note that most member states have not been able to opt out of global economic initiatives. Altmann Borbón argues that the pragmatism of ALBA members contrasts with the ideological objectives of the organization.[37] None of the ALBA member countries has broken its existing

---

[34] See Daniele Benzi and Ximena Zapata, "Geopolítica, Economía Y Solidaridad Internacional En La Nueva Cooperación Sur-Sur: El Caso De La Venezuela Bolivariana Y Petrocaribe," *América Latina Hoy*, 63 (2013), pp. 76–7.

[35] See SUCRE, "Informe de Gestión," (2012), www.sucrealba.org/images/informes/informe_2012.pdf.

[36] Toro asserts that ALBA has successfully functioned as a form of "soft balancing" against U.S. power in the region, in security, development, and finance. Alfredo Toro, "El Alba Como Instrumento De 'Soft Balancing'."

[37] Josette Altmann Borbón, "Alba: From Integration Alternative to Political and Ideological Alliance," p. 187.

ties with the United States, international financial institutions or other trading blocs. Nicaragua, for example, while part of ALBA, has pragmatically maintained its status as a member of DR-CAFTA – effectively straddling diametrically opposed integration projects. Moreover, although there is meaningful solidarity-based exchange taking place, the South-South cooperation emphasized by ALBA is neither purely altruistic nor fully grounded in a confluence of object-ive economic interests: it is most fundamentally a political project, animated primarily by the geostrategic and ideological agendas of the present government of one member state (Venezuela).

III HUMAN RIGHTS, DEMOCRACY, AND "TWENTY-FIRST-CENTURY SOCIALISM"

The Bolivarian Alternative's most provocative challenge to the global normative order pertains to questions of human rights and democ-racy. The Venezuelan government has set itself most directly against mainstream human rights institutions, having broken relations with both Human Rights Watch (expelling the organization after a critical report in 2008) and the Inter-American Commission on Human Rights (IACHR) (giving notice in 2012 of its withdrawal from the American Convention on Human Rights, effective as of September 2013). It has met the critical reports of those organizations,[38] not only with fierce recriminations,[39] but with a competing vision. Far from

---

[38] See for example "Human Rights Watch, a Decade Under Chávez: Political Intolerance and Lost Opportunities for Advancing Human Rights in Venezuela" (2008), available at www.hrw.org/sites/default/files/reports/venezuela0908web.pdf; Inter-American Commission on Human Rights (IACHR), "Democracy and Human Rights in Venezuela," OEA/Ser.L/V/II, Doc. 54 (December 30, 2009).

[39] See for example James Suggett, "Venezuela Rejects Inter-American Human Rights Commission Report," *Venezuelanalysis.com: News, Views, and Analysis* (May 12, 2009), venezuelanalysis.com/print/4438. The Venezuelan Foreign Relations Ministry alleged political bias, contrasting the roughly 150 IACHR cases brought against Venezuela from 1999 to 2009 with the total number brought during the period of previous governments from 1977 to 1999: six,

renouncing human rights and democracy as such, the Venezuelan leadership – along with other ALBA leaders, such as Nicaraguan President Daniel Ortega – has claimed the high ground in these areas, reviving normative controversies of an earlier era – an era that included the initial period of Sandinista rule in Nicaragua (1979–90).[40]

It is commonplace to speak of three "generations" of human rights: (1) the civil and political rights that have pride of place in international human rights instruments and Western liberal-democratic constitutions, emphasizing negative governmental duties to avoid impositions on individuals; (2) economic and social rights, sometimes included but typically subordinated within international human rights instruments, emphasizing governmental duties to secure access for all persons to the material conditions of a dignified human existence (without which civil and political rights cannot be effectively enjoyed); and (3) rights to underlying structural conditions that, while

notwithstanding that the period included mass killings by government forces during the 1989 "Caracazo" disturbances.

[40] One must be cautious, however, about identifying the current period of Sandinista rule (since 2007) with the previous one. Political alliances have shifted – many old anti-Sandinistas have now aligned with Ortega, whereas key figures from the Sandinista government of the 1980s are now in fierce opposition – and the character of governance has changed in important respects: collective leadership has given way to the personal authority of Ortega and his wife, Rosario Murillo; repression (albeit measured, and largely prompted by armed insurgency) has given way to more indirect means of sidelining critics; and the once-well-regarded electoral apparatus has become mired in charges of non-transparency and vote tampering. However one evaluates the difference, the current Ortega government, owing principally to ALBA subsidies, has been incomparably more successful in achieving the social goals that the Sandinista movement has championed. In the words of one-time adversary Arturo Cruz Sequeira, Ortega "has used the resources from Venezuela to resolve multiple immediate needs of the country and at the same time, within the formal budget, he has handled the economy with great responsibility, within the IMF program," and has achieved "an equilibrium, satisfying the immediate needs of the people without risking the macroeconomic future," thus effectuating a "responsible populism." NicaNet Nicaragua News Bulletin (May 20, 2014), www.nicanet.org/page=blog&id=26683 (citing *Informe Pastran* (May 14, 2014) and *La Prensa* (May 14, 2014)).

indispensable to individual well-being, are cognizable only as entitlements of collective entities vis-à-vis the global order, such as the right to development and the right to a safe and healthy environment. The mainstream human rights movement acknowledges all three categories, and frequently characterizes them as interdependent and mutually reinforcing. But for mainstream human rights advocates, second- and third-generation rights tend to be relegated to a supporting role; when these advocates decry false trade-offs, it is typically in the context of insisting categorically on negative governmental duties (the "thou shalt nots" of the natural rights tradition) and thus, effectively, positing a categorical priority for first-generation rights.[41]

The "hard Left" has long complained of the skewed effects of the equal application of civil and political rights in unequal economic and social conditions. As one of this chapter's authors has noted elsewhere, "rights can function as shields behind which privileged elites, when confronted by governments bent on economic and social reform or transformation, can act to mobilize resistance and to generate economic chaos."[42] A textbook illustration of this phenomenon, charge *chavistas*, is the provocative role of opposition television stations in the incidents surrounding the abortive April 2002 Venezuelan

---

[41] The conventional wisdom can be summed up as follows: "the real test of a belief in human rights comes when the goals of the struggle or strategy come into conflict with the defence of rights claims." Steven Lukes, *Moral Conflict And Politics* (1991), p. 188. This assertion rests on a controvertible proposition: that "the defence of rights claims" is qualitatively different from, and therefore capable of taking categorical priority over, "the goals of a struggle or strategy." The struggle or strategy may be indispensable to establishing conditions of a dignified human existence, by reference to which human rights are (by any modern method) deduced. A clash of human rights-based considerations cannot be excluded *a priori*, even if experience teaches skepticism about claims (whether from the Left or the Right) for the practical necessity of ruthless tactics. (An *a priori* insistence on the primacy of negative over affirmative duties – i.e., deontological morality – might still be defensible, but only on distinct grounds pertaining to the duty-bearer rather than to the right-bearer.) Brad R. Roth, "Retrieving Marx for the Human Rights Project," *Leiden J. Int'l L.*, 17 (2004), pp. 33–51.

[42] Ibid., p. 57.

coup d'état.[43] Alliance governments have resorted to seemingly heavy-handed measures against opponents (e.g., the withdrawal of television licenses, prosecutions of journalists for criminal libel), supporters assert, only to counter – in relatively restrained ways – the efforts of entrenched elites to derail transformative policies that implement the human rights of the underprivileged.

The Alliance governments and their sympathizers have led the way in redirecting human rights discourse toward the conditions facing those most deprived of both basic material needs and inclusion in social institutions. From this perspective, economic and social rights are both foundational to human dignity and the *sine qua non* of the equal and effective enjoyment of civil and political rights.

The *chavista* period in Venezuela has been marked by a substantial reorientation of resources in favor of long-neglected portions of the population, with major reported gains in poverty reduction, adult and childhood education, and health, as well as greatly increased access of the lower classes to higher education.[44] Similarly dramatic social improvements have been reported (and in some cases verified by

---

[43] This interpretation of events is the centerpiece of the well-known pro-Chávez documentary, "The Revolution Will Not Be Televised"(Power Pictures, 2003). For detailed allegations of media collaboration with the coup-plotters, see Maurice Lemoine, "Venezuela's Press Power: How Hate Media Incited the Coup against the President," *Le Monde Diplomatique* (Eng. ed., August 2002), available at http://mondediplo.com/2002/08/10venezuela.

[44] A typical list of claims for the Chávez government's material accomplishments reads as follows:

– About 1.5 million Venezuelans learned to read and write thanks to the literacy campaign ... In December 2005, UNESCO said that Venezuela had eradicated illiteracy.

– The number of children attending school increased from 6 million in 1998 to 13 million in 2011 and the enrollment rate is now 93.2 percent ... [T]he rate of secondary school enrollment rose from 53.6 percent in 2000 to 73.3 percent in 2011 ... [T]he number of [post-secondary] students increased from 895,000 in 2000 to 2.3 million in 2011, assisted by the creation of new universities.

– From 1999 to 2011, the poverty rate decreased from 42.8 percent to 26.5 percent and the rate of extreme poverty fell from 16.6 percent in 1999 to 7 percent in 2011.

United Nations agencies and other well-regarded international institutions) for other ALBA countries, such as Nicaragua.[45] Although some such improvements might have been expected to accompany the surge in resources available in that period to an oil-exporting country and its beneficiaries, and although these improvements have coincided with social improvements elsewhere in Latin America, the gains have been noteworthy, especially relative to the markedly lackluster social performance of predecessor governments of the participating states.[46]

It is difficult to assess the extent (if any) to which these gains were made possible only by a brand of politics that has narrowed space for opposition participation and that has rendered adversaries vulnerable to governmental and government-inspired reprisals.[47] It is also

- In the rankings of the Human Development Index (HDI) of the United Nations Program for Development (UNDP), Venezuela jumped from 83 in 2000 (0.656) at position 73 in 2011 (0.735), and entered into the category Nations with "High HDI."
- The GINI coefficient, which allows calculation of inequality in a country, fell from 0.46 in 1999 to 0.39 in 2011. According to the UNDP, Venezuela holds the lowest recorded Gini coefficient in Latin America, that is, Venezuela is the country in the region with the least inequality.
- Child malnutrition was reduced by 40 percent since 1999.
- In 1999, 82 percent of the population had access to safe drinking water. Now it is 95 percent.

Salim Lamrani, "50 Truths about Hugo Chávez and the Bolivarian Revolution," *Venezuelanalysis.com: News, Views, and Analysis* (March 9, 2013), http://venezuelanalysis.com/analysis/8133 (bullet point numbering omitted).

[45] See Thomas Muhr, "(Re)constructing Popular Power in Our America."

[46] For an account of the shortcomings of the pre-Chávez political order in addressing the needs and aspirations of the less well-off sectors of Venezuelan society, see Richard S. Hillman, *Democracy For The Privileged: Crisis And Transition In Venezuela* (1994).

[47] See for example Human Rights Watch, "Venezuela: Chávez's Authoritarian Legacy: Dramatic Concentration of Power and Open Disregard for Basic Human Rights," (March 5, 2013), www.hrw.org/news/2013/03/05/venezuela-chavez-s-authoritarian-legacy; IACHR, "Democracy and Human Rights in Venezuela," p. 290 ("citizens and organizations that make their disagreement with governmental policies public often become victims of retaliation, intimidation, disqualification, exclusion, discrimination in the workplace, and

difficult to match what has been gained against what has been lost, especially given questions about the sustainability of present levels of social spending and the susceptibility of newly unchecked concentrations of power to being deployed more abusively as political challenges mount.[48] History teaches that measures originally rationalized as directed against "enemies of the revolution" tend over time to become directed against erstwhile supporters whose dissidence becomes regarded as "objectively" in league with revolution's enemies, and then against professed loyalists who nonetheless express disapproval of intolerant policies, and so on *ad infinitum*. The undermining of such safeguards as judicial independence augurs potentially deleterious developments.[49]

---

in some instances are even subject to legal attack and deprived of their liberty. Thus, reprisals levied against dissenters have left certain sectors of society stripped of the means to protect their interests, to protest, to criticize, to propose, and to exercise their role as overseers of the democratic system").

[48] These challenges came to the fore in the wave of militant opposition demonstrations that Venezuela experienced for several months beginning in February 2014. To be sure, hardline oppositionists employed a combination of peaceful and violently disruptive means to underscore their provocative demands for "*La Salida*" – "the exit" (of a government that had just won three elections in fourteen months) – in an effort perceived to mimic the run-up to the attempted coup of 2002. The government's responses, however, were problematic: large numbers of arrests; severe beatings of detainees by members of the National Guard; the filing of questionable charges against a handful of opposition leaders; and several shootings of demonstrators that appear to have been perpetrated by members of pro-government groups ("*colectivos*"). Even controlling for the international media coverage's neglect of facts inconsistent with the anti-government narrative – for example, the number of deaths on the pro- and anti-government sides were roughly equal, and over a dozen National Guardsmen were arrested on charges of excessive use of force – the overall performance of Venezuelan institutions in the crisis raised serious questions about the rule of law. For detailed and nuanced coverage of these events, see the archives of *Venezuelan Politics and Human Rights*, a blog hosted by the Washington Office on Latin America (WOLA), at http://venezuelablog.tumblr.com/.

[49] Human Rights Watch, "Venezuela: Chávez's Authoritarian Legacy," reports as follows:

The same quandary that marks the evaluation of human rights performance attends any discussion of democracy in Venezuela and its emulators. Left-populist governments in Venezuela, Bolivia, Ecuador, and Nicaragua have maintained electoral success – probably reflecting actual majorities, even where, as in Nicaragua, significant electoral improprieties have been charged.[50] Critics complain of the substantial erosion of procedural mechanisms associated with liberal-democratic governance, applying such terms as "competitive authoritarianism."[51] But supporters identify democracy, not with procedures designed to reduce the stakes of political contestation, but with the affirmative use of political power to advance a democratic social reality in the face of concentrated wealth, entrenched privilege, and pronounced social stratification; in this view, an evaluation of democratic performance, far from being neutral with respect to

In 2009, Chávez publicly called for the imprisonment of a judge for 30 years after she granted conditional liberty to a prominent government critic who had spent almost three years in prison awaiting trial. The judge, María Lourdes Afiuni, was arrested and spent more than a year in prison in pretrial detention, in deplorable conditions. She remains under house arrest.

The circumstances surrounding this troubling incident are not unambiguous, as the judge was alleged to have corruptly arranged the bank fraud suspect's release through irregular proceedings conducted in the prosecutors' absence. See Ian James, "Jailing of Judge Provokes Debate in Venezuela," *Associated Press* (December 16, 2009), available at www.law.com/jsp/law/international/LawArticleFriendlyIntl.jsp?id=1202436355382.

[50] For serious charges of electoral irregularities, see EU Election Observation Mission, "Nicaragua 2011: Final Report on the General Elections and Parlacen Elections" (2012), available at www.eueom.eu/files/dmfile/moeue-nicaragua-final-report-22022012_en.pdf.For 2011 pre-election polling data forecasting the landslide Sandinista victory, see CID-Gallup, "Ortega Se Consolida en Ultima Encuesta de CID Gallup Previa a Elecciones" (October 2011), available at www.cidgallup.com/Documentos/Boletin%20Nicaragua%20Octubre%202011.pdf.

[51] Enrique Peruzzotti, "Elected Authoritarianism in South America: Argentina, Venezuela and Ecuador, "Center for Hemispheric Policy, University of Miami (July 2, 2013), available at https://umshare.miami.edu/web/wda/hemisphericpolicy/Task_Force_Papers/PERUZZOTTI%20%20The%20Future%20of%20Democracy%20and%20Emergin%20Markets%20in%20Latin%20America%20Task%20Force.pdf.

substantive outcomes, should credit the establishment, by whatever means, of egalitarian social policies.[52] Where disagreement about the substance of democracy reaches a certain threshold of intensity, partisans (on both sides) inevitably become more prone to reconsider adherence to procedures designed to arbitrate disagreement.

IV THE REASSERTION OF SOVEREIGNTY ON BEHALF OF THE GLOBAL SOUTH

A common theme in the discourse of Alliance members is the reassertion of the sovereign equality of the lesser developed countries. Although a movement to coordinate national economies, ALBA eschews models of economic integration that circumvent or subvert state authority. Christopher Absell thus refers to ALBA as a form of "political and economic integration that forgoes the formation of supra-national institutions in favor of the maintenance of State sovereignty."[53] A principal goal of ALBA, having arisen in reaction against the proposed FTAA, is to reduce the power of transnational corporations vis-á-vis capital-importing states, a goal that has led Venezuela,

---

[52] As one of the authors of this chapter has put it:"Egalitarian social policies – policies oriented toward greater economic equality, material security, and access to the institutions of civil society – are essential to democracy in three ways: (1) They *enable* democracy by providing the material base for meaningful and effective political participation, so that less advantaged sectors can advance their self-conceived interests in the political arena on the same terms as social elites. (2) They *reflect* democracy, for they are evidence – perhaps the only truly persuasive evidence – of the real weight of popular sectors in political decisionmaking. (3) The *embody* the essence of democracy in that they empower less advantaged sectors with respect to social decisions taken outside of the political realm – decisions likely to have the greatest concrete effect on people's lives." Brad R. Roth, "Evaluating Democratic Progress: A Normative Theoretical Perspective," *Ethics & Int'l Aff.*, 9 (1995), p. 65.

[53] Christopher David Absell, "The ALBA-TCP: Looking with Keen Eyes," p. 6 (online English version).

Bolivia, and Ecuador to withdraw from the International Convention on the Settlement of Investment Disputes (ICSID).[54]

On another front, ALBA governments have emerged as a distinctive, but ultimately ambiguous, voice in global climate change negotiations. The leading ALBA states, while vigorously emphasizing dimensions of the climate issue that implicate global distributive justice, are suspected of defending their interests as major fossil fuel producers. At the December 2009 Copenhagen Conference of the Parties of the United Nations Framework Convention on Climate Change, Venezuela and Bolivia pressed vociferously for binding emissions reductions on the part of the most developed countries, but are best remembered for blocking the formal adoption of the accord on which most of the participants had agreed, prompting many diplomats and observers to characterize them as "spoilers."[55]

More broadly, ALBA members have seized the international stage to denounce what they regard as new forms of North American and Western European domination, and to reinvigorate long-standing demands for North-to-South economic redistribution. This effort achieved its greatest prominence when the ALBA governments successfully engineered the election of former Nicaraguan Foreign Minister Miguel d'Escoto Brockmann as UN General Assembly President for the 2008–9 session. While d'Escoto's performance drew repeated criticism from Western diplomats for violating the neutrality of that role,[56] he initiated two notable "Interactive Thematic Dialogues,"

---

[54] For an argument that withdrawal from ICSID fails to address the fundamental imbalances of the international investment order and leaves states subject to even more disadvantageous dispute settlement mechanisms established under bilateral investment treaties (BITs), see Diana Marie Wick, "The Counter-Productivity of ICSID Denunciation and Proposals for Change," *J. Int'l Business & L.*, 12 (2012), p. 239.

[55] See for example Daniel Bodansky, "Current Developments: The Global Climate Change Conference: A Postmortem," *Am, J. Int'l L.*, 104 (2010), p. 231.

[56] These criticisms did not always lack validity, as when d'Escoto openly sided with Russia against Georgia during the South Ossetia conflict. On the other hand, d'Escoto's July 2009 accompaniment of ousted and exiled Honduran

one on the "World Financial and Economic Crisis and Its Impact on Development" and the other on the "Responsibility to Protect" ("R2P"), featuring prominent critics of present global power dynamics (e.g., Joseph Stiglitz and Noam Chomsky, respectively).[57] These conclaves elevated the profile of long-standing grievances. Ultimately, however, they failed to galvanize support for alternative approaches; indeed, participating states generally reaffirmed the R2P formula for humanitarian intervention.

D'Escoto's "Concept Note" on the Responsibility to Protect doctrine complained of the uncontrolled prerogatives of the Security Council and its veto-holders, and inveighed against the use of the doctrine to circumvent UN Charter strictures against the use of force.[58] Yet ironically, d'Escoto and his allies seemed caught between

President Manuel Zelaya on an unauthorized (and ultimately abortive) return by air to Tegucigalpa substituted a courageous expression of resolve for the emptiness of international rhetoric (of GA Res. 63/301 (2009)). See Mark Lacey and Ginger Thompson, "Honduras Is Rattled as Leader Tries Return," *New York Times* (July 6, 2009), available at www.nytimes.com/2009/07/06/world/americas/06honduras.html.

[57] President of the 63rd Session, United Nations General Assembly, "Interactive Thematic Dialogue of the UN General Assembly on the World Financial and Economic Crisis and Its Impact on Development" (March 25–27, 2009), available at www.un.org/ga/president/63/interactive/worldfinancialcrisis.shtml; President of the 63rd Session, United Nations General Assembly, "Interactive Thematic Dialogue of the United Nations General Assembly on the Responsibility to Protect" (July 23, 2009), available at www.un.org/ga/president/63/interactive/responsibilitytoprotect.shtml.

[58] D'Escoto stated as follows:

Colonialism and interventionism used responsibility to protect arguments. National Sovereignty in developing countries is a necessary condition for stable access to political, social and economic rights and it took enormous sacrifices to recover this sovereignty and ensure these rights for their populations. As the U.S. Declaration of Independence says, the people have the right to get rid of their government when it oppresses them and has thereby failed in its responsibility to them. The people have inalienable rights and are sovereign. The concept of sovereignty as responsibility either means this and therefore means nothing new or it means something without any foundation in international law, namely that a foreign agency can exercise this responsibility. It should not become a "jemmy in the door of national sovereignty." The

championing the Charter system's default rule of non-intervention and denouncing the privilege embodied in the Permanent Five's veto, which effectively bolsters that default rule by requiring consensus among non-like-minded states. Nor is the tension within the legal argument purely abstract: when a *coup d'état* in ALBA member Honduras overthrew a Chávez and Ortega ally, President Manuel Zelaya, neither d'Escoto nor the Venezuelan and Nicaraguan governments adhered to the non-intervention language they invoke in other contexts (including, more recently, as to Libya and Syria). Even more incongruously, Venezuela and Nicaragua were among the only states in the world to recognize the statehood of Abkhazia and South Ossetia, de facto entities whose secession from Georgia is almost universally attributed to inadmissible Russian armed intervention.

On the whole, the Alliance's rhetoric on the question of intervention reflects more an expression of political resentment of a Great-Power-oriented double-standard than an affirmation of the legal principle of sovereign equality. Worse, the Venezuelan, Bolivian, Ecuadorean, Nicaraguan, and Cuban governments have called into question their commitment to humane values by taking the hardest of anti-interventionist lines in General Assembly votes on the Syrian conflict in 2012 and 2013. In doing so, they have found themselves aligned only with Russia, China, and five marginalized states: Belarus, Iran, North Korea, Zimbabwe, and Syria itself.[59]

concept of responsibility to protect is a sovereign's obligation and, if it is exercised by an external agency, sovereignty passes from the people of the target country to it. The people to be protected are transformed from bearers of rights to was of this agency.

Office of the President of the General Assembly, "Concept Note on Responsibility to Protect Populations from Genocide, War Crimes, Ethnic Cleansing and Crimes against Humanity" (July 23, 2009), pp. 1–2, available at www.un.org/ga/president/63/interactive/protect/conceptnote.pdf.

[59] See "General Assembly Adopts Text Condemning Violence in Syria, Demanding That All Sides End Hostilities," GA/11372 (May 15, 2013) (vote on GA Res. 67/262), www.un.org/News/Press/docs//2013/ga11372.doc.htm. See also GA Res. 66/253 www.un.org/News/Press/docs//2013/ga11372.doc.htm. See also GA Res. 66/253 (August 3, 2012).

While the ALBA governments have given renewed voice to Third World concerns about the basic structure of the global order, they have not succeeded in changing the terms of the international conversation. The credibility of their efforts has suffered from the tendency to indulge knee-jerk reactions against dominant global forces, at the expense of thoughtful and workable alternatives to prevailing normative trends.

V CONCLUSION

The Bolivarian Alliance has drawn sharply contrasting reactions from progressive commentators. For its staunchest supporters, it is the long-awaited model of a counter-hegemonic, participatory alternative to capitalistic globalization: "Breathing life into the dormant ideology of the Third World project, ALBA actualises the dreams of collaborative and state-specific development according to people-, not market-, based targets."[60] For its harshest critics, ALBA's programs of trade, investment and assistance are an unsustainable artifact of *chavista* political maneuvering; for them, the Chávez legacy reduces to the "dramatic concentration of power and open disregard for basic human rights."[61]

Although this brief treatment cannot hope to adjudicate a controversy in which so many essential facts are in dispute, some observations can be ventured. Massive oil subsidies (however obfuscated by non-market-based barter schemes) do not amount to a generalizable alternative to incorporation within a capitalistic global economy, but they may allow particular recipient states to invest in productive capacities – including human capital, through improvements in health and education – that will outlive the subsidies. Even if ALBA programs end up being sharply curtailed, they will potentially have made a permanent contribution to economic development in the poorer member states and in the member states of associated formations

---

[60] Mohsen Al Attar and Rosalie Miller, "Towards an Emancipatory International Law," p. 353.
[61] Human Rights Watch, "Venezuela: Chávez's Authoritarian Legacy."

such as Petrocaribe. And while the Alliance has not succeeded, by and large, in assuming a leadership role among the lesser developed countries (which encompass the widest range of interests and values),[62] it has renewed the presence of Third World militancy, disrupting global capitalism's aura of inevitability and creating space for more nuanced forms of resistance to unbalanced trade and investment regimes and to the dominant global political elites.[63]

As to their internal governance practices, Chávez and his allies present a mixed picture. Whatever their unsavory elements, the Alliance governments have provided substantial and hitherto-unknown gains to underprivileged sectors of their societies, in terms of both material improvements and meaningful inclusion in social institutions. For all of the erosion of institutional integrity and procedural correctness (and to some extent, civil liberty), there have been countervailing improvements for large numbers of people who had been denied not only rudimentary economic and social rights, but consequently the equal and effective enjoyment of civil and political rights, under more certifiably liberal-democratic predecessor governments.[64] The Alliance governments' *asistencialismo* cannot be dismissed as a political "dirty trick," since the conferral of benefits on previously ignored constituencies amounts to a democratic gain. Regardless of the genuineness of newfangled vehicles of popular

---

[62] It is noteworthy that outside of Venezuela and Nicaragua, Chávez lacked the broad popularity among Latin Americans that he so clearly craved. See "Latinobarómetro: Opinión Pública Latinoamericana, Informe Flash: La Imagen de Hugo Chavez, 1995–2011" (March 7, 2013), available at www.latinobarometro.org/latino/LATContenidos.jsp.

[63] Such opening of space might help to explain the appreciation for Chávez expressed by former Brazilian President Lula da Silva. Luiz Inacio (Lula) Da Silva, "Latin America After Chávez," *New York Times* (March 6, 2013), available at www.nytimes.com/2013/03/07/opinion/latin-america-after -chavez.html.

[64] See Ewan Robertson, "Analysts Confused as Venezuelans Say Their Country is Second Most Democratic in Region," *Venezuelanalysis.com*, (July 11, 2014), available at http://venezuelanalysis.com/news/10786 (reporting *Latinobarometro* poll showing the top five Latin American countries in popular assessment as democratic to be Uruguay, Venezuela, Argentina, Ecuador, and Nicaragua).

participation, the material interests of the popular classes have had unprecedented weight in political decision-making under the present governments of Venezuela, Nicaragua, Bolivia, and Ecuador, and this development promises to be difficult to reverse.

None of this is to overlook or to excuse the diminutions of transparency and accountability – and the attendant corruption and autocracy – that have come to be associated with the Alliance governments. But in a region marked by concentrated wealth, entrenched privilege, and pronounced social stratification, the term "democracy," if it is to be accorded moral weight, must be seen as having substantive as well as procedural requisites. If nothing else, the Bolivarian Alternative has prominently restored the socioeconomic component to the international conversation about democracy and human rights – a component that had been effectively relegated to the margins for nearly a generation.

8 GLOBAL CRISIS AND THE LAW OF WAR

Jeanne M. Woods

INTRODUCTION

The title of this collection invokes Sigmund Freud's celebrated critique of modernity[1] and Joseph Stiglitz's contemporary reprise.[2] The theme of discontent invites us to deconstruct discourses of power: discourses of civilization, globalization, and international law. Our task is to probe the lacunae between the emancipatory promises of transformative new orders and their ultimate malaise; to expose the desertification that mocks distant shimmering oases; and to radically channel the discontent that surfaces when the paradigms inevitably fail to keep their immanent promises. Instead of human happiness, prosperity, justice, and peace, these universalist narratives produce their opposites: misery, poverty, death.

It is significant that Freud penned *Civilization and its Discontents* in the interwar years. The unprecedented savagery of the First World War informed his critical assessment of the fruits of modernity: art, technology, order;[3] the social contract, law, justice.[4] Freud posits the goal of civilization as the subjugation of man's instinctual desire for aggression and self-destruction. This project is undermined, however, by its assumption of the right to employ violence to defend its achievements.[5] Paradoxically, then, violence is both a hallmark of civilization and its most formidable obstacle.[6]

---

[1] Sigmund Freud, *Civilization and its Discontents* (Martino Publishing Co., CT, 2010).

[2] Joseph Stiglitz, *Globalization and its Discontents* (Norton, 2003).

[3] Sigmund Freud, *Civilization and its Discontents* , p. 56.   [4] Ibid. , p. 59.

[5] Ibid., pp. 85–7.   [6] Ibid., pp. 99, 102.

In *Globalization and its Discontents*, Joseph Stiglitz offers a tentative insider challenge to the neoliberal phase of the global expansion of capitalism. Stiglitz acknowledges that the hegemony of market fundamentalism has enriched elites at the center of the global economy while immiserating the masses on its periphery. Yet he maintains that globalization, if properly "managed," has the potential to "enrich everyone in the world."[7]

International law embodies similar paradoxes: the presumption of righteousness implicit in law; the brutal injustice inherent in universalist conceits. This chapter explores the intersection of three such universalist paradigms: civilization, globalization, and the international law of war. As Foucault observed, dominant discourses from the sixteenth century onward posited "perpetual war" as the template of all social interaction.[8] War constructed territorially defined states in Europe,[9] carried them on a bloody mission to "civilize" the unknown world. Through war the state produced and reproduced itself as a legal entity; through civilization it constituted a legal regime to legitimate its violence.[10] Law promised to distinguish between "just" and "unjust" slaughter; to establish rules to apportion the savagery; to create remedies to rehabilitate the dead. This legal embrace of violence – the violence-as-normative paradigm – is a primal feature of the civilized state.

The violence-as-normative paradigm ensures the structural domination of a few militarily powerful states.[11] The discourse of civilization

---

[7] Joseph Stiglitz, *Globalization and its Discontents* , p. i.

[8] Michel Foucault, *Society Must Be Defended* (Lectures at the College de France 1975–76), David Macey (trans.), (Picador, NY, 2002).

[9] Max Weber, "What is Politics," in Charles Lemert (ed.), *Social Theory: The Multicultural & Classic Readings* (4th ed., 2010), p. 115(defining a state as a "human community that (successfully) claims the monopoly of the legitimate use of physical force within a given territory").

[10] See for example Bastiaan de Gaay Fortman, "The Dialectics of Western Law in a Non-Western World," in Jan Berting et al., *Human Rights in a Pluralist World: Individuals and Collectivities* (NY: RSC/Meekler, 1990), p. 242 (arguing that "[l]aw legitimates. It legitimates behavior of individuals and groups[;] it also legitimates public action including the use of force").

[11] See for example National Security Council, Executive Office of the President, "2002 National Security Strategy of the United States," available at http://

has provided ubiquitous rationalizations for this paradigm, from the conquest of the Americas to the recent Euro-American interventions in North Africa. The narrative is consistent, whether it is denominated the civilizing mission or the human rights movement; natural rights to trade or rights to democratic governance; the "clash of civilizations" or the war on terror.[12]

This chapter seeks to unpack this narrative. An historical analysis of these discourses, widely separated in time, reveals their intimate interconnections. Such an approach is absent from the Freudian critique. Steeped in the liberal tradition, Freud fails to situate modernity in the context of its historical antecedent: what, for Europeans, was a glorious age of discovery and enlightenment; what, for the Global South, meant invasion, genocide, conquest, and enslavement. Similarly, Stiglitz's analysis of contemporary globalization does not touch upon previous phases of the global expansion of capitalism – the trans-Atlantic slave trade, colonialism, the Scramble for Africa[13] – upon which the present order is built.[14] His assessment is further weakened by the presumptive legitimacy of liberal constructs: social contract, growth, development, poverty, free trade, rule of law.[15] This liberal discourse legitimates the international financial institutions Stiglitz purports to critique; reifies the Rawlsian myth that "the poor" share in the social contract;[16]

georgewbushwhitehouse.archives.gov/nsc/nss/2002/ (announcing U.S. intention to wage war unilaterally and preemptively, and to prevent the rise of a rival military power.).

[12] See for example Samuel Huntington, "The Clash of Civilizations and the Remaking of World Order," (Simon & Schuster, 1996) (positing that the clash of radically differing cultures, rather than ideologies or economics, will dominate future global politics); National Security Strategy of the United States, ("Bush Doctrine")(referring to the "enemies of civilization").

[13] "The Scramble for Africa" is the term used to describe the period between 1884 and 1914, when European powers rapidly colonized most of Africa. It was preceded by the Berlin Conference of 1884, when European states carved up the continent among themselves.

[14] See Samir Amin, *The Liberal Virus: Permanent War and the Americanization of the World* (NY: Monthly Review Press, 2004), p. 23.

[15] Joseph Stiglitz, *Globalization and its Discontents* , pp. 65, 78.   [16] Ibid.

and fails to wonder whether anyone would freely enter into a social contract wherein her poverty is a given.

A deconstruction of contemporary discourses of power must take into account the continuing resonance of history – of pre-Westphalian norms articulated by theorists such as Vitoria and Grotius that fashioned the foundations of international law,[17] launched a global civilizing mission, and legitimized the violent process of "accumulation by dispossession."[18] As a vehicle for accumulation by dispossession, nascent international legal norms facilitated the construction of a relentlessly expansionist system that situated the conquering powers of Europe at its center and the dominated peoples of the South on its periphery, enabling the emergence of capitalism as a global order.[19]

This system is in crisis. Its logic promotes accumulation (euphemistically "growth") for its own sake, subordinating competing social values. Today profits are highest in the voluble financial sector. In the productive sector profits are maximized by exporting manufacturing from the center to the low-wage periphery while dismantling small-scale agriculture. Through the reduction of the human person to passive consumer and spectator in a minimalist democracy, political elites dismantle social safety nets and the middle classes in the Euro-American center. In the periphery, global corporations pit impoverished workers against each other in a vicious race to the bottom. The exploitation of the periphery and pacification of domestic polities renders violence indispensable to the maintenance of the system, thus mandating its normative status.

This chapter posits that the current structural crisis portends an escalation of violence that could lead to wide-scale global war. Part II describes the geopolitical destabilization brought on by the

---

[17] Antony Anghie, "Francisco de Vitoria and the Colonial Origins of International Law," in *Imperialism, Sovereignty and the Making of International Law* (Cambridge University Press, 2005).

[18] I borrow this term from Egyptian scholar Samir Amin; see Samir Amin, *Global History: A View from the South* (UK: Fahamu/Pambazuka, 2011), pp. 7–8.

[19] Ibid. The core–periphery model was developed by the Dependency School, associated most closely with Andre Gunder Frank and *Walter Rodney*.

crisis. Part III surveys the recurrent use of the discourse of civilization to justify military aggression; Part IV retraces the evolution,
devolution, and resurrection of just war theory, and its role in both
the early construction of global capitalism and its contemporary
phase.

I ECONOMIC CRISIS AND GEOPOLITICS

The global financial meltdown denominated the Great Recession was
the latest in a series of economic crises to erupt since the 1970s. In
Freudian terms, these recurrent financial crashes epitomize the
human instinct to self-destruct. It is widely recognized that economic
volatility is a major risk factor for political upheaval and violent
reaction.[20] The consequences of economic crises for the majority of
people – increased unemployment, poverty, and despair – are omin-
ous threats to the status quo.[21] The Great Recession exacerbated
domestic political conflicts throughout the world, exemplified by the
so-called Arab Spring. At the same time, according to Dennis Blair,
former Director of U.S. National Intelligence, the crisis reduced the
credibility of U.S. management of the global economy and put U.S.
hegemony at risk.[22] Harvard historian Niall Ferguson concurs with

---

[20] According to a recent report by the U.S. intelligence community the crisis-
prone global economy will alter the global balance of power and trigger radical
economic and political changes at a speed unprecedented in modern history.
See National Intelligence Council Report, "Global Trends 2030: Alternative
Worlds," p. 14, available at http://globaltrends2030.files.wordpress.com/
2012/11/global-trends-2030-november2012.pdf.

[21] Niall Ferguson, "Foreign Policy Implications of the Global Economic Crisis,"
Remarks Prepared for the U.S. Senate Comm. on Foreign Relations
Roundtable, February 11, 2009.

[22] Dennis C. Blair, Director of National Intelligence, "Annual Threat
Assessment of the Intelligence Community," Unclassified Statement for the
Senate Select Comm. on Intelligence 2 (February 12, 2009)(stating that the
"widely held perception that excesses in U.S. financial markets and
inadequate regulation were responsible [for the crisis] has increased criticism
about free market policies [and] already has increased questioning of U.S.
stewardship of the global economy and the international financial structure").

Blair's assessment and anticipates a rise in conflicts with rival powers such as Russia and China over global resources and influence.[23]

The depth of the crisis – the first synchronized global downturn since the Great Depression – underscored the instability of late-stage capitalism, an era characterized by the subordination of the productive economy to highly profitable but dangerously speculative financial markets.[24] The chain reaction that began in the U.S. securitized mortgage market spread throughout the international banking system,[25] causing a decline in global production and trade and a sharp rise in protectionism.[26] These same economic indicators were major precipitating factors in the two global conflagrations of the twentieth century.[27]

Ferguson has labeled the financial crisis a crisis of globalization.[28] This frenzied liberalization and expansion of global production, trade, and financial markets that began in the late 1970s was a reaction to the "stagflation" earlier in the decade. As in earlier ages of expansion – ages of discovery and colonialism – globalization was

---

[23] Niall Ferguson, "Foreign Policy Implications of the Global Economic Crisis."

[24] Between 2000 and 2006 the assets of large global banks more than doubled – from $10 trillion to $23 trillion. James Crotty, "Structural causes of the global financial crisis: a critical assessment of the 'new financial architecture'," *Cambridge J of Econ.*, 33 (2009), p. 569.

[25] Niall Ferguson, "The Axis of Upheaval," *Foreign Policy Online* (February 16, 2009), available at www.foreignpolicy.com/articles/2009/02/16/the_axis_of_upheaval.

[26] According to Global Trade Alert (2013), over 3,330 new government protectionist measures, such as trade remedies, local content requirements, and discriminatory regulatory practices, have been reported since 2008, with 431 measures imposed during the year May 2012 to June 2013 alone – the highest in a single period to date. According to the International Labor Organization, global unemployment has increased by 28 million since the onset of the crisis. International Labor Organization, "Global Unemployment Trends 2013," available at www.ilo.org/wcmsp5/groups/public/–dgreports/—dcomm/—publ/documents/publication/wcms_202215.pdf.

[27] See generally, Andrew J. Crozier, *The Causes of the Second World War* (Blackwell Publishers Ltd., Oxford, 1997).

[28] For a comprehensive definition of globalization see Comm. on Economic, Social and Cultural Rights, Rep. on its 18th Sess., "Globalization and the Enjoyment of Economic, Social and Cultural Rights," ¶ 2, UN Doc. E/1999/22 (May 11, 1998).

facilitated by technological advancements in transportation and communications. The contemporary phase was accelerated by the opening of new markets in China and Eastern Europe. Guided by neoliberal ideology – the new *laissez-faire* – this expansion entailed the removal of local government controls over international flows of goods, services, technology, and capital, and the privatization of former state functions and public assets.

As neoliberalism minimized the regulatory intervention of the state,[29] it placed private corporations at the forefront of global economic expansion. Many global corporations have evolved into titans with economies rivaling those of small countries. Of the largest economies in the world, more than half are corporations.[30] Comparing GDP and sales, General Motors is now bigger than Denmark, Wal-Mart is bigger than Poland, and Exxon-Mobil is bigger than South Africa.[31] Their dominance gives them vast political power, evoking the role of private commercial enterprises in colonial expansion;[32] the legal subjectivity that enabled the first corporations to shape the international legal order is prominently absent from the prevailing Westphalian narrative.

In the new *laissez-faire* global economy state actors are relegated to supporting roles;[33] rather than protecting workers, consumers, and communities, they use their authority to reduce legal restrictions on

---

[29] See for example Susan Strange, *The Retreat of the State: the Emergence of Private Authority in Global Governance* (Cambridge University Press, 2002).

[30] For example, in 2000 Exxon-Mobil's gross sales were $210.3 billion while Indonesia's GDP was $153 million. See Frank R. Lopez, "Corporate Social Responsibility in a Global Economy after September 11: Profits, Freedom, and Human Rights," *Mercer L. Rev.*, 55 (2004), pp. 739–40. The size of corporations, measured by sales and the number of employees, is staggering. For example, Wal-Mart's workforce has grown from 62,000 employees in 1983 to 1,140,000 in 1999. Ibid. In terms of sales, it is now the largest company in the world.

[31] Ibid.

[32] See generally Stephen R. Brown, *Merchant Kings: When Companies Ruled the World, 1600–1900* (Thomas Dunn Books, NY, 2009).

[33] See for example Robin F. Hansen, "Multinational Enterprise Pursuit of Minimized Liability: Law, International Business Theory and the Prestige Oil Spill," *Berkeley J. Int'l L.*, 26 (2008), pp. 424–5.

the activities of corporations. States also have at their disposal a network of powerful postwar multilateral institutions with a mission to promote globalization;[34] at the same time, these institutions can be manipulated or circumvented should they become obstacles to profit maximization. For example, the United States and the EU utilize free trade agreements that allow them to impose trade concessions on weaker states outside of the consensus strictures of the WTO, while using NATO to sideline the United Nations – as Germany, Italy, and Japan sidelined the League of Nations in the prelude to the Second World War.

According to political economist James Crotty, these developments accelerated the ascendency of finance capital:

> Several decades of deregulation ... grossly inflated the size of financial markets relative to the real economy. The value of all financial assets in the US grew from four times GDP in 1980 to ten times GDP in 2007. In 1981 household debt was 48% of GDP, while in 2007 it was 100%. Private sector debt was 123% of GDP in 1981 and 290% by late 2008 ... The share of corporate profits generated in the financial sector rose from 10% in the early 1980s to 40% in 2006, while its share of the stock market's value grew from 6% to 23%.[35]

The reign of finance capital ensures that its interests prevail over the public interest. Therefore, in the wake of a crisis of its own creation, finance capital is immunized from its catastrophic consequences – its private liabilities are nationalized by compliant political elites who bail out banks while imposing austerity measures to balance the books on the backs of the public.[36] Hence a "jobless recovery" can coexist with massive financial sector earnings, generating an unprecedented growth of income inequality.[37] One scholar has described finance capitalism

---

[34] For example the United Nations (UN), the Bretton Woods Institutions, the World Trade Organization, a plethora of Bilateral Investment Treaties (BITs), and regionally based Free Trade Agreements (FTAs).
[35] James Crotty, "Structural causes of the global financial crisis," p. 575.
[36] Joseph Stiglitz, *Globalization and its Discontents*, p. 209.
[37] Professor David Moss of Harvard Business School found that income disparities between rich and poor widened as government regulations eased and bank failures rose. See Louise Story, "Income Inequality and Financial

as a "vampire economy that competes with and sucks the blood of the real or productive economy. The logic of the vampire economy is that while it lives on the real economy, it will eventually take it down."[38]

The predominance in an economy of a sector that produces only debt is inherently irrational, and is symptomatic of the deepening structural crisis of global capitalism, reflected in the intermittent sovereign debt crises. The irrationality of the system is further demonstrated by the failure of the leading economies to redress the destruction of the life-support system of the planet in favor of accelerated commodification of its resources – perhaps more support for Freud's theory that humanity is driven by a self-destructive instinct.[39] Basic needs are subordinated to corporate profits as national social contracts are shredded and social safety nets, education, health care, and even rudimentary infrastructure are abandoned.

For the peoples of the periphery – 80 percent of the world's population – these conditions have long been a way of life. The crisis hit the poorest countries in Africa and Latin America especially hard because of their export-dependent economies.[40] For them the crisis means increased misery, increased dependence, and increased violence.

As law evolves in the context of crisis its tendency is to regress. Decades of deregulation to promote corporate hegemony has reduced the role of the state to its police function. In the United States, we are witnessing growing repression and attacks on democratic forms, from voter suppression measures to outright corporate takeover of

Crises" (August 21, 2010), www.nytimes.com/2010/08/22/weekinreview/22story.html?_r=0.

[38] Anthony Monteiro, "The Existential Crisis of Capitalism," available at http://blackagendareport.com/print/content/existential-crisis-us-capitalism.

[39] See Sigmund Freud, *Civilization and its Discontents*, pp. 97–8 (discussing the "death instinct").

[40] Desmond Lachman, American Enterprise Institute, "Foreign Policy Implications of the Global Economic Crisis," Senate Foreign Relations Comm. Roundtable, February 11, 2009, available at www.aei.org/article/foreign-and-defense-policy/foreign-policy-implications-of-the-global-economic-crisis/.

economically depressed communities. The intersection of the state
with finance capital was epitomized when two dozen people were
arrested at a Citibank in Manhattan for attempting to close their
accounts![41]

A state of emergency declared more than twelve years ago
remains in place.[42] This legal *status quo* countenances violent repression of political protest;[43] unprecedented mass surveillance on a
global scale; and aggressive militarism in the form of a Hobbesian
permanent "war on terror." An old, discredited theory – the "just
war" doctrine – has been revived to legitimate this war and other
questionable uses of force.

---

[41] See www.dailykos.com/story/2011/10/15/1026740/-Breaking-30-Citibank
    -customers-arrested-for-closing-their-account-With-Citibank-Statement
    -Update.
[42] For the Executive Order issued by President George W. Bush declaring a
    national state of emergency following the September 11 attacks, see 66 Fed.
    Reg. 48201 (September 14, 2001). The Order has been reaffirmed annually
    by Barack Obama. For the 2013 Order see www.whitehouse.gov/the-press
    -office/2013/09/10/notice-continuation-national-emergency-notice.
[43] See for example "Take Back the Streets: Repression and Criminalization of
    Protest Around the World," an ACLU collaborative effort, October 2013,
    available at https://www.aclu.org/files/assets/global_protest_suppression_
    report_inclo.pdf. Police responses to the nonviolent Occupy movement are
    emblematic of a disturbing pattern of government conduct: the tendency to
    transform individuals exercising a fundamental democratic right – the right to
    protest – into a perceived threat that requires a forceful government response.
    The case studies detailed in this report, each written by a different domestic
    civil liberties and human rights organization, provide contemporary examples
    of different governments' reactions to peaceful protests. They document
    instances of unnecessary legal restrictions, discriminatory responses,
    criminalization of leaders, and unjustifiable – at times deadly – force. An FBI
    document dated October 19, 2012, released pursuant to a Freedom of
    Information Act request, contained the following statement: "An indentified
    (*sic*)(unknown) received intelligence that indicated that protestors in New
    York and Seattle planned similar protests in Houston, Dallas, San Antonio,
    and Austin, Texas. (Unknown) planned to gather intelligence against the
    leaders of the protest groups and obtain photographs, then formulate a plan to
    kill the leadership via suppressed sniper rifles."

II WHAT'S PAST IS PROLOGUE: THE STRANGE CAREER OF CIVILIZATION

As Freud theorized, civilization employs violence to suppress the "primitive." The discourse of civilization was elaborated by western scholars from the fifteenth through the nineteenth centuries to justify the violent dispossession of "primitive" peoples, the accumulation of their lands and resources, and their annexation to the emergent sovereign states. The new sovereignty discourse defined "civilized" in accordance with the religion, culture, and political organization of Europe, constructing racist doctrines of discovery, conquest, and statehood.[44] As Justice Joseph Story noted, "[a]s infidels, heathens, and savages [non-Europeans] were not allowed to possess the prerogatives belonging to . . . independent nations."[45] Ironically, successful violence would eventually allow some "infidels" to attain these prerogatives; in the nineteenth century victory in war against European states was the price of admission for Japan and Turkey into the exclusive "family of civilized nations."[46]

Accumulation by violent dispossession was promoted by both religious and secular authorities. In *Inter Caetera*, or the Bull of Demarcation, Pope Alexander VI proclaimed the newly "discovered" lands of the Americas the property of the Spanish and the Portuguese. Sixteenth-century theologian Thomas More asserted a right to wage war "[i]f the natives won't do what they're told," especially if they deny settlers their "natural right" to indigenous lands.[47] In his seminal study of the work of Francisco Vitoria, Professor Antony Anghie located the emergence of modern international law in this

[44] See Robert Williams, *The American Indian in Western Legal Thought: The Discourses of Conquest* (1990), p. 15.

[45] Joseph Story, "Commentaries," §152, reprinted in M. F. Lindley, *The Acquisition and Government of Backward Territory in International Law* (1926), p. 29.

[46] Turkey was admitted to the Concert of Europe through the 1856 Treaty of Paris after defeating Russia in the Crimean War; Japan became officially "civilized" in 1905 after defeating Russia in the war over Manchuria, becoming the first Asian state in modern times to defeat a European power.

[47] Thomas More, *Utopia* (1516) (1965), pp. 79–80.

pre-Westphalian discourse.[48] Anghie demonstrated that the international legal regime was constructed to provide the rules of engagement for "accumulation by dispossession" by the rival European powers.[49] Proto-capitalist theories of property rights informed the discourse of civilization, rationalizing the conquest of "primitive" lands.[50] Locke argued that property rights should be denied to "the wild Indian, who knows no enclosure, and is still a tenant in common."[51] Vattel built on Lockean property rights theory to legalize annexation of territory inhabited by "savages."[52] Critiquing this expansion of the doctrine of *terra nullius* (the right to annex land belonging to no one) Sir William Blackstone (1723–1780) wrote:

> [H]ow far the seising on countries already peopled, and driving out or massacring the innocent and defenceless natives, merely because they differed from their invaders in language, in religion, in custom, in government, or in colour; how far such a conduct was consonant to nature, to reason, or to Christianity, deserved well to be considered by those, who have rendered themselves immortal by thus civilizing mankind.[53]

III JUST WAR THEORY: "WAR IS PEACE"[54]

Just war theory was an indispensable instrument of the civilizing mission. This legal rationalization of state violence evolved from the

---

[48] Antony Anghie, "Francisco de Vitoria and the Colonial Origins of International Law," in *Imperialism, Sovereignty and the Making of International Law* (Cambridge Univ. Press, 2005).

[49] Ibid., pp. 331–3. See also *Johnson* v. *M'Intosh*, 21 U.S. 543, 573 (1823) (defining the doctrine of discovery).

[50] John Locke, *Second Treatise of Government* ¶31.   [51] Ibid. at ¶25.

[52] William Blackstone, *Commentaries on the Laws of England* (17th ed., 1830) Book I, Ch. XVIII, §205 – §209.

[53] Ibid., Book II, Ch.1, p. 7.

[54] George Orwell, 1984 (Signet Classic, 1950), p. 6. Augustine theorized that the purpose of a just war is to promote peace. See John Mark Mattox, *Saint Augustine & the Theory of Just War* (Continuum Books, 2006), pp. 45–60; Mark Evans, "Moral Theory and the Idea of a Just War," in Mark Evans (ed.) *Just War Theory: A Reappraisal* (Edinburgh University Press,

works of Aristotle,[55] Augustine of Hippo,[56] and Thomas Aquinas.[57] The two latter theorists wrote to refute the early Christian doctrine that eschewed recourse to war and violence.[58] Following the official embrace of Christianity by the Roman Emperor Constantine, the universalist themes of the new faith were deployed in furtherance of Empire. Christian leaders modified their pacifist views as they reimagined the Roman Empire as a "divinely approved political vehicle for the furthering of the Christian faith."[59] Thus, Augustine and Aquinas argued that Christians should use force despite biblical calls to pacifism, asserting a *duty* to wage war akin to domestic law enforcement.[60] Aquinas emphasized the naturalness of just war.[61] The doctrine venerated the eternal battle between good and evil, conflating concepts of vengeance, punishment, and defense.[62] As Jonathan Bush explains, just war grew to legitimate "centuries of Crusades against Muslims ... Baltic pagans [and] dissidents ... wars of reconquest against breakaway Protestant kingdoms, systematic

---

2005), pp. 1, 9, and 15 (arguing that "the goal of a just war is a just peace"); and Joseph L. Falvey, Jr., "Our Cause is Just: An Analysis of Operation Iraqi Freedom Under International Law and the Just War Doctrine," *Ave Maria L. Rev.*, 2 (2004), p. 67.

[55] Aristotle, *Nicomachean Ethics*, Terence Irwin (trans.), (Hackett Publishing, 1991).

[56] Augustine, "Contra Faustum," in E. M. Atkins and R. J. Dodaro (eds.), *Political Writings* (Cambridge University Press, 2001).

[57] Thomas Aquinas, *On Law, Morality and Politics*, Richard J. Regan and William P. Baumgrath (eds.), (2nd ed., 2003).

[58] Stephen C. Neff, *War and the Law of Nations: A General History* (Cambridge University Press, 2005), p. 38.

[59] Ibid., p. 46.

[60] Augustine, "Contra Faustum." Aquinas argued that "[j]ust as it is lawful for [rulers] to have recourse to the sword in defending [the] common weal against individual disturbances, so too it is their business to have recourse to the sword of war in defending the common weal against external enemies." Thomas Aquinas, *On Law, Morality and Politics* , pp. 221–2.

[61] Frederick H. Russell, *The Just War in the Middle Ages* (Cambridge University Press, 1975), p. 300.

[62] Ibid., p. 305.

atrocities against Jews, and wars of expansion against indigenous peoples in the New World, Africa and Asia."[63]

Vitoria and Grotius took just war from theology to law. As a legal construct, the doctrine situated the war power exclusively in the hands of the sovereign.[64] Thus, just war theory was the midwife of the infant state. Invoking the discourse of civilization and the universalist claims of natural law, Vitoria united just war theory with the emergent sovereignty discourse to construct the state as an exclusively European, Christian entity. He theorized a law of nations that recognized only Christians as having the capacity to engage in just war and hence claim sovereignty.[65] At the same time, this law of nations established universally binding norms that conferred upon Europeans the right to travel and reside in Indian lands; to engage in trade and make a profit in their territory; to exploit their gold and other natural resources; to acquire citizenship; and to proselytize.[66] Within Vitoria's universalism, the imprimatur of the "civilized states" overrode the customs, rights, and wishes of the indigenous people. Indeed, dire consequences – war, plunder, enslavement – attended any rejection of Europeans' natural rights.[67] Vitoria expressly invoked a concept of humanitarian intervention "[i]f the Indians ... prevent the Spaniards from freely preaching the Gospel." In that case he argued that, "in favor of those who are oppressed and suffer wrong, the Spaniards can make war [and] seiz[e] the lands and territory of the natives."[68]

---

[63] Jonathan A. Bush, "'The Supreme ... Crime' and its Origins: The Lost Legislative History of the Crime of Aggressive War," *Colum. L. Rev.*, 102 (2002), p. 2330.

[64] Ibid., p. 221.

[65] Franscisi de Vitoria, *De Indis Et De Ivre Belli Reflectiones*, James B. Scott and Ernest Nys (eds.), John P. Bate (trans.) (1917; written 1532, published 1557), ¶435, p. 173.

[66] Ibid., pp. 151–4.

[67] According to Vitoria, "when the Indians deny the Spaniards their rights under the law of nations they do them a wrong. Therefore, if it be necessary, in order to preserve their right, that they should go to war, they may lawfully do so." Ibid., p. 154.

[68] Ibid., p. 157.

A century later, in the face of growing discontent with just war theory,[69] Dutch jurist Hugo Grotius waged a polemic against pacifism,[70] further refining the doctrine. Grotius affirmed the legality of the conquest of territory by force[71] and elaborated a theory of private property that privileged such conquest.[72] The Grotian rights of conquest included *inter alia* the right to employ force and terror;[73] to capture property *even if the war is not just*;[74] to enslave prisoners of war;[75] and to exercise dominion over the conquered territory and peoples.[76]

Thus was the state born in the flames of war. Conquest, plunder, and enslavement were made formal legal tools of state- and empire-building.[77] The Hobbesian construction of internal sovereignty imagined permanent war necessitating a powerful absolutist state.[78] The role of force in constructing external sovereignty is pithily

---

[69] See Mark W. Janis, "Religion and the Literature of International Law: Some Standard Texts," in Mark W. Janis and Carolyn Evans (eds.), *Religion and International Law* (1999), pp. 121–2. See also Jann K. Kleffner and Carsten Stahn (eds.), *Jus Post Bellum: Towards a Law of Transition From Conflict to Peace* (T. M. C. Asser Press, 2008), p. 15.

[70] Ibid., p. 54.

[71] Hugo Grotius, *De Jure Belli ac Pacis* (The Rights of War and Peace) (1625) Book III, Ch. VI.

[72] Ibid., Ch.II, Book II, §II.

[73] Ibid., p. 294. ("Wars ... must employ force and terror as their most proper agents.")

[74] Ibid., p. 335 ("[A]ccording to the law of nations, not only the person who makes war upon just grounds; but anyone whatever, engaged in regular and formal war, becomes absolute proprietor of everything which he takes from the enemy.").

[75] Ibid., p. 346.   [76] Ibid., p. 348.

[77] As Tilly writes, "all of Europe was to be divided into distinct and sovereign states. ... Over the next three hundred years [after Westphalia] the Europeans and their descendants managed to impose that state system on the entire world." Charles Tilly, "Reflections on the History of European State-Making," in Charles Tilly (ed.), *Formation of National States in Western Europe* (Princeton University Press, 1975), pp. 45–6.

[78] Thomas Hobbes, *Leviathan* (1651), (Legal Classics Library, 2012), pp. 96, 128.

summarized by Charles Tilly: "War made the state and the state made war."[79]

In the European center, the territorial state evolved to become the dominant form of political organization. In the colonized periphery polities that were independent sovereign entities before the European confrontation became vassals tied to their "mother" countries. Once consolidated, the European states formally outlawed mercenaries, pirates, and private war.[80] Today, as the territorial state devolves, mercenary private contractors are once again legitimate actors, waging war in the periphery.[81] The former colonies, though juridical states, remain de facto protectorates under the tutelage of the western-dominated international financial institutions. These weak states are ever vulnerable to the threat of violence.

According to recent scholarship, civil war has replaced inter-state war as the dominant contemporary manifestation of the violence-as-normative paradigm.[82] Most of these deadly conflicts are taking place

---

[79] Charles Tilly (ed.), *Formation of National States in Western Europe* , p. 44. See also Robert C. Stacey, "The Age of Chivalry," in Michael Howard, George J. Andreopoulos, and Mark R. Shulman (eds.), *The Laws of War* (Yale University Press, 1994), p. 39.

[80] See generally Janice E. Thompson, *Mercenaries, Pirates and Sovereigns: State-Building and Extraterritorial Violence in Early Modern Europe* (Princeton University Press, 1994).

[81] In a sobering study, Joseph Stiglitz details the prominence of private mercenary contractors. See Joseph E. Stiglitz and Linda J. Blimes, *The Three Trillion Dollar War: The True Cost of the Iraq Conflict* (W.W. Norton & Co., 2008).

[82] See generally P. Collier, A. Hoeffler, L. Elliot, H. Hegre, M. Reynal-Querol and N. Sambanis, *Breaking the Conflict Trap: Civil War & Development Policy* (Oxford University Press, 2003); Paul Collier and Anke Hoofer, "The Challenge of Reducing the Global Incidence of Civil War," Center for the Study of African Economies, Dept. of Economics, Oxford University, March 26, 2004, available at www.copenhagenconsensus.com/Files/Filer/CC/Papers/Conflicts_230404.pdf.; Paul Collier and Nicholas Sambanis (eds.), *Understanding Civil War (Volume I: Africa): Evidence & Analysis* (2005); Paul Collier and Nicholas Sambanis (eds.), *Understanding Civil War (Volume II: Europe, Central Asia, & Other Regions): Evidence & Analysis* (2005); Michele D'Avolio, "Regional Human Rights Courts & Internal Armed Conflicts," *Intercultural Hum. Rts. L. Rev.*, 2 (2007), p. 261; and Emily Crawford,

in former colonial territories.[83] The erasure of the sovereignty of the multiplicity of indigenous peoples forcibly incorporated into colonial regimes[84] ensures the persistence of violent conflict.[85]

Globalization has further eroded stability in the postcolony through the imposition of market fundamentalism. The work of Jean Comaroff and John Comaroff documents how the deregulation of state functions together with the economic immiseration of these polities has created a sinister new version of the violence-as-normative paradigm: "violence as a means of production."[86] Under this paradigm ruling regimes "cede[] their monopoly over coercion to private contractors, who plunder and enforce at their behest,"[87] a phenomenon that resembles the use of chartered companies by European states in the pre-colonial period.

IV JUST WAR: THE RESURRECTION

Post–Cold War discourse on the law of war evidences a tendency – sometimes overt, sometimes subtext – to posit the arrival of a

---

"Unequal before the Law: The Case for the Elimination of the Distinction between International & Non-International Armed Conflicts," *Leiden J. Int'l L.*, 20 (2007), p. 441.

[83] In Africa alone, devastating civil wars were responsible for the deaths of over 12 million people between 1963 and 2002. United Nations Development Programme [UNDP], "Armed Violence in Africa: Reflections on the Costs of Crime and Conflict," October 2007 (prepared by Robert Muggah), available at www.undp.org/cpr/documents/armed_violence/AV_crime_conflict.pdf. More than five million people have died in the Congolese civil war, making it the deadliest conflict since World War II. BBC, "DRC Death Toll More Than 5 Million," available at http://news.bbc.co.uk/2/hi/africa/7202384.stm.

[84] See Makau Wa Mutua, "Why Redraw the Map of Africa: A Moral and Legal Inquiry," *Mich. J. Int'l L.*, 16 (1995), pp. 1138–40; and James Thuo Gathii, "International Law & Eurocentricity," *Eur. J. Int'l L.*, 9 (1998), p. 187.

[85] See Obiora Chinedu Okafor, *Re-defining Legitimate Statehood International Law and State Fragmentation in Africa* (Martinus Nijhoff, 2000), pp. 35–9.

[86] Jean Comaroff and John L. Comaroff, "Law and Disorder in the Postcolony: An Introduction," in Jean Comaroff and John Comaroff (eds.), *Law and Disorder in the Postcolony* (2006), pp. 2–6.

[87] Ibid., p. 9.

"Grotian moment" – a historic rupture from the past as a new, transformative norm is born.[88] The proposed new norm would privilege uses of force that are not countenanced by the United Nations Charter. The timing of this new moment is no accident; military intervention furthers neoliberal globalization, allowing the penetration of regions previously inaccessible to capital or not accessible on its terms.[89] Anne Orford points out: "[t]he narrative of intervention masks the involvement of international economic institutions and development agencies in shaping those societies that later erupt into humanitarian and security crises."[90] Central to this law of war discourse is the assertion of universal moral principles that proponents argue should override positive law, such as Anne-Marie Slaughter's contention that the NATO bombing of Yugoslavia was "illegal but legitimate."[91] Lillich argues that there has been a political evolution that has changed the meaning of Article 2(4) to allow humanitarian interventions. He attempts to parse Articles 2(4) and 51 of the UN Charter, arguing that humanitarian intervention does not violate the territorial integrity or political independence of a state, or that pre-emptive military action is encompassed within the inherent right of self-defense preserved in

---

[88] See Saul Mendlovitz and Mary Datan, "Judge Weeramantry's Grotian Quest," *Transnational L & Contemporary Problems*, 7 (1997), p. 402 (defining the term "Grotian moment"). See also Boutros Boutros-Ghali, "The Role of International law in the Twenty-first Century: A Grotian Moment," *Fordham Int'l L.J.*, 18 (1995), p. 1613 (describing the creation of ad hoc war crimes tribunals as such a transformational moment).

[89] See James Thuo Gathii, *War, Commerce, and International Law* (Oxford University Press, 2010), p. 199. ("Wars over resources in [postcolonial] countries coincide with the promotion of free markets in mineral-extractive activities.")

[90] Anne Orford, *Reading Humanitarian Intervention* (Cambridge University Press, 2003), p. 188.

[91] See Anne-Marie Slaughter, "Good Reasons for Going Around the U.N.," *New York Times*, March 18, 2003, available at www.nytimes.com/2003/03/18/opinion/good-reasons-for-going-around-the-un.html. See also Bruno Simma, "NATO, the U.N. and the Use of Force: Legal Aspects," *European J Int'l L.*, 10 (1999), p. 1; and Michael J. Glennon, "The New Intervention: the Search for a Just International Law," *Foreign Affairs*, 78 (1999), p. 2.

Article 51.[92] Some scholars have offered post hoc arguments that intervention that achieves more good than harm ought to be considered legitimate.[93] Others argue that force used to protect human rights is consistent with the Charter.[94] A United Nations high-level panel embraced a collective "responsibility to protect" [95] as an

[92] See Richard B. Lillich, "Intervention to Protect Human Rights," *McGill L.J.*, 15 (1969), pp. 211–12. Two arguments are used to justify such a political evolution: first, that it does not impair the political independence or territorial integrity of a state, and second that, in any event, when it comes to the protection of nationals abroad intervention is permissible as an extension of the concept of self-defense in Article 51.

[93] See for example Jane Stromseth, "Rethinking Humanitarian Intervention," in J. L. Holzgrefe and Robert O. Keohane (eds.), *Humanitarian Intervention: Ethical, Legal, & Political Dilemmas* (Cambridge University Press, 2003), p. 267–9.

[94] See for example Fernando R. Teson, *Humanitarian Intervention: an Inquiry into Law and Morality* (3rd rev. ed., 2005), p. 217.

[95] The Responsibility to Protect is set forth in paragraphs 138 and 139 of the 2005 World Summit Outcome Document:

"Each individual State has the responsibility to protect its populations from genocide, war crimes, ethnic cleansing and crimes against humanity. This responsibility entails the prevention of such crimes, including their incitement, through appropriate and necessary means. We accept that responsibility and will act in accordance with it.

The international community, through the United Nations, also has the responsibility to use appropriate diplomatic, humanitarian and other peaceful means, in accordance with Chapters VI and VIII of the Charter, to help protect populations from genocide, war crimes, ethnic cleansing and crimes against humanity. In this context, we are prepared to take collective action, in a timely and decisive manner, through the Security Council, in accordance with the Charter, including Chapter VII, on a case-by-case basis and in cooperation with relevant regional organizations as appropriate, should peaceful means be inadequate and national authorities manifestly fail to protect their populations from genocide, war crimes, ethnic cleansing and crimes against humanity."

This text was adopted by the General Assembly in Resolution 60/1. 2005 World Summit Outcome, A/RES/60/1, at ¶¶138–139 (October 24, 2005). The Security Council endorsed the text of the Outcome Document in Resolution 1674: "The Security Council ... [r]eaffirms the provisions of paragraphs 138 and 139 of the 2005 World Summit Outcome Document

emerging customary norm that could justify military intervention.[96] The discursive shape-shifting oscillates from defense of allies to humanitarian intervention to "R2P." [97]

regarding the responsibility to protect populations from genocide, war crimes, ethnic cleansing and crimes against humanity." S.C. Res. 1674, UN Doc. S/RES/1674 (April 28, 2006).

[96] A More Secure World: Our Shared Responsibility, Report of the High-Level Panel on Threats, Challenges and Change, UN Doc. A/59/565 at paras. 202, 201 (2004), available at www.un.org/secureworld/report.pdf. But see Carsten Stahn, "Responsibility to Protect: Political Rhetoric or Emerging Legal Norm?", *Am. J Int'l L*., 101 (2007), p. 120 (concluding, after reviewing propositions asserted by proponents, that responsibility to protect is "in many ways still a political catchword rather than a legal norm").

[97] States contesting the R2P trajectory argue that serious procedural irregularities taint its unanimous adoption at the UN Global Summit. The meeting notes at the 60th session indicate that no debate was held prior to taking the Outcome Document to a vote. Opponents argue that the final draft was delivered to delegates immediately before the vote, contrary to UN rules, and that only a small number of Members were involved in its drafting. The first open debate on the responsibility to protect did not take place until June 2006, eight months after its adoption by the General Assembly. See Press Release from the S.C. (SC/8763), "More Progress Needed to Ensure Better Protection for Civilians in Armed Conflict" (June 28, 2006). States critical of the doctrine include Venezuela and Cuba, see UN GAOR, 60th Sess., 8th plen. mtg., UN Doc. A/60/PV.8 (September 16, 2005); China, see Press Release from the S.C. (SC/8763), "More Progress Needed to Ensure Better Protection for Civilians in Armed Conflict" (June 28, 2006); The Russian Federation, see Press Release from the S.C. (SC/884), "United Action Needed to Protect Civilians in Armed Conflict" (December 4, 2006); Mexico, see Press Release from the S.C. (SC/9057), "More and More Innocent Civilians Caught In Conflict, Not Enough Being Done to Provide Protection for Defenceless" (June 22, 2007); Sudan, see Press Release from the S.C. (SC/9571), "Security Council, in Presidential Statement, Reaffirms Commitment to Protection of Civilians in Armed Conflict" (January 14, 2009); Sri Lanka, see Press Release from the S.C. (SC/9786), "Security Council, Expressing Deep Regret Over Toll On Civilians in Armed Conflict, Reaffirms Readiness to Respond to their Deliberate Targeting" (November 11, 2009); and Malaysia, see Press Release from the S.C. (SC/9786), "Security Council, Expressing Deep Regret Over Toll On Civilians in Armed Conflict, Reaffirms Readiness to Respond to their Deliberate Targeting" (November 11, 2009); India, Egypt, and Pakistan, see General Assembly 64th Session, The United

In essence, these commentators are reasserting the doctrine of the "just war." Significantly, as with just war doctrine, proponents of this "new" norm seek to transform military aggression into a legal duty. For such a norm to be successfully implemented, intra-state violence must be normatively re-framed: internal armed conflict or civil war must be re-characterized as genocide or crimes against humanity, implicating post-war international criminal law.[98] This transformation was heralded when the Security Council began unilaterally to expand its mandate after the Cold War.

The "Grotian moment" was endorsed in U.S. President Barack Obama's Nobel Prize acceptance speech,[99] which sought to provide an *opinio juris* for a norm of military intervention. Obama's speech made clear his commitment to defending capitalism against the barbarians at the gate. He invoked the Hobbesian conception of human nature, arguing that "force is sometimes necessary [because of] the imperfections of man and the limits of reason." He echoed Aquinas when declaring that war is natural, at times "morally justified," a "necessity" and "an expression of human feelings."[100] Like its medieval counterpart, the Obama Doctrine dangerously frames the debate in terms of an existential contest between good and evil, a struggle that by definition can never end.

Nations (July 12, 2011), www.un.org/webcast/ga2009.html (Video of the debate available for download).

[98] For example, in Security Council Resolution 1556, demanding that the Sudanese government disarm the Janjaweed militias, the Council declared that "the Government of Sudan bears the primary responsibility to respect human rights while maintaining law and order and protecting its population within its territory." S.C. Res. 1556 (July 30, 2004). In 2011, U.S. President Barak Obama defended NATO intervention in the Libyan civil war by claiming that there was a "looming genocide" in Benghazi. www.nytimes .com/2011/03/29/world/africa/29prexy.html?pagewanted=all?_r=0.

[99] See U.S. President Barack Obama, 2009 Nobel Prize Acceptance Speech: A Just & Lasting Peace (December 10, 2009)("Obama Doctrine"), available at www.nobelprize.org/nobel_prizes/peace/laureates/2009/obama-lecture .html.

[100] Ibid., p. 3.

This argument segues neatly into the narrative of the war on terror, a narrative that mirrors just war doctrine, swathed in righteousness and laced with the discourse of civilization. The interminable nature of the war reprises Vitoria, for whom war against non-Christians is "perpetual and [the pagans] can never make amends for the wrongs and damages they have wrought."[101] Indeed, in "the case of the unbeliever ... it is useless ever to hope for a just peace on any terms."[102] Under just war theory the war on terror becomes a juridical institution: justice assumes legality, while war is the ultimate enforcement mechanism.

The renaissance of just war theory can be traced to Michael Walzer's philosophical treatise *Just and Unjust Wars,* a reassertion of this once-discredited doctrine in liberal clothing.[103] The resurrected just war doctrine retains its ontological underpinnings, while like the early natural law theorists, its proponents claim to be informed by a universal objective morality.[104]

Contemporary just war advocate Mark Evans crafts a secular restatement of Augustine's dichotomous "City of God" and "City of Man," positing just war as non-ideal but necessary in an imperfect

[101] Franscisi de Vitoria, *De Indis Et De Ivre Belli Reflectiones,* ¶453, p. 181.

[102] Ibid. at ¶457, p. 183.

[103] See Michael Walzer, *Just And Unjust Wars: A Moral Argument With Historical Illustrations* (3rd ed., 2000), p. 85. Walzer and other commentators argue that the human rights corpus would be meaningless if no implicit power of collective or individual enforcement were read into them. Ibid., p. 107. Others argue that unilateral interventions should be acceptable within zones of influence or when necessary to gather evidence in international proceedings. See Myres S. McDougal and W.Michael Reisman, "Response by Professors McDougal and Reisman," *Int'l Law.,* 3 (1969), pp. 438, 442–4 (arguing that humanitarian intervention is a well-established principal of customary international law).

[104] Mark Evans, "Moral Theory and the Idea of a Just War," pp. 1, 8 (arguing that "the morality from which [just war] draws its theory of justice ... holds that there are right and wrong answers to the moral questions it poses and thus rejects the idea of moral relativism. ... A concomitant feature of just war theory's moral objectivism is its universalism ... applicable to all human societies and situations and provid[ing] a shared basis from which the morality of all conflicts may be assessed.")

world.[105] (Illegal but legitimate?)[106] His reformulation retains the medieval conflation of *jus ad bellum* and *jus in bello*,[107] allowing a just warrior to selectively apply humanitarian law.[108] Indeed, under Evans's "supreme emergency exemption" the core value of IHL, the principle of distinction, may be suspended.[109] In the same vein, Vitoria argued that "it is indubitably lawful to carry off both the children and women of the Saracen [Muslim] into captivity and slavery."[110] As Anghie observed, it is the construction of the barbarian through the discourse of civilization that rationalizes such exceptions.[111] The war on terror as juridical institution re-constructs the Islamist as barbarian; thus the use of weaponized drones that kill innocent civilians has gone effectively unchallenged by the international community.[112] In a war against the uncivilized there are no innocents.

---

[105] Ibid., p. 9.

[106] See Anne-Marie Slaughter, "Good Reasons for Going Around the U.N."

[107] Aquinas contended that it is the justness of the initial resort to war that governs what is lawful conduct in war. Judith Gail Gardam, "Proportionality and Force in Int'l Law," *Am. J. Int'l L.* (1993), p. 395. See also Robert C. Stacey, "The Age of Chivalry," p. 30 ("Theology, prior to the 16th century concentrated almost exclusively on the right to declare war."). These elements were separated by jurists such as Vitoria and Grotius. Theodor Meron, "Common Rights of Mankind in Gentile, Grotius & Suarez," in *War Crimes Law Comes of Age: Essays* (Oxford University Press, 1998), p. 122.

[108] "One must observe all national and international laws governing the conduct of war *which do not fundamentally conflict* with the theory's *other moral requirements*." Mark Evans, "Moral Theory and the Idea of a Just War," p. 13 (emphasis added)("other requirements" include a "preference for democracy").

[109] Ibid., pp. 12–13.

[110] Franscisi de Vitoria, *De Indis Et De Ivre Belli Reflectiones*, ¶453, p. 181.

[111] Antony Anghie, "Francisco de Vitoria and the Colonial Origins of International Law," p. 333.

[112] But see Mary Ellen O'Connell, "Unlawful Killing with Combat Drones: A Case study of Pakistan 2004–2009," in Simon Bronitt et al. (eds.), *Shooting to Kill: Socio-Legal Perspectives on the Use of Lethal Force* (Hart Publishing, 2012). At the behest of U.S. Director of National Intelligence James Clapper, the Senate Intelligence Committee dropped legislation that would have provided public disclosure of the number of people killed in drone strikes and

In his modern restatement Evans substitutes a "democratic bias" in lieu of an explicitly racist standard.[113] Geoffrey Robertson is not so oblique. He bravely proclaims that human rights advocates "will call a savage a savage, whether or not he or she is black."[114]

The discourse of civilization underlies all pro-war discourse. It is an essential part of the process of dehumanization that allows the killing of fellow human beings. Colonial powers advanced explicitly racist arguments against extending the protections of the nascent *jus in bello* to peoples of the periphery. For example, in objecting to a proposed ban on expanding bullets, Britain argued that they were needed in colonial wars in Africa. Explained Sir John Ardagh:

> In civilized war a soldier penetrated by a small projectile is wounded, withdraws to the ambulance, and does not advance any further. It is very different with a savage. Even though pierced two or three times, he does not cease to march forward ... but continues on, and before anyone has time to explain to him that he is flagrantly violating the decision of the Hague Conference, he cuts off your head.[115]

Similarly, Germany's genocide of the Herero people in its colony of South West Africa (Namibia) – a tragedy foreshadowing the Holocaust – was dismissed as necessary native pacification, a domestic act

---

the circumstances of their deaths. www.commondreams.org/headline/2014/04/29.

[113] Mark Evans, "Democracy and the Right to Wage War," in Mark Evans (ed.) *Just War Theory: A Reappraisal*, p. 89, n. 13.

[114] Geoffrey Robertson, *Crimes Against Humanity: the Struggle for Global Justice* (Ringwood, 1999), p. 453. One wonders whether Robertson would use such language regarding Robert McNamara and Henry Kissinger (war crimes in Vietnam); Tony Blair and George W. Bush (waging an illegal war of aggression); Donald Rumsfeld (torture, rendition, indefinite detention); or President Barack Obama (drone assassinations).

[115] Chris af Jochnick and Roger Normand, "The Legitimation of Violence: A Critical History of the Laws of War," *Harv. Int'l L.J.*, 35 (1994), p. 73, n. 107. See also James B. Scott (ed.), *The Hague Peace Conferences of 1899 & 1907*, (1909), p. 343.

not governed by the law of war.[116] But this racist barometer was not confined to the colonial context. In both 1935 and 1937, Ethiopia, a sovereign state and member of the League of Nations,[117] presented evidence to the League of Italian war crimes, including the use of mustard gas,[118] bombing of Red Cross hospitals and ambulances, and extra-judicial killings. But the League took no action. Following the war Britain actively opposed the prosecution of these atrocities as war crimes, and Ethiopia was forced to give up its claim.

Obama's Grotian moment is, sadly, a continuation of this racist legacy. From an instrumentalist perspective it is a transparent effort to justify U.S. interventions in the Global South: Iraq, Afghanistan, Libya, Somalia,[119] and Uganda.[120] Normatively, his just war seeks to legitimate military aggression, torture, renditions, indefinite detention, forced feedings, warrantless surveillance, and drone assassinations – non-ideal but necessary measures against the tenacious new/old barbarians. As Issa Shivji poignantly observed, "in the human rights crusade it [is] fair to protect rights while napalming the humans."[121]

---

[116] See Antony Anghie, Bhupinder Chimni, Karin Mickelson and Obiora Okafor (eds.), *The Third World and International Order: Law, Politics and Globalization* (Martinus Nijhoff, 2004), p. 195.

[117] Richard Pankhurst, "Italian Fascist War Crimes in Ethiopia: A History of their Discussion from the League of Nations to the United Nations (1936–1949)," *Ne. Afr. Stud.*, 6 (1999), p. 83, available at http://muse.jhu.edu/journals/northeast_african_studies/v006/6.1pankhurst.html.

[118] Mustard gas was outlawed in the 1907 Hague Convention (IV) on the Laws and Customs of War on Land. Hague Convention (IV) Respecting the Laws and Customs of War on Land, Annex I, art. 23, October 18, 1907, 36 Stat. 2277, 205 Consol. T.S. 277, reprinted in Dietrich Schindler and Jiri Toman (eds.), *The Laws of Armed Conflict: A Collection of Conventions, Resolutions, and Other Documents* (1988), pp. 102–3.

[119] Obama Doctrine, pp. 3–4.

[120] "U.S. Support to Regional Efforts to Counter the Lord's Resistance Army," U.S. State Dept. Press Release, March 23, 2012, www.state.gov/r/pa/prs/ps/2012/03/186732.htm. See also Richard Downie, "The Lord's Resistance Army," Center for Strategic & International Studies (October 18, 2011), http://csis.org/publication/lords-resistance-army.

[121] Issa G. Shivji, *The Concept of Human Rights in Africa* (Codesria, 1989), p. 3.

Invocations of humanitarianism to justify military interventions are inherently political calculations, with indeterminate legal standards.[122] They have historically provided a façade for the advancement of the economic or strategic interests of powerful states. As we have seen, Vitoria justified the rape of the Americas on humanitarian grounds.[123] In the lead-up to World War II, both the Germans and the Japanese attempted to justify their invasions of weaker states on humanitarian grounds.[124] Subsequently, Cold War logic – defense of allies against the "communist menace" – formed the rationale for military interventions. Post–Cold War trends such as the Euro-American interventions in Libya, Cote d'Ivoire, and Mali, clothed in humanitarian rhetoric, mirror classic colonialist claims to geo-political spheres of influence.

The new just war theory retains the medieval conflation of defense, vengeance, and punishment. As the just war was designed to punish sin,[125] so Obama claimed to seek vindication for an asserted universal norm in his plea that the righteous international community must "punish" Syria.[126] In the lead-up to the invasion of Iraq, U.S. President George Bush and British Prime Minister Tony Blair advanced a justification of preemptive self-defense. This pretext was, correctly, widely rejected. When no weapons of mass destruction were found, humanitarian rhetoric began to supplement the failed legal argument,[127] with a subtext of punishment for past

[122] See Thomas M. Franck and Nigel S. Rodley, "After Bangladesh: The Law of Humanitarian Intervention by Military Force," *Am. J. Int'l L.*, 67 (1973), p. 284 (concluding that "a usable general definition of 'humanitarian intervention' would be extremely difficult to formulate and virtually impossible to apply rigorously").

[123] Franscisi de Vitoria, *De Indis Et De Ivre Belli Reflectiones* (arguing that "in favor of those who are oppressed and suffer wrong, the Spaniards can make war . . . seizing the lands and territory of the natives").

[124] See Thomas M. Franck and Nigel S. Rodley, "After Bangladesh ," p. 284.

[125] Frederick H. Russell, *The Just War in the Middle Ages*, p. 292.

[126] See for example Steve Holland and Susan Cornwell, "As Obama pushes to punish Syria, lawmakers fear deep U.S. involvement," September 2, 2013 www.reuters.com/article/2013/09/02/us-syria-crisis-usa-idUSBRE97T0NB 20130902.

[127] See Jeanne M. Woods and James M. Donovan, "Anticipatory Self Defense and Other Stories," *Kansas J of Law & Public Pol'y*, 14 (2005), pp. 487–501.

use of chemical weapons and vengeance against Muslims for the September 11 attacks.

In the face of the apparently overwhelming victory, however, the UN Security Council caved to U.S. military might. Succumbing to the bombastic and premature declaration of "Mission Accomplished" the Security Council effectively ratified the invasion, legitimized the U.S. occupation and provided assistance to the occupation forces in suppressing Iraqi resistance.[128] As with Vitoria's injunction to Native Americans that resistance to Spanish incursions would violate natural law, so these resolutions rendered resistance to the "coalition of the willing" tantamount to terrorism.[129]

But unlike the colonial enterprise, the goal of these interventions is not to assert sovereignty but to put in place compliant indigenous regimes, enabling the further penetration of markets and the plunder of the countries' natural resources. The systematic imposition of military control is particularly important for control of the oil and gas resources of western and central Asia and Africa.[130] Such regimes

---

[128] See SC Res 1483, UNSCOR, 58th sess., 4761st mtg., UN Doc S/RES/1483 (May 22, 2003)(recognizing the United States and the United Kingdom as occupying powers). The Coalition Provisional Authority relied on this resolution when enacting Order No. 39, which dramatically broadened the ability of foreign countries to invest in Iraq without reinvesting any profits in the national economy. Foreign Investment, CPA/ORD/19 (September 2003). See also SC Res. 1500, UN SCOR, 58th sess. 4808th mtg., UN Doc S/RES/1500 (August 14, 2003)(endorsing the "broadly representative Governing Council of Iraq"); and SC Res 1511, UN SCOR, 58th sess., 4844th mtg., UN Doc S/RES/1511 (October 13, 2003)(authorizing a "multinational force under unified command to take *all necessary measures* to contribute to the maintenance of security and stability in Iraq")(Emphasis added. This language is typically used when the Council authorizes military action).

[129] Antony Anghie, "Francisco de Vitoria and the Colonial Origins of International Law," p. 328.

[130] See generally, Jeanne M. Woods, "Impunity or Accountability in the Extractive Industries: Reform, Regulation, or Resistance?" *African Y.B. Int'l L.*, 15 (2008), p. 207. In a December 2000 CIA report, analysts speculated about the future supply of African oil. In his May 2001 Report on U.S. energy policy, former Vice-President Richard Cheney highlighted the new

must be content to remain obedient, subordinate, and peripheral in the global economy. The inevitable rejection of these terms by oppressed peoples will lead to endless cycles of civil war and military intervention under the auspices of NATO.

significance of African oil for U.S. markets. National Energy Policy Development Group, Executive Office of the Vice-President, National Energy Policy Report 8.11 (May 2001). Eight months later, the Institute for Advanced Strategic and Political Studies (IASPS), a neoconservative thinktank based in Israel (according to the website of the IASPS, its mission is to save Western society from the "[c]onvergence of Islam and Western Elites"), held a symposium in Washington, D.C. entitled "African Oil: A Priority for U.S. National Security and African Development." See Institute for Advanced Strategic & Political Studies, "The Institute's Mission," 2004, www.iasps.org/mission.php. Speakers included U.S. diplomatic and intelligence officials, members of Congress, and energy industry executives. The symposium spawned a working group, the African Oil Policy Initiative Group (AOPIG), which issued recommendations for U.S. policy. Asserting a convergence of U.S. energy security interests and African economic development goals, the AOPIG proposed a "historic, strategic, alignment with West Africa," with the Gulf of Guinea emerging as a "vital U.S. interest." African Oil Initiative Policy Group, "African Oil: A Priority for U.S. National Security & African Development" (2002), p. 18, available at www.iasps.org/strategic/africanwhitepaper.pdf. The 2002 Bush Administration's National Security Strategy, in which the doctrine of preemptive military action was announced, asserted that Africa's "disease, war, and desperate poverty" threatens a U.S. strategic priority: "combating global terror." "Bush Doctrine," p. 7. In 2004 a Congressionally-appointed panel proposed a "conceptual shift to a strategic view of Africa." Walter H. Kansteiner III and J. Stephen Morrison, Center for Strategic & International Studies, "Rising U.S. Stakes in Africa: Seven Proposals to Strengthen U.S.-Africa Policy" (2004), available at www.allafrica.com/sustainable/resources/view/00010230.pdf. The Administration's 2006 National Security Strategy identifies Africa as "a high priority" and – in a resurrection of the doctrine of *terra nullius* – "recognizes that [U.S.] security depends upon ... strengthening fragile and failing states and bring[ing] ungoverned areas under the control of effective democracies." National Security Council, Executive Office of the President, National Security Strategy of the United States, at 37 (2006), available at http://georgewbush-whitehouse.archives.gov/nsc/nss/2006/. In February 2007, President Bush announced the formation of AFRICOM, Press Release, Office of the Press

In its 2002 National Security Strategy the United States proclaimed that it would not tolerate the existence of any other global military power.[131] While Obama's humanitarian rhetoric may be more palatable than Bush's preemption claims, they are not mutually exclusive. In fact, the Bush and Obama Doctrines are mutually reinforcing, as evidenced by the justification proffered for the NATO intervention in Libya: preemptive defense against genocide.[132]

V THE *JUS IN BELLO*: WAR IS TERROR

With the ascendency of legal positivism in the nineteenth century, even the malleable just war doctrine was rejected as an unwarranted intrusion on sovereignty.[133] The subsequent codification of rules purporting to "humanize" war is emblematic of Freud's thesis that civilization seeks to constrain instinctual aggression while paradoxically giving violence normative status. A comprehensive study of the *jus in bello* by Jochnick and Normand persuasively demonstrates that the project of codification functions more to legitimate violence than to restrain it.[134]

Secretary, Executive Office of the President of the United States, "President Bush Creates a Department of Defense Unified Combatant Command for Africa" (February 6, 2007), a new unified combatant command to "protect U.S. national security objectives in Africa and its surrounding waters," Lauren Ploch, Congressional Research Service, "Africa Command: U.S. Strategic Interests & the Role of the U.S. Military in Africa" (July 6, 2007) available at http://assets.opencrs.com/rpts/RL34003_20070706.pdf.

[131] "Bush Doctrine" (announcing intent to act unilaterally and preemptively, and to "dissuade future military competition").

[132] Similarly, in one appeal to Congress and the American public, President Obama exclaimed that he had "decided the United States should take military action against" Syria in order to "deter [the use of chemical weapons] and degrade [Assad's] capacity to carry it out." www.politico.com/story/2013/08/obama-to-speak-on-syria-96122.html.

[133] Emmerich de Vattel, *The Law of Nations* (1758) in *The Classics of International Law*, Bk. III, chs. iii and xii (Washington, 1916).

[134] Chris af Jochnick and Roger Normand, "The Legitimation of Violence," p. 57. ("By endorsing military necessity without substantive limitations, the

Modern rules of war were rooted in chivalric mythology, a customary regime that entitled nobles to kill peasants, non-Christians, and other civilians.[135] Given such dubious origins it is unsurprising that humanitarian law still permits the taking and maiming of human life. Its core principle, the principle of distinction, countenances the killing of non-combatants – women, children, the elderly –under the state-centric doctrine of military necessity. A vague and indeterminate state prerogative, military necessity operates as an exception to most humanitarian rules, and has been embodied in all formulations of the *jus in bello* from the Lieber Code to the Geneva Conventions and its Protocols.[136] By

laws of war [provide] a powerful rhetorical tool to protect . . . controversial conduct from humanitarian challenges.")

[135] Robert C. Stacey, "The Age of Chivalry," p. 30. See also Chris af Jochnick and Roger Normand, "The Legitimation of Violence," p. 61.

[136] Military necessity is defined in the Lieber Code as "those measures which are indispensable for securing the ends of the war, and which are lawful." General Orders No. 100 (1863), reprinted in Richard S. Hartigan (ed.), *Lieber's Code & the Law of War 1*, (1983), art. 14. It is also embodied in arts. 15–19 and 29, Ibid. Similarly, the Saint Petersburg Declaration, drafted at the first international conference on the laws of war convened by Czar Alexander II of Russia in 1868 permitted belligerents to inflict "necessary" suffering. "Declaration Renouncing the Use, in Time of War, of Explosive Projectiles Under 400 Grammes Weight," December 11, 1868, 138 Consol. T.S. 297, reprinted in Dietrich Schindler and Jiri Toman (eds.) *The Laws of Armed Conflict: A Collection of Conventions, Resolutions, and Other Documents* (1988), pp. 102–3. See also the Hague Conventions, in which military necessity conditions restrictions on the methods of war. The Hague Convention (II) with Respect to the Laws and Customs of War on Land, July 29, 1899, 32 Stat. 1803, 187 Consol. T.S. 429, reprinted in Dietrich Schindler and Jiri Toman (eds.), *The Laws of Armed Conflicts* (4th ed., 2004), p. 60 ("inspired by the desire to diminish the evils of war *so far as military necessities permit*." [emphasis added]); and Hague Convention (IV) Respecting the Laws and Customs of War on Land, Annex, October 18, 1907, 36 Stat. 2277, 205 Consol. T.S. 277, reprinted in *The Laws of Armed Conflicts*, pp. 66, 67, 73, 80, articles 5, 23, and 54.

The 1954 Hague Convention includes the principle of military necessity as a justification for the waiving of protective measures for cultural property. United Nations Educational, Scientific and Cultural Organization, Convention for the Protection of Cultural Property in the Event of Armed Conflict, May 14, 1954, 249 U.N.T.S. 215 reprinted in *The Laws of Armed*

codifying the doctrine of military necessity the *jus in bello* elevated the philosophy of *kriegsraison* – a once-controversial extremist proposition that a ruthless war is quicker and therefore more humane[137] – to the status of credible legal principle.

The Lieber Code, the first legal regulations to be employed during wartime, provided that "the more vigorously wars are pursued, the better it is for humanity."[138] For Lieber "vigorous pursuit" included starvation of civilians, bombardment of civilians without warning, and destruction of all armed enemies and enemy property.[139] Nearly a century later U.S. President Harry Truman deployed this same rationale to justify the use of atomic bombs against civilian populations in Hiroshima and Nagasaki.[140] Incredibly, the tactic of mass starvation and policies of deliberate "morale bombing"– attacking populated areas to spread terror – were expressly upheld by the war crimes tribunals at Nuremberg and Tokyo.[141] The chief U.S.

Conflicts, p. 999. Furthermore, the Geneva Conventions of 1949 contain several provisions which allow military necessity to justify waiver of express rules. See Geneva Convention on the Amelioration of the Condition of the Wounded and Sick in Armed Forces in the Field arts. 12, 42, August 12, 1949, 6 U.S.T. 3114, 75 U.N.T.S. 31, reprinted in *The Laws Of Armed Conflicts*, pp. 459, 465, 475; Geneva Convention Relative to the Treatment of Prisoners of War arts. 8, 23, 76, 126, August 12, 1949, 6 U.S.T. 3316, 75 U.N.T.S. 135, reprinted in *The Laws Of Armed Conflicts*, pp. 507, 515, 521, 538, 556; Geneva Convention Relative to the Protection of Civilian Persons in Time of War arts. 49, 83, 12 Aug. 1949, 6 U.S.T. 3516, 75 U.N.T.S. 287 [Hereinafter Geneva Convention (IV)], reprinted in *The Laws Of Armed Conflicts*, pp. 575, 594, 604. In particular, Article 27 of Geneva IV provides that, "the Parties to the conflict may take such measures of control and security in regard to protected persons as may be necessary as a result of war."

[137] *Kriegsraison* means "the necessities of war are prior to the customs of war." Chris af Jochnick and Roger Normand, "The Legitimation of Violence," p. 63 n. 53.

[138] Lieber Code, art. 29.

[139] Chris af Jochnick and Roger Normand, "The Legitimation of Violence," pp. 65–6.

[140] Ibid., p. 88. ("The logic of terror bombing led inexorably to the use of atomic bombs in Hiroshima and Nagasaki.")

[141] *United States* v. *List* (Case No. 7), in 11 War Crimes Comm'n, U.N. Trials of War Criminals Before the Nuremberg Tribunals Under Control Council

Prosecutor at Nuremberg argued that "aerial bombardment of cities and factories has become a recognized part of modern warfare as carried on by all nations."[142] The Tribunal condoned the bombardment of civilians to induce surrender, "whether with the usual bombs or by atomic bomb."[143]

The 1949 Geneva Conventions left many of these prerogatives in place. Despite the subsequent adoption of Protocol I,[144] which sought to ameliorate some of the most heinous practices, humanitarian concerns remain subordinate to military objectives. Thus, as the new millennium dawned, an international tribunal upheld aerial bombing of civilian areas in the 1999 NATO attack on Yugoslavia, relying on principles of proportionality: some 500 civilian deaths were deemed acceptable relative to the "military advantage" gained in the

Law No. 10 759, at 1253–54 (1950) In *List*, a German general ordered the removal of the entire civilian population and the destruction of all food and shelter, leaving "some sixty-one thousand men, women and children homeless, starving and destitute." Although the Tribunal found that these orders served no military purpose, it nevertheless ruled that since the accused believed they might slow the enemy's advance, the commands were not criminal. See Also *United States* v. *von Leeb*, in 11 War Crimes Comm'n, U.N. Trials of War Criminals Before the Nuremberg Tribunals Under Control Council Law No. 10 563 (1950). ("The cutting off of every source of sustenance from without is deemed legitimate. It is said that if the commander of a besieged place expelled the noncombatants, in order to lessen the number of those who consume his stock provisions, it is lawful, though an extreme measure, to drive them back so as to hasten the surrender.")

[142] W. Hays Parks, "Air War and the Law of War," *A.F. L. Rev.*, 32 (1990), p. 37 (quoting Telford Taylor, Final Report to the Secretary of the Army on the Nuremberg War Crimes Trials Under the Control Council Law No. 10 (1949)).

[143] *United States* v. *Ohlendorf* (Case No. 9), in 4 War Crimes Comm'n, U.N. Trials of War Criminals Before the Nuremberg Tribunals Under Control Council Law No. 10 1, (1948), p. 467.

[144] Protocol Additional to the Geneva Conventions of 12 August 1949, and relating to the Protection of Victims of International Armed Conflicts (Protocol I), 8 June 1977, Arts. 35–60, 1125 UNTS 3/ 1991 ATS No 29/ 16 ILM 1391 (1977).

attack.[145] More recently, a German court dismissed a case brought in the killing of nearly a hundred civilians in a 2009 NATO airstrike, on the ground that the officer who ordered the strike was following protocol. The officer was subsequently promoted to the rank of Brigadier-General.[146] Notably, the United States, the world's pre-eminent military superpower, has not ratified Protocol I. As the burgeoning deployment of drone technology demonstrates,[147] the *jus in bello* still fails to protect individuals from horrific new weapons, while safeguarding the prerogatives of powerful states. The deployment of terror by the state – advocated by Grotius in the seventeenth century –remains a legal option today.

With the end of the Cold War and the acquisition of unipolar hegemony by the United States, the Security Council began to utilize ad hoc Tribunals to further elaborate the *jus in bello,* arguably an ultra vires expansion of its Chapter VII powers.[148] Critics have challenged the undemocratic nature of formulating purportedly universal norms

---

[145] See International Criminal Tribunal for the Former Yugoslavia [ICTY], "Final Report to the Prosecutor by the Committee Established to Review the NATO Bombing Campaign Against the Federal Republic of Yugoslavia," 39 I.L.M. 1257, at ¶ 56 (June 8, 2000). ("The committee agrees there is nothing inherently unlawful about flying above the height which can be reached by enemy air defences. [I]t appears that with the use of modern technology, the obligation to distinguish was effectively carried out in the vast majority of cases during the bombing campaign.") It has been reported that between 489 and 528 Yugoslav civilians were killed in the bombing. Heike Krieger, *The Kosovo Conflict and International Law* (Cambridge University Press, 2001), p. 323.

[146] "Case of German-ordered US strike that resulted in death of more than 90 civilians dismissed over lack of evidence," www.aljazeera.com/news/asia/2013/12/german-court-rejects-afghan-airstrike-case-201312111344393 50883.html.

[147] See for example Jordan Paust, "Propriety of Self-Defense Targetings of Members of Al-Qaeda and Applicable Principles of Distinction and Proportionality," *ILSA J. Int'l & Com. L.,* 18 (2012), p. 575 (applying a narrow formalist reading of human rights obligations in connection with targeted drone killings and creating an artificial dichotomy between the "law of self-defense" and the law of war).

[148] Tribunals have been established to prosecute war crimes in the former Yugoslavia, Rwanda, and Sierra Leone. See Leila Sadat Wexler, "The

through such a patently political process.[149] On the substance of international criminal law – a wholly new discipline – the Tribunals were informed by the Nuremberg and Tokyo Tribunals.[150] This body of law was already problematic because of concerns regarding the principle of legality and "victors' justice." Similar concerns are raised by the Tribunals established pursuant to the Security Council's Chapter VII powers, a process that remains dominated by the same powerful states.[151]

The permanent International Criminal Court created through the Rome Treaty[152] is similarly problematic. Its mandate is to try the "most serious crimes," including genocide, crimes against humanity, war crimes, and crimes of aggression, although crimes of aggression are not yet actionable.[153] However, its legitimacy is severely compromised by the consent-based character of the Court.[154] Of particular concern is the fact that only two permanent members of the

Proposed Permanent International Court: An Appraisal," *Cornell Int'l L.J.*, 29 (1996), pp. 671–2.

[149] See for example Antony Anghie and B. S. Chimni, "Third World Approaches to International Law and Individual Responsibility in Internal Armed Conflict," in Stephen R. Ratner and Anne-Marie Slaughter (eds.), *The Methods of International Law* (2004), p. 210.

[150] Cassandra Jeu, "A Successful, Permanent, International Criminal Court ... 'Isn't it Pretty to Think So?'" *Hous. J. Int'l L.*, 26 (2004), p. 426.

[151] For a well-documented assessment of the Rwandan Tribunal as victors' justice, see Luc Reydams, "Let's Be Friends: The United States, Post-Genocide Rwanda, and Victor's Justice in Arusha" (January 1, 2013), available at http://papers.ssrn.com/sol3/papers.cfm?abstract_id=2197823.

[152] Rome Statute of the International Criminal Court, July 17, 1998, Art. 1, 37 I.L.M. 999, 1003. The ICC is a consent-based regime; it assumes jurisdiction over natural persons in four ways: 1) the country in which an alleged crime was perpetrated is a party state, 2) the alleged perpetrator of a crime is a national of a party state, 3) the United Nations Security Council refers the case to the ICC, or 4) a non-party state voluntarily submits itself to ICC jurisdiction for the purposes of a particular matter.

[153] Ibid., Art. 5. Crimes of aggression will not become actionable until at least January 2017. Rev. Conf. of the Rome Statute, 13th plenary meeting, June 11, 2010, I.C.C. Doc. RC/Res. 6 (June 16, 2010).

[154] See Rome Statute, Arts. 12–13.

Security Council are parties to the Treaty.[155] The absence of the world's major military powers from the ambit of the Court's jurisdiction inescapably politicizes the Court.[156] As at Nuremberg and Tokyo, the crimes of the superpowers – including those committed in the course of the "war on terror" – will be immune from prosecution.[157]

Other arguments concerning the potential politicization of the Court have focused on the fact that thus far the prosecutor has issued indictments only in Africa.[158] Proponents counter that of the eight investigations launched, four were requested by the governments of the states

---

[155] While the United Kingdom and France have both ratified and signed the Treaty, the United States, the Russian Federation and China remain outside of its purview. Other major non-party states include Israel and India. "The States Parties to the Rome Statute, International Criminal Court," available at www.Icc-cpi.int.

[156] The U.S. in particular waged a relentless campaign to pressure states parties, under threat of sanctions, to sign Bilateral Immunity Agreements to prevent Americans from being brought before the court. See "Campaign for Immunity," available at www.amicc.org/usicc/biacampaign.

[157] Moreover, despite the relatively bright-line definitions of offenses, the inevitable judicial interpretation and policymaking lead to concerns about the transparency of norm promulgation. See for example Jared Wesell, "Judicial Policy-Making at the International Criminal Court: An Institutional Guide to Analyzing International Adjudication," *Colum. J. Transnat'l L.*, 44 (2006), p. 386.

[158] See for example Charles Chernor Jalloh, "Africa and the International Criminal Court: Collision Course or Cooperation?" *N.C. Cent. L. Rev.*, 34 (2012), pp. 209–10 ([S]ome African nations ... are increasingly questioning what they perceive as an insensitive application of the international criminal law instrument to indict only weak individuals from generally poor African states. For example, President Paul Kagame of Rwanda has gone so far as to suggest that the ICC is a "fraudulent institution" reminiscent of "colonialism" and "imperialism" that is seeking to undermine and to control Africa. Although Rwanda is not a member of the ICC, his position is echoed by others, such as President Thomas Yayi of Benin, who lamented the "harassment" of African leaders and concluded that "[w]e have the feeling that this court is chasing Africa." See also Allison Marston Danner, "Enhancing the Legitimacy and Accountability of Prosecutorial Discretion at the International Criminal Court," *Am. J. Int'l L.*, 97 (2003), pp. 536–7.

in question.[159] However, rather than resolving the issue of impartiality, this leaves open the possibility that the Court is actually taking sides in ongoing civil wars, potentially propping up dictators friendly to the West. Thus, the ICC can be perceived as just another technology that can be deployed in furtherance of intervention and hegemony.[160]

VI CONCLUSION

Throughout history, ruling classes in crisis have invented external enemies to divert attention and unify the populace. As late-stage capitalism confronts multiple intersecting crises – of debt, energy, climate, inequality – it has reconstructed a paradigm of permanent war. Following the collapse of the USSR a new enemy was needed to replace the "communist menace."[161] As Morton Halperin and

[159] "Situations and Cases," International Criminal Court, available at www.icc-cpi.int.

[160] Harold Koh, Legal Advisor to the United States Department of State, led a U.S. delegation to the 2010 ICC Review Conference in Kampala. At the conclusion of the Conference, Koh stated that the Obama Administration is considering a request from Prosecutor Luis Ocampo to deploy AFRICOM – the U.S. military command for Africa – to assist in the enforcement of ICC warrants. Harold Koh, Legal Advisor U.S. Dept. of State, and Stephen J. Rapp, Ambassador-at-Large for War Crimes Issues, Special Briefing: U.S. Engagement With the ICC & the Outcome of the Recently Concluded Review Conference (June 15, 2010) (transcript available at www.state.gov/j/gcj/us_releases/remarks/2010/143178.htm). Furthermore, Rapp stated that the United States, while still unwilling to become a party to the Rome Treaty, would cooperate with the ICC "when it is in the U.S. interests" to do so. Ibid. In 2011, the United States initiated "Operation Lightning Thunder" which resulted in a failed military attempt to capture Ugandan rebel leader Joseph Kony, pursuant to an ICC arrest warrant. Richard Downie, "The Lord's Resistance Army," Center for Strategic & International Studies (October 18, 2011), http://csis.org/publication/lords-resistance-army. An indictment was issued against former Libyan leader Moammar Kadafi prior to the NATO intervention in that country.

[161] See S.C. Res. 1744 ¶ 4, UN Doc. S/RES/1744 (2007) (authorizing a peacekeeping mission in support of the Transitional Federal Government of the Republic of Somalia).

I predicted in 1991, terrorism, drugs and economic espionage have emerged to justify escalating military expenditures and a massive intelligence network.[162] At the same time an evolving *corpus* of human rights and international criminal law is being mobilized to further the civilizing mission. As Anne Orford points out, "the revolutionary potential of human rights is radically circumscribed when rights become an apology for state violence."[163] As in the Cold War, our predecessor battle against an enemy ideology, law is appropriated to repress domestic dissent;[164] like the Cold War the battlefield is located primarily in the Global South, where the resources and markets of the future await capture.

But law is a site of resistance as well as a tool of oppression.[165] International capital has been forced to adjust to social and political movements, for example the national liberation movements of the 1950s and 1960s. Other peoples' movements like the environmental movement and the fight to maintain democracy and expand it beyond minimalism can also produce meaningful change. President Obama was prevented from bombing Syria as a consequence of world public opinion, manifested in the refusal of the British Parliament and the U.S. Congress to endorse the action.

In a prescient observation – before the Final Solution, before Hiroshima, before Global Warming – Freud noted that man's obsession with controlling nature could "very easily exterminate [civilization] to the last man."[166] Yet Freud believed that this destructive instinct "can be tempered and harnessed."[167] For Freud, interdependence is the "means to hold aggression in check."[168]

---

[162] Morton Halperin and Jeanne M. Woods, "Ending the Cold War at Home," *Foreign Pol'y*, 81 (1990–1), pp. 138–43.

[163] Anne Orford, *Reading Humanitarian Intervention*, p. 187.

[164] See Mary L. Dudziak, *War-Time: An Idea, Its History, Its Consequences* (Oxford University Press, 2012), pp. 79–85.

[165] See generally, Jeanne M. Woods, "Theorizing Peace as a Human Right," *Human Rights & Inter'l Discourse*, 7 (2013), p. 178; and Jeanne M. Woods, "Theoretical Insights from the Cutting Edge," *Proceedings of the 104th Annual Meeting of the American Society of International Law* (2010), p. 389.

[166] Sigmund Freud, *Civilization and its Discontents* , p. 86.   [167] Ibid., p. 101.

[168] Ibid., p. 107.

Stiglitz sees the forces of globalization increasing that interdependence.[169] The innovative technologies that enable capital to penetrate markets across the globe – that made globalization possible – also connect its victims – human beings – in unprecedented ways. We can use this technology to exploit or to organize; to isolate or to unite; to retreat into our hypnotically addictive toys; or to change the world.

---

[169] Joseph Stiglitz, *Globalization and its Discontents*, p. 224.

INDEX

1949 Geneva Conventions, 280
1998 Summit of the Americas, 227
2001 Americas Summit in Quebec, 227
2002 US National Security Strategy, 277
2009 Copenhagen Conference of the
    Parties of the United Nations
    Framework Convention on Climate
    Change, 243

Absell, Christopher, 242
accumulation by dispossession, 260
*Aftershock, the Next Economy and America's
    Future*, 197
Agamben, Giorgio, 116
age of high mass consumption, 97
age of imperialism, 189
Agenda 21, 42
aggregate demand, 198
aggregate global welfare, 186
Alston, Philip, 9
Alternative consumption, 82
American Society of International Law, 135
Anghie, Antony, 2
Annual Meeting of the American Society of
    International Law, 1
Anthropocene, 51
Arab Spring, 253
Archibugi, Daniele, 212
Argentina v. NML Capital Ltd.
    US Supreme Court, 17
Asian menace, 106
Association of Caribbean States, 227
attainability critique, 142
Augustine, 261
authoritarianism, 215

Barrio Adentro, 231
basic needs, 32
Bear Sterns, 3
binge development, 28, 53, 67, 109
biodiversity, 54

biophysical
    constraints, 53
    consumption, 40
    needs, 34
biosphere, 54
Bitcoin mining, 40
Bitcoins. *See* cryptocurrencies
Blackstone, Sir William, 260
Blair, Dennis, 253
Blair, Tony, 274
Bolivarian Alliance for the Peoples of Our
    America (ALBA), 221
Bolivarian Alternative for the Americas
    (ALBA), 15
Bookchin
    Murray, 101
Bookchin, Murray
    ecologist, 10
Borbón, Altmann, 234
Bretton Woods Institutions, 57, 137
Bretton Woods organizations, 208
BRICS
    Brazil, Russia, India, China and South
    Africa, 161
Brockmann, Miguel d'Escoto, 243
Brundtland Report, 54
Buen Vivir, 110
Bull of Demarcation. *See* Inter Caetera
Bush, Laura W., 125
Bush Doctrine, 277

Campaign for a United Nations
    Parliamentary Assembly, 212
Capital in the Twenty-First Century
    by Thomas Piketty, 4
Caribbean Court of Justice, 94
Castro, Fidel, 222
Castro, Raul, 222
Chavez, Hugo
    President, Venezuela, 15
chavismo, 226

chavistas, 237
citizen-consumer, 49
City of God, 270
City of Man, 270
civil society
    and participation in the international
        system, 205
Civilization and its Discontents, 194
clash of civilizations, 251
classical economic theory, 198
coalition of the willing, 275
Cocoyoc Declaration, 103
Cold War, 149
Cold War logic, 274
colonial governance, 115
colonialism, 104
Comaroff, Jean, 265
Comaroff, John, 265
commodification of nature, 76
common heritage, 152
communist, 199
Community of Latin American and
        Caribbean States (CELAC), 232
competitive authoritarianism, 241
Conference on Population Problems, 106
Connelly, Matthew, 106
consumer, 37
    choice, 55
    confidence, 40
    society, 33
    identity, 49
consumerism, 106
consumers' republic, 96
Consumption, 39
consumption-led global economic model,
        78
continuous bargaining, 177
Convention Against All Forms of
        Discrimination Against Women
        (CEDAW), 148
Convention on the Rights of the Child, 148
*Convention on Wetlands of International
        Importance especially as Waterfowl
        Habitat*
    Ramsar Convention, 93
corporate actors, 180
corporate hegemony, 257
corporate rule, 183
corporate social responsibility, 43
Correa, Rafael, 222
cosmopolitan democracy, 212
cost neutrality, 44
countercyclical, 141
counter-neoliberal, 130
crisis governance, 127
crisis logic, 135
critical faith, 18, 20

critical instability, 135
cryptocurrencies, 39

d'Escoto, Miguel
    President, UN General Assembly, 8, 163
de Gaulle, Charles, 207
De Schutter, Olivier
    UN Special Rapporteur on the Right to
        Food, 146
de Vattel, Emmerich, 74
de Vitoria
    Francisco, 71
de Zayas, Alfred, 214
Deaton, Angus
    economist, 4
decolonized, 97
democracy, 14
democracy deficit', 196
Deng Xiaoping, 199
desirability critiques, 142
developed
    countries, 45
    world, 48
developing world, 44
development, 141
    international, 56
    sustainable, 27, 52, 61
disaster capitalism, 20, 130
discipline of crisis, 116
divine plan, 74
Dodd-Frank reform law, 164
domestic trafficking, 128
Dyer, Gwynne, 106

Earth Summit, 51
easy consumption, 46
Eccles, Marriner, 197
Eco-efficiency, 42
ecological equilibrium, 105
ecological footprint, 48
economic
    contraction, 26
    crises, 13
    development, 10
    growth, 36, 44
    instability, 13
    prosperity, 18
    stability, 171
    stagnation, 32
Economic and Social Council of the United
        Nations, 96
economic architecture, 1
Economic Covenant, 148
economic equality, 199
economy
    global, 26, 38
ecosystem people, 86

efficiency gains, 44
Einstein, Albert, 194
Emperor Constantine, 261
end-consumer, 46
energy
  efficiency, 42
  grabs, 66
  security, 83
Enlightenment, 174
environmental
  awareness, 94
  burdens, 11
  collapse, 107
  crisis, 10, 26
  degradation, 56, 63, 101
  harm, 11, 85
  justice, 10
  protection, 60, 88
  sustainability, 10
environmentalism
  mainstream, 11
  modern, 10
equality
  gender, 17
Equilar 100 C.E.O. Pay Study
  conducted by the New York Times, 4
eternal Eros, 109
European Central Bank, 151
European Commission, 151
European Court of Human Rights, 155
European Parliament, 165
European Union, 6, 207
exclusive economic zone, 90
extreme poverty, 7
Exxon-Mobil, 255

fair trade, 82
Falk, Richard, 13, 212
famines, 32
feminists, 153
Final Solution, 285
Financial institutions, 162
finitude, 33
firm, 179
First World War, 249
food security, 83, 161
Ford, Henry, 41
fossil fuel, 243
Foucault, Michel, 177
fragmentation, 137, 157
free trade, 95
Free Trade Area of the Americas (FTAA),
  227
Freefall
  by Joseph Stiglitz, 3
Frente Amplio, 230
Freud, Sigmund, 194

Frías, Hugo Chávez, 221
Friedman, Milton, 20
Friedman, Milton
  economic rationalist, 130
functionalism, 195, 206

G20, 204
Galbraith, John Kenneth, 197
GDP, 39
gender, 11
  identities, 118
  roles, 125
  transgressions, 118
General Agreement on Tariffs and Trade,
  95
General Motors, 255
general welfare, 172
Geneva Conventions, 278
Gini Coefficient, 199
Gini, Corrado, 199
Glass-Steagall, 165
global
  crisis governance, 121
  economic crisis, 9, 26
  economic governance, 8
  economic order, 13
  economy, 163
  governance, 196
  inequality, 14
  neoliberal governance, 121
  North, 107
  operations, 182
  Parliamentary Assembly (GPA), 14, 209
  political economy, 192
  regime, 196
globalization, 21, 138
Globalization and its Discontents, 250
Goldman Sachs, 150
Great Recession, 2, 26, 201, 253
green consumption, 19
Grotian moment, 269
Grotius, 252
Grotius, Hugo, 74

Harvard School of Public Health, 12
*Havana Charter for an International Trade
  Organization*, 96
Held, David, 212
hetero-normative, 12, 128
heteronormativity, 134
Hobbes, Thomas, 195
home mortgage loans, 201
Homophobia, 128
housing bubble, 3
human
  civilization, 85
  condition, 195

human (cont.)
  rights, 121
  rights and labour paradigm, 131
Human Rights Watch, 235
humanitarian intervention, 262
Hume, David, 195
hydroelectricity, 87
hyper-consumerist, 28
hyper-consumption, 67

immiseration, 56
imperial actuality, 134
income inequality, 5, 197
industrial revolution, 32
Industrial Revolution, 98
industrialization, 10, 85
Inter Caetera, 259
Inter-American Commission on Human
    Rights (IACHR), 235
Inter-American Court of Human Rights,
    155
international
  commerce, 9, 30, 70
  community, 11, 57
  development, 71
  terror, 130
  trade, 39, 71
International Bank for Reconstruction and
    Development, 95
International Civil Aviation Organization,
    196
International Convention on the Settlement
    of Investment Disputes (ICSID), 243
international criminal law, 282
international environmental law, 10
International Labour Organization, 204
International Law Commission, 137
International Monetary Fund (IMF), 95,
    151
international organizations, 206
international peace and security, 95
international system
  and participation of civil society, 205
International Trade Organization, 95
international transparency, 165
interwar period, 94
investment banks, 3

jobless recovery, 256
jus ad bellum, 271
jus in bello, 271
Just and Unjust Wars, 270
just war, 258
Justice Department, 162

Kant, Immanuel, 195
Keohane, Robert, 196

Keynes, John Maynard, 197
kriegsraison, 279

land grabs, 66
Langton, Marcia
  aboriginal activist, 130
law
  armed conflict, 15
  international human rights, 12
  women's human rights, 12
League of Nations, 208
learned helplessness, 109
Lehman Brothers, 3
Lenin, V.I., 189
liberal environmentalism, 99, 101
Lieber Code, 278
Limits to Growth movement, 60
Living Goods, 159
lobbying, 179
Locke, John, 260
logic of capitalism, 181

Machiavelli, Niccolo, 195
Mackenzie Valley Pipeline Inquiry, 88
Maduro, Nicolás, 225
mainstream social norms, 118
Malthus, Thomas, 63
manufacturing, 45
market failures, 173
market fundamentalism, 250
masculinist, 128
mass consumption, 96
mass unemployment, 94
Maya Leaders Alliance, 93
meeting of federal and provincial ministers,
    87
Merkel, Angela
  German Prime Minister, 151
Mickelson, Karin, 10
middle class, 32
Miéville, China
  Marxist international lawyer, 134
Milanovic, Branko
  economist, 4
military
  hegemony, 15
  intervention, 269
  necessity, 278
Millennium Development Goals (MDGs),
    6, 105, 155
mimetic desire, 35
Minority Rights Group, 92, 100
"Mission Accomplished", 275
Mitrany, David, 195
modern global economy, 39
modern political economy, 174
Morales, Evo, 222

More, Thomas, 259
mother, 126
Mullainathan, Sendhil
    Harvard economist, 9
mysogyny, 128

nation state, 13
National Climate Assessment, 16
national self-reliance, 104
nation-building, 87
nation-state, 188
NATO, 276
natural law, 74
natural resource depletion, 63
need, 30
need-generating, 34
neo-colonial protectionism, 131
neo-functionalism, 207
neoliberal expansionism, 116
neoliberal globalization, 200
neoliberalism, 18
neo-Malthusian, 60
New Development Bank, 161
new global sovereign, 184
New International Economic
    Order, 51
Nietzsche, Friedrich, 195
non-governmental organizations (NGOs),
    156
Nuremberg, 279
Nye, Joseph, 196

Obama Doctrine, 269
Obama, Barack, 269
Ocean acidification, 54
Oliver, Joe
    Canada's Minister of Natural Resources,
    87
opinio juris, 269
Orford, Anne, 266
organic farming, 82
Organization of American States and the
    United Nations, 94
organized citizenry, 211
Ortega, Daniel, 222
Our Common Future. *See* Brundtland
    Report
Our Synthetic Environment, 101
outsource, 45
over-consumption, 53, 107

Pauly, Daniel
    fisheries scientist, 90
pecuniary business principles, 189
Permanent Five, 245
pervasive scarcity, 66
Petrocaribe, 231

Piketty, Thomas
    economist, 4
pink-washing, 130
polarization critique, 141
political communities, 36
polities. *See* political communities
polyarchy, 229
Pope Alexander VI, 259
postwar
    economic order, 95
    multilateral institutions, 256
    world, 94
power of consumption, 47
President Dwight Eisenhower
    US President, 96
principle of distinction, 278
private economic actors, 172
private ordering, 13
privatized foreign aid, 158
procyclical measures, 141
progress narrative, 78
Progressives, 171
Protocol I, 280
public goods, 172
public oversight, 171

Rajan, Raghuram, 197
Rawls, John, 202
reciprocity, 77
redistributionist policies, 204
regimes, 137
regulatory advantages, 183
regulatory failure, 173
Reich, Robert, 197
Remittances, 3
renewable resources, 55
Report on the Fragmentation of
    International Law, 137
resource extraction, 88
Responsibility to Protect (R2P), 244
Rio Declaration, 42
Rome Treaty, 282
Roosevelt, Franklin, 212
Rostow, W.W., 97
Rubin, Gayle, 117
Run for Congo Women, 159

Sandinista Front (FSLN), 229
scarcity, 28, 35
scarcity postulate, 48
Scramble for Africa, 251
Second World War, 94
security state, 25
self-interested, 172
September 11th, 2001, 25
sex trafficking, 121
sex work, 118

sexual
  exploitation, 121, 124
  negativity, 123
  panic, 121
sexuality, 12
Shafir, Eldar
  Princeton economist, 9
shrinking women, 146
Slaughter, Anne-Marie, 266
Smith, Adam, 172
social
  construct, 37
  dislocation, 94
  ecology, 102
  justice, 80
  media, 49
sovereign immunity, 17
Soviet Union, 149
specialization, 45
stagflation, 254
Standard & Poors, 3
State of the World's Fisheries report, 91
State of World Fisheries and Aquaculture
  report, 89
Stiglitz, Joseph, 1, 250
stimulus capital, 26
Story, Joseph, Justice, 259
strategies of disruption, 18
Strauss, Andrew, 13
structural reform, 18
subprime mortgage market, 2
Sucre
  electronic currency, 231
supersalaries, 4
supreme emergency exemption, 271
surplus people, 50
sustainability
  environmental, 10
sustainable
  consumption, 42
  development, 16
  production, 42
sustainable fisheries, 90

tariffs, 95
tax havens, 165
Telesur, 231
terra nullius, 260
territorial state, 264
terrorism, 25
terrorist, 157
The First CEDAW Impact Study, 147
The Future of an Illusion
  by Sigmund Freud, 85
The International Bill of Rights, 149
The Lancet, 7
The World Federalists, 195

The World's Women, 147
Third World Approaches to International
  Law (TWAIL), 10
Third World Approaches to International
  Law, 103
Third World militancy, 247
Thomas Aquinas, 261
Tokyo Tribunals, 282
toxic assets, 3
traditional society, 97
transnational regulatory institutions, 185
Transnational solidarity, 18
Truman, Harry, 279

U.N. Climate Panel, 16
U.N. Security Council, 275
UN Commission of Experts on Reforms of
  the International Monetary and
  Financial System, 8, 163
*UN Resolution on the World Economic
  Crisis*, 6
Union of South American Nations
  (UNASUR), 232
United Nations, 208
United Nations Conference on
  Environment and Development, 99
United Nations Conference on
  Environment and Development
  (UNCED), 52
United Nations Conference on the Human
  Environment, 98
*United Nations Convention on the Law of the
  Sea* (UNCLOS), 90
United Nations Human Rights Council,
  213
Universal Declaration of Human Rights,
  137
utopian optimism, 63

vampire economy, 257
violence-as-normative paradigm, 250
virtual trading, 40
Vitoria, 252
Vivir Bien, 110

Wal-Mart, 255
war against nature, 10, 85, 111
war on terror, 251
War on Terror, 25
Washington Consensus, 142
weapons of mass destruction, 274
Western hegemony, 15
Western lifestyle, 142
Wilson, Woodrow, 206
women, 11
  height, 12
Women, 152

women's agency, 120
women's human rights, 138
Women's human rights, 153
worker protections, 204
world authority, 194
world capitalism, 189
World Commission on Environment
    and Development (Brundtland
    Commission), 99
World Economic Forum at Davos, 162
world federalists, 196

World Health Organization, 208
World Summit on Sustainable
    Development, 42
World Trade Organization, 204
world's poor, 56

Xenos, Nicholas, 32

youth literacy rates, 147

Zelaya, Manuel, 245

CPSIA information can be obtained at www.ICGtesting.com
Printed in the USA
BVOW08*2241270415

397724BV00005B/32/P